Higher Self Yoga

Book I

Higher Self Yoga

Book I

Published by Inner Journey Publishing
A division of
Higher Self Yoga, Inc.

ISBN 978-0-989-4682-0-6

Design by Kathy Crowe

Cover art by Eleanor Goud

Dedicated to RHH, my spiritual teacher
and
My Master, MM, who inspired this book and the
creation of the Higher Self Yoga teaching.

Their love and guidance made this possible.

Acknowledgements

I want to thank our main editor, Will Marsh, for his excellent work and our indexer, Victoria Baker. In addition, Judy Bach, Olga Denisko, and Sharon Magruder edited the material as it was developed. Their work was very special in making the final edit an easier one to do.

Also thanks to Ursula Velonis and Laura Williams for their work on the glossary.

The main person who has my gratitude is Kathy Crowe, the Co-President of Inner Journey Publishing. She edited, designed the book and made the changes that were needed, keeping everything in order and coordinating all the work of the others. She has been more than instrumental in making this book become a reality.

I also want to acknowledge the other Co-President of Inner Journey Publishing, Laraine Lippe, who handled the finances and much more that were needed to publish this book.

And thanks to the wonderful artist Eleanor Goud for the use of her Higher Self paintings on the cover of this book and other Higher Self Yoga materials.

Table of Contents

Introduction
About Higher Self Yoga..iii
Working with the Higher Self...vi
Higher Self Exercises..x

Chapter 1
In the Beginning There Was the Word 1

Chapter 2
First There Was the Word, Then There Was Vibration 23

Chapter 3
After the Word and Vibration Came the Light...............................34

Chapter 4
When Humans Were Formed 44

Chapter 5
Letting Go of Old Concepts 55

Chapter 6
Choosing the Right Path 63

Chapter 7
Finding Your Teacher 80

Chapter 8
Looking at Obstacles 89

Chapter 9
Letting Your Intuition Decide 104

Chapter 10
Inside the Subtle World...112

Chapter 11
When You Reach an Impasse that Stops Movement 123

Chapter 12
Looking at the End of Life 146

Chapter 13
When You Are Feeling the Sadness of Life 157

Chapter 14
Holding the Wisdom..166

Chapter 15
Obstacles That Impede Spiritual Growth....................................177

Chapter 16
Facing Truth 192

Chapter 17
When Life Is Lacking in Love 203

Chapter 18
When You Think You Are Doing Well...216

Chapter 19
The Importance of Boundaries 227

Chapter 20
Seeing the God Within.. 238

Chapter 21
Dealing with the Outside World 245

Chapter 22
Letting Go of Expectations...261

Chapter 23
When You Feel Lost.. 286

Chapter 24
The Journey.. 307

Glossary...321

About the Author.. 324

Index 325

Introduction
About Higher Self Yoga

The Higher Self, sometimes called the Wise Being within, is part of you and also part of the Source—the unknown, the ultimate Reality, the energies that have no beginning and no end. As humans, we strive to return to the Source. It does not matter whether we see the Source as a Being, or simply as energy. Returning to the Source is the path of spiritual people.

The Higher Self is the accumulation of all of your positive characteristics. When you activate it, you awaken the spirit within. The more you use the Higher Self to guide you, the more you become one with the higher energies. The Higher Self will help you see and transmute those characteristics that impede your spiritual growth. It takes you on the path to wholeness. It leads you into your true potential, and helps you discover who you really are.

When you bring your Higher Self into your full consciousness, you are then totally connected to the Source and have the ability to experience truth and wisdom. To become one with the Higher Self—through practice, discipline, and self-awareness—is the goal of this teaching.

In the West, most people think of yoga as a physical exercise, but in the East yoga is understood as a method of union with the Source. Bhakti Yoga, for instance, is about linking to the Source using the heart. So Higher Self Yoga is about linking to the Source using the Higher Self.

Both the casual reader and the serious student will find much of value in these pages, although Higher Self Yoga is not a simple teaching. It consolidates the teachings of most of the world religions into a method of assimilation. It expands the concepts of many religions by developing methods to connect to nature and the kingdoms that operate in nature. It combines the concepts of working with the heart and mind to achieve balance. It explores the meaning of reincarnation and karma and how to overcome karmic influences. It brings new concepts of how to work with energies and how the energies affect not only you, but also the community, the nation and the planet. It explores ways to help others on the path.

This teaching is based on the ancient teachings given to humankind thousands of years ago. It is designed for spiritual growth, for striving for higher knowledge and wisdom. It is a teaching that makes no distinction between man, woman, race, sexual orientation, or cultural background. It is a path that teaches how to overcome challenges.

In this teaching psychological growth is emphasized. With the use of experiential exercises it helps those who are willing to heal psychological wounds and emotional attachments, and who are ready to open their hearts to Love. Love is a far greater concept in this teaching than is defined in the worldly sense. It is not in any way an emotional love. It is the ultimate Source. It is Wisdom.

The Higher Self can help you in your daily life, whether it's in your work or in your relationships. Working with the Higher Self keeps you focused, calm during times of adversity, and open to change. It frees you from emotions that can keep you from moving forward. If you work consciously with the Higher Self, It can aid you in making decisions. For example, if you need to resolve mundane problems, the Higher Self can help you. If you are having difficulty with someone, the Higher Self will advise you how to approach the person. If you need creative inspiration in your work, the Higher Self is the direct source.

Working with the Higher Self is always a wonderful experience. The more you work with it the more you will experience joy in your life.

Note: Rather than say "he or she," throughout the book odd number chapters use "he" and even number chapters use "she," but of course the material applies to both genders.

Working with the Higher Self

When you start to work with the Higher Self it often is personified in a form that appears as a woman or man. The gender does not have to relate to the gender of the person contacting It.

The Higher Self can also take on the form of an angel, a mystical animal, a light or color, or even energy experienced in the body. The most common form is human, which is why these exercises mention seeing the Higher Self as a figure, but for you the figure may just be a shaft of bright light and that is perfectly fine.

In doing the exercises, be aware that everyone is unique and experiences visualization differently. Some people can see the scenes in their mind's eye, whereas others just feel or sense what's happening. Some people are auditory; they hear sounds and voices. Others experience a combination of sensory impressions. Therefore, when you communicate with the Higher Self, It may send you impressions that appear as thoughts in your mind or you may hear Its voice. It can also send body sensations that relay messages.

Sometimes personal desires can interfere with the message. Therefore, it is best to have the answer come by the use of signals. For instance, if you see the Higher Self, ask It to show you a visual signal for "yes," "no," and "maybe." A "yes" or a "no" signal may simply be the shaking of Its head "yes" or "no." If your experience with the Higher Self is more sensory, you may feel a twitch in your left leg for a "yes" answer and a "no" may be a twitch in your right leg. Then ask questions accordingly. At the end of the meditation you can ask the Higher Self to tell you more and receive a message either verbally or through impressions.

The Higher Self will always reach you in some manner. You may ask a question and not receive an answer at the time, but later when you are walking down the street, the answer may pop into your head, or you may have a dream in which you receive the answer.

Since the Higher Self is your Wise Self and is part of you, It knows everything about you and everything about your personal evolution. It therefore can help you in all of your life's problems, from the most mundane to the most profound. Using It to help you makes It stronger, until you will begin to bring the Higher Self into your consciousness in your everyday life. Eventually, you will not even see a form but simply feel It in your heart as being one with you. Remember, Its role is to not only help you with problems, but also to guide you spiritually so that eventually you become a Wise Being in all your thoughts and actions.

 The more you use the Higher Self, the stronger is the pull of the shadow side of the personality. Consequently, the shadow side, which is also part of you and part of the unconscious, will begin to fight back in a negative manner. Be aware that you may suddenly have negative thoughts and feelings that you have never experienced before. Try to look at them in a detached, or disidentified, manner, and even see them as a black ball that you will give to your Higher Self to transmute.

Working with the Higher Self is a process. There will be times when you experience It fully in the meditation and at other times nothing happens. When first contacting the Higher Self It can be very evasive. It may appear and then quickly disappear. The more you persist in contacting It, the stronger It will become. If It should disappear when you are communicating with It, just link with your heart chakra (a center located in the middle of your chest), repeat the end of the meditation, and literally demand that It return.

In all Higher Self meditations, remember to shine light on the Higher Self when you first experience It. Sometimes desires coming from your personality will impersonate the Higher Self. Shining light on It is a way to verify It is indeed your Higher Self. When the rays of light shine on the Higher Self, if It is truly the Higher Self, It will either stay the same or become brighter. If it is something else, it will disappear or turn dark. If this happens, and it happens to everyone at some time or other, simply tell it to leave and repeat the end of the exercise. If during the exercise you experience blocks or fears, see these as a black ball that you give to your Higher Self, saying, "Please take these away from me temporarily, so that I can receive clear answers from You."

After doing this, again shine light down onto the Higher Self to be certain It is still truly there. Do this at least once during the communication just in case some inner desire has replaced It.

If you only experience body impressions of the Higher Self, always keep connecting with the heart chakra. The Higher Self should convey a warm expansive feeling. Its energy is never cold, so if you are experiencing a sudden cold feeling in the chest, reconnect with the heart chakra and ask the Higher Self to come back.

Working with the Higher Self is always a wonderful experience. Its wisdom and humor make a magical combination. Sometimes It will take on other forms to indicate something you need to do. For example, It may appear as a frolicking child or an elf, indicating you need to have more fun or play with your inner child. It will even take on other nationalities and appear in different genders. If It suddenly changes from what you are used to seeing, ask It why It has taken on this new form.

It will sometimes appear as one of your past lives, usually a life that was deeply spiritual, like a monk or lama.

Sometimes the Higher Self will play games with you. For example, It may show you a symbol that you don't understand. It's important then, at a later time, to take the symbol and visualize it in your heart chakra and ask to see or receive more information about it.

Always the Higher Self works with your whole being. It will never reveal information to you that you are not ready to receive. It will never hurt you or scare you. It is gentle and loving at all times. It always knows what's best for you, and It will never deceive you. If that ever happens, be aware that it's coming from something other than your Higher Self.

These exercises will introduce you to your Higher Self. The more you work with the Higher Self, the easier it becomes to contact It. You may then eliminate most of the exercise and start with a point toward the end. With some people the Higher Self will appear just by linking with the heart chakra. Remember It always operates through the heart.

The more you use your heart chakra in your everyday life, using it in all your relationships and using it with yourself, the stronger the Higher Self will become. You will find your heart opening and your feelings toward others becoming more compassionate. These are not sentimental feelings, but strong, simple feelings of genuine love.

Each of us is capable of opening our heart, and becoming one with our Higher Self, but it requires discipline and practice. It is an ongoing process that develops one's spiritual nature. When blocks and fears arise, as they surely will, look at them as obstacles you need to work through. Break down the fears and see the root of them. Ask for a process from your Higher Self that will help you go through the blocks, starting with a first step. Work with that step and ask for another one.

You may want to ask the Higher Self to show you a symbol that represents It. Take the symbol and draw it, keeping it in front of you during the day to remind you to link with the Higher Self.

Remember the Higher Self is your inner guide. It will lead you through the obstacles and help you awaken your spiritual and creative nature. Acknowledge the Higher Self when you do acts of love and kindness. We criticize ourselves when we make mistakes, but how often do we acknowledge our good qualities?

Within the Higher Self sleeps the spirit of the individual. When you activate the Higher Self, you awaken the spirit. The more you use the Higher Self to guide you in all your decisions, the more you become one with higher forces and energies.

The Higher Self will help you see and transmute those characteristics that impede your spiritual growth. It takes you on the path to wholeness, It leads you into your true potential, and It helps you discover who you really are.

Higher Self Exercises

The following are Higher Self exercises. I suggest you do all of them one at a time, on a different day, to determine which one works best for you:

The Mountain Exercise:
Sit down in a comfortable chair.

Close your eyes and feel your whole body relaxing. First your feet are going to relax, then your legs, your thighs, your stomach, chest, shoulders and arms, your neck and head. Now your whole body is feeling relaxed.

Take some deep breaths and center yourself by linking with your heart chakra, which is located in the center of your chest.

With each breath feel the cares of the day dissolving into nothing and try to let go of any thoughts and feelings.

Now imagine you are standing in a meadow and right in front of you is a mountain. You are going to climb the mountain. It will be a very easy climb, and at the very top you will meet your Higher Self.

For now you start to walk on the path, which is in front of you. Almost immediately you enter a forest. It's a forest of tall pines and other evergreen trees. As you walk upward on the path, you can smell the pine, feel the pine needles under your feet, and hear the birds singing.

And as you slowly climb upward, rays of sunlight break through the branches and light your way.

Now you are leaving the forest, and you continue climbing upward on the path. There are scattered trees and rocks and grass, and as you climb you can feel the warmth of the sun on your shoulders. It's a beautiful summer day, with a gentle breeze blowing. You continue to climb upward.

Suddenly, you hear the sound of a waterfall. You leave the path and go over to the side of the cliff and look up toward the top of the mountain and see a beautiful waterfall cascading down. As the water hits the rocks nearest you, feel the wet spray on your face and you hear the roar of the water as it hits the rocks beneath you.

You turn now and go back to the path and continue climbing upward. Now there are no more trees, just big boulders and scrub brush and sand. You stop for a minute and see that there are other mountain ranges on either side. You can look down and see the meadow where you started.

You turn and continue climbing upward. Now you are coming to the top of the mountain, and as you go around a bend you see at the very top a flat plateau of land and on the plateau is a bench. Sit down on the bench and take a moment to look around you. Experience the beautiful view of mountains all around you.

As you sit there feel the warmth of the sun on top of your head. Now look up at the sun, which is directly above you. As you look, a figure is going to appear and slide down on a sunbeam and stand in front of you. The figure is your Higher Self. You may also experience It as a light or a feeling of warmth and expansion in your heart chakra. When you feel you are experiencing It, imagine the sun shining down on It and notice if It changes. If It stays the same or gets brighter, then It is your Higher Self. If it disappears or gets dark, tell it to leave, and try the exercise again.

If you see It as a figure, imagine reaching out and holding the hands of your Higher Self, linking your heart to Its heart. Feel Its energy flowing to you. How does it feel?

When you feel connected, ask the Higher Self questions that can be answered with a signal for a "yes" answer, a "no" answer, or a "maybe" answer.

When you feel ready to end the conversation, ask the Higher Self if It has anything else it needs to tell you. Listen to Its answer, which may take the form of actual words, thoughts, or impressions. Then thank your Higher Self and write down everything that has happened.

The Meadow Exercise

Sit down in a comfortable chair.

Close your eyes and feel your whole body relaxing. First your feet are going to relax, then your legs, your thighs, your stomach, chest, shoulders and arms, your neck and head. Now your whole body is feeling relaxed.

Take some deep breaths and center yourself by linking with your heart chakra, which is located in the center of your chest.

With each breath feel the cares of the day dissolving into nothing and try to let go of any thoughts and feelings.

Now imagine yourself standing in the middle of a meadow. It is a beautiful summer day, the sun is shining brightly and there is a soft breeze blowing.

Experience the meadow around you—the trees, the green grass with wildflowers growing, and the mountains in the distance.

You can smell the sweetness of the air and feel the warmth of the sun and the gentleness of the breeze.

You may want to take your shoes off and feel the grass under your feet.

In the distance, across the meadow, a figure appears and slowly walks toward you. You know the figure is your Higher Self. As It comes closer, try to sense what It looks like. Is It a man or a woman? Is It just a light or is It a body feeling? The Higher Self will come to a stop in front of you.

When you feel you are experiencing It, imagine the sun shining down on It and notice if It changes. If It stays the same or gets brighter, then It is your Higher Self. If it disappears or gets dark, tell it to leave, and try the exercise again.

If you see It as a figure, imagine reaching out and holding the hands of your Higher Self, linking your heart to Its heart. Feel Its energy flowing to you. How does it feel?

When you feel connected, ask the Higher Self questions that can be answered with a signal for a "yes" answer, a "no" answer, or a "maybe" answer.

When you feel ready to end the conversation, ask the Higher Self if It has anything else it needs to tell you. Listen to Its answer, which may take the form of actual words, thoughts, or impressions. Then thank your Higher Self and write down everything that has happened.

The Garden Exercise

Sit down in a comfortable chair.

Close your eyes and feel your whole body relaxing. First your feet are going to relax, then your legs, your thighs, your stomach, chest, shoulders and arms, your neck and head. Now your whole body is feeling relaxed.

Take some deep breaths and center yourself by linking with your heart chakra, which is located in the center of your chest.

With each breath feel the cares of the day dissolving into nothing and try to let go of any thoughts and feelings.

Imagine you are entering a walled garden. The entrance has a trellis of climbing roses over it. As you enter you see two paths. The one on the left continues to follow beds of roses. The one on the right has a variety of flowers arranged by color. Some beds are golden, full of lilies and smaller orange and yellow flowers. There are also beds of blue and purple hyacinth and iris. Imagine your favorite flowers in the beds. This path continues down to a small paved circle of stone with a bench on it. You sit down on the bench. Your Higher Self is coming down the opposite path and sits down next to you on the bench.

When you feel you are experiencing It, imagine the sun shining down on It and notice if It changes. If It stays the same or gets brighter, then It is your Higher Self. If it disappears or gets dark, tell it to leave, and try the exercise again.

If you choose to walk down the path of rose beds you will see all varieties and colors of roses. This path also comes to a round paved circle of stones with a bench on it, and you also see the Higher Self coming down the opposite path to sit down next to you on the bench.

When you feel connected, ask the Higher Self questions that can be answered with a signal for a "yes" answer, a "no" answer, or a "maybe" answer.

When you feel ready to end the conversation, ask the Higher Self if It has anything else it needs to tell you. Listen to Its answer, which may take the form of actual words, thoughts, or impressions.

Then thank your Higher Self and write down everything that has happened,

The Lake Exercise

Sit down in a comfortable chair.

Close your eyes and feel your whole body relaxing. First your feet are going to relax, then your legs, your thighs, your stomach, chest, shoulders and arms, your neck and head. Now your whole body is feeling relaxed.

Take some deep breaths and center yourself by linking with your heart chakra, which is located in the center of your chest.

With each breath feel the cares of the day dissolving into nothing and try to let go of any thoughts and feelings.

Pretend you are in a boat on a beautiful lake. You are rowing or paddling toward an island. You pull up to the island and dock your boat.

You get out of the boat and walk down a path that takes you to a pavilion that overlooks the lake. There is a bench where you wait for the Higher Self. You see It is in a boat on the lake, and It comes to a dock in front of you and gets out and meets you on the pavilion.

When you feel you are experiencing It, imagine the sun shining down on It and notice if It changes. If It stays the same or gets brighter, then It is your Higher Self. If it disappears or gets dark, tell it to leave, and try the exercise again.

When you feel connected, ask the Higher Self questions that can be answered with a signal for a "yes" answer, a "no" answer, or a "maybe" answer.

When you feel ready to end the conversation, ask the Higher Self if It has anything else it needs to tell you. Listen to Its answer, which may take the form of actual words, thoughts, or impressions. Then thank your Higher Self and write down everything that has happened

The House Exercise

Sit down in a comfortable chair.

Close your eyes and feel your whole body relaxing. First your feet are going to relax, then your legs, your thighs, your stomach, chest, shoulders and arms, your neck and head. Now your whole body is feeling relaxed.

Take some deep breaths and center yourself by linking with your heart chakra, which is located in the center of your chest.

With each breath feel the cares of the day dissolving into nothing and try to let go of any thoughts and feelings.

Imagine you are sitting in your home meditating. The doorbell rings and you go to the door and open it. On the other side is your Higher Self. It enters and sits down across from you.

When you feel you are experiencing It, imagine the sun shining down on It and notice if It changes. If It stays the same or gets brighter, then It is your Higher Self. If it disappears or gets dark, tell it to leave, and try the exercise again.

When you feel connected, ask the Higher Self questions that can be answered with a signal for a "yes" answer, a "no" answer, or a "maybe" answer.

When you feel ready to end the conversation, ask the Higher Self if It has anything else it needs to tell you. Listen to Its answer, which may take the form of actual words, thoughts, or impressions. Then thank your Higher Self and write down everything that has happened.

Chapter 1

In the Beginning There Was the Word

When the Word was pronounced, its sound followed the contours of the planet and gave forth vibrations that activated the mineral and plant kingdoms. Its vibration contains energy, and this energy is the source of life itself.

What is meant by sound? How does it affect nature? How does it affect animals? How does it affect humans?

When you speak, the sound goes forth as vibrations in the subtle worlds. It produces good or negative vibrations depending on its content. If the sound is laughter, it produces millions of vibrations that resound in positive motion. Similarly, a sound of anger produces millions of vibrations that resound in negative motion or chaos. The subtle world contains billions of vibrations of both. Along with actions, it is these sound vibrations that cause karma.

Sound is far more effective than anyone can imagine. Just as thoughts have enormous pupation, sound also travels faster than scientists have calculated. Since the invention of radio and television, sounds that are even more penetrating, such as cell phones and cell towers, have polluted the atmosphere. Imagine a space filled with discordant sounds flying so fast it is impossible to retain even one note. These sounds can only be moderated and lessened by the elementals that work constantly to change and clear the vibrations in the subtle worlds.

When you chant sacred sounds in a group, these vibrations help clear the chaos. Chanting AUM is very important because the vibrations have healing effects on all the planes of the subtle world, especially when AUM is chanted correctly, pronouncing the A, not just the OM, as in ahh-ohh-mmm.

As a yogi, it is important to keep your words grounded in truth. Any untruth uttered by a yogi pollutes the atmosphere even more than that spoken by an ordinary person. You need to be careful of your temperament, and not speak with anger, intolerance, irritation, or simply words that are fickle or scattered. Your responsibility is far more than you realize. You affect not only the people you speak to but also the elementals around you and the subtle planes where your sounds vibrate.

Another example: When someone talks negatively about another person, not only do those negative words affect the listener but they also vibrate to the person being talked about. The vibrations of those words surround the person and penetrate his subtle body, and consequently they can affect the physical body.

This may seem exaggerated to you, but it is true. Obviously, some people are more sensitive than others to sound vibrations. They will pick up the chaos and even respond to it defensively. Such people are more telepathic and need to learn ways to prevent sound from penetrating their physical bodies. Others can throw the vibrations off in their aura; but if they feel tired or irritated, they too can be affected.

There are ways to express feelings about someone without causing sound vibrations to affect them. First, of course, it is best to talk to the person. Not only is this more direct, but the sound is taken in immediately by the person and does not linger around the subtle body. Second, if for some reason you find it too difficult to speak directly to the person, you can say to a friend that you need to talk about someone, and then direct the sound by asking beforehand that your words stay only with you and not in any way travel to the other person. This frees you to discuss your problem with a friend, especially if you need advice on how to deal with the person in question.

By commanding the sounds of your words to stay with you, you are not only containing them, you are also working with controlling the vibrations that emanate from you. As a yogi you are responsible for all the vibrations you produce and send.

Think of yourself as a violin. Your sounds flow forth to others who listen to you and to the currents in the air as well as the hidden currents surrounding you. If you play the violin with skill and produce beautiful sounds, you affect others in a positive way. If, instead, you are not trained and make mistakes, you produce discordant sounds that negatively affect everyone around you. As a violinist, it is important to moderate your playing until you are skillful enough to play beautifully. You can practice by playing in a soundproof room so others cannot hear you.

Similarly, you can contain your words by envisioning the room you are in as having metal walls and commanding your words to stay only in the room. After meeting with a friend with whom you are discussing a problem you have with another person, or after meeting with the person in question, you can cleanse the room with incense or sage. If, as you talk, you are walking in nature, you need to consciously send the words to a container that you envision, and ask that the container be destroyed in the sunlight.

When you talk negatively about someone on the phone, you produce a different kind of vibration. Not only do the vibrations go to the person you're speaking about, but they also travel through communication lines and affect the atmosphere around the planet. If you can only talk by phone, inwardly ask that the words stay in your room and also clearly imagine a bell around the phone receiver so that the person you're speaking to can still hear you, but the vibrations will not go into the receiver.

Conscious speaking is difficult to remember and to do. It takes much practice and skill. Question yourself all the time about it.

If you are with someone who doesn't understand this, and the person needs to talk to you about someone he is having difficulty with, then it is up to you to ask inwardly that the person's words stay in the room and not travel to the person in question.

This is about awareness. The number one step is to become aware of words, of thoughts, and of actions. Awareness is the first step on the path. Higher Self Yoga is about awareness of the ego self, the lower self, and, most of all, the Higher Self. Your Higher Self is conscious of your words, thoughts, and actions, and will try to direct you in becoming more mindful of these.

When you are aware of every word you speak, you will find that you speak fewer words and the words you do speak will take on more meaning because they are carefully thought out. It doesn't matter if you speak rapidly or slowly—what is important is the tone of voice and the words and their connotations. If your words have hidden meanings that could be interpreted adversely, then you have not thought out the proper words to speak.

Words can convey many different meanings, and often the same word has two, three, or even more meanings. It's important to have a strong enough vocabulary that you choose a word that is clearly defined, a word that can be taken in the right manner.

For example, in the use of the word "good," if you say to someone, "You have a good way of expressing yourself," that can be taken in a number of ways. First, it can be taken literally, referring to a statement the person just made. It can also be more general, meaning the person always expresses himself in a clear and articulate way. If the person was making a negative remark, your statement could be a sarcastic reply. The word good can also refer to what you think is good. In fact, the person could be expressing dislike or a prejudice that you agree with but others might not consider good. So this sample sentence looks literal but in fact has several interpretations.

Another example is the word "spiritual." Someone may tell you that you are spiritual and that he likes that about you. But what does this mean? Spiritual to you may mean something totally different from the speaker's meaning. Spiritual can denote a churchgoer, a kind person, a religious person who may or may not be spiritual, a zealot, or even someone who believes in psychic phenomena but never practices anything that would be considered spiritual.

Words not only produce vibrations but also have meanings far outweighing their dictionary definitions. A word to one person may have an entirely different meaning to someone else. Therefore, it is very important to use the right word and explain what you mean by that word if there is any question of misinterpretation. This is especially true when you are in a foreign country and are engaged in conversation in a language that is not native to you.

Many mistakes with words have caused conflicts between peoples and nations. In the future, language will be spoken through the heart and then misinterpretation will not exist.

If you think about each word you use, that would be very burdensome. Focus solely on what you mean to convey and then choose words that are simply understood.

For example, you want to convey to someone that you feel he has done something that has consequences of which he is not aware. How can you best convey this without making him feel wronged or criticized or even angry?

You can say, "When you did such and such, I felt you meant well and your intentions were really fine ones. But what occurred to me was the way other people may take your actions. For instance, another person, who isn't aware of your true feelings, could think you are doing such and such from hidden motives. Maybe you can somehow express more of your feelings so that your intention is not misunderstood. I would be happy to help you do this. I know it may seem odd to you, but it is important to me that you are not misunderstood."

This is a little exaggerated to show how you can make a person feel you are not being critical but, in fact, have positive feelings toward him.

So many times words are misconceived and take on new energies because of this. The energy around words can also give them new meanings. For instance, if you say, "I really care about you" to someone, and if the energy is one of caring, the person will feel it in the heart. If, instead, your statement is coming before criticizing someone, the person will feel you are going to be critical and close down. Energy is always the predominant thing. If someone tries to manipulate you with indirect words, you know it right away, even if the words sound correct. Tones of voice, looks, ways of moving, all of these accompany words and make them take on strong, hidden meanings.

If someone is controlling and says, "This is for your own good," you know it really is in the speaker's interest, not yours.

Question anyone who uses indirect ways of asking for something. Ask, "What is it you really want?" Confront the person, and force clarity if you have to.

If you're speaking to someone who is a pleaser, be aware that he may offer to help you but really doesn't want to. Clarify that the offer is truly coming from the heart, not from a wish to be liked. Often people accept help, knowing the person is a pleaser, because, after all, a pleaser can always be counted on to offer help! The motives are wrong and eventually the pleaser will start to feel used, even when he has offered all along.

It's always best to question someone like this; otherwise it could hurt your friendship. When you do this, make certain you have first formed the words in your heart. Take your time, and give your heart a chance to bring up the right words. Patience is a virtue, something that is very important to learn in this teaching. Having patience means using time with care, not being rushed, but giving yourself and others time to think clearly.

Now, it is time to give you an exercise.

Exercise One:
Link with your Higher Self by connecting to your heart, and ask:
- *What in my language needs to change?*
- *Do I use words that are unclear and misleading?*
- *How can I become more direct and loving in speaking?*
- *Is there a practice that I can do to learn to speak from the heart?*
- *Give me a process that will help me do all of the above.*

It is important to learn the ability to mirror others. The best way to do this is to link with your Higher Self, and then ask your Higher Self to link with the other person's Higher Self. Linking in this way each time you speak will help you to hear the person with discrimination, understanding, and knowledge of what he is really saying. Try this every time you talk to someone, and notice if there is a change in your language. If you are doing the process correctly, there should be no misunderstandings and the words should be direct and clear.

Let's now look at words themselves. Words are energy. Their meanings can vary but the energy does not change unless a new energy is added to them. For instance, if you say to someone, "I really care about you," you could be saying this with truth or you could be saying it because you feel the person wants to hear it. You also could be saying this because you are planning to ask for something or to criticize the person. In all of those instances you are transmitting energy into the words that do not originate in the words themselves. The words themselves have good, quiet, vibrations. The added energies can vary from love to dislike and have many hidden motivations.

To be aware of this is step one. To design a different way of conveying truth is step two, and to find the right words is step three. If you are saying the words "I really care about you" and you mean them, then those are the proper words to use. If, instead, you are saying those words to prepare the ground for something else you want to say, then it's best not to use them. Instead, words that convey your true feelings should be used. For instance, if you want to convey criticism, you need to choose words that are open and nonjudgmental, yet clearly express what is bothering you. It is best, then, to say how you are feeling and why, placing the emphasis on yourself and your feelings and not all on the other person. For example, "It really bothers me when you do such and such."

If you truly dislike a person and have to interact with him, it's best to choose words that are direct, simple, and clear. Their meanings should not be harsh or judgmental but very concise and business like. Try to avoid emotional content in the words; otherwise your true feelings will lace the words with vibrations that he will pick up.

You will inevitably encounter people you have been with in past lives. Many of these people will be from hurtful karmic relationships that bring up negative feelings. It is important to be aware of this from the start.

Take time to see if the karmic exchange is coming from truth in the present life, or simply reflecting the old life.

Remember, an old life is simply that, old. Meeting people you knew in past lives can be positive or negative. They have learned lessons along the way and as a consequence may be different today. Knowing about karma is helpful because you can distance yourself and maintain your awareness during any exchanges. If the karma has primarily been negative, then it is best to be cautious and not become involved with the person until you can determine if he has changed. If the karma is positive, then it is easier to become friends and link into the good feelings toward each other. Sometimes, karma, even if it is negative, needs to be played out and end. In the playing out, be careful to stay disidentified from the feelings. Having a focused mind is of the utmost importance in such a relationship.

Never begin a close relationship until you are totally aware of your karma with the person. Too often karma can hook you into an intimacy that will produce negative results. Always proceed carefully when you feel a great attraction toward someone. Negative and positive karma attract in a similar manner. The results come much later, after you are enmeshed. A yogi needs to always be aware of karmic relationships. One negative karmic relationship can pull a yogi off the path, and the loss will be felt not only in this life but in future ones as well.

When you first meet someone, be aware of your first thoughts. Your intuition will always recognize a past connection. Listen to it. It will clearly send you a feeling that will indicate whether the karma is more positive or more negative. Usually, karma is mixed, but it will lean toward one side. Be certain that you know which side it leans toward.

If you meet someone with whom you have difficult karma, you will often feel a very strong attraction. When this happens, always check it out with your Higher Self. Positive karma can be strong at first or can gradually grow stronger as the relationship develops.

The words you use with someone can also be an indication of negative karma. If you notice your words are negative, take time to observe your interactions carefully. The words you use often bring up old feelings from past lives. So it is wise to watch your words to see if there are hidden meanings and vibrations. Even if your words are not negative, you can be giving ordinary words negative vibrations if the karma is negative. Be certain to be totally disidentified when dealing with such a karmic relationship.

Words are the key to karma. When they are spoken, they bring up feelings and reactions that play into karma or make new karma. That is why it is so important to choose your words carefully, to speak them purely, and to use heart energy at all times to cloak the words.

Karma is created instantly. It's important to keep karma in higher awareness in relationships. Although you must be vigilant at all times in relationships, the best way to balance this vigilance is through meditation.

Freeing the mind of words is freeing the spirit. When words intrude into meditations, they create vibrations that keep the spirit from soaring. I am speaking now of words coming from your own thinking, not those sent from a higher source. Freeing the mind of words allows your mind to rest; such stillness opens the channels to the higher worlds.

The resting mind is the doorway to the inner mind, which is connected to the Higher Self and leads to the higher states of consciousness. When you have changed your words to convey positive meanings, then you are crossing the threshold to the inner mind. The energy of positive words encompasses the higher vibrations, and those vibrations help the spirit to strive upward.

Exercise Two:
Ask your Higher Self to let you feel the vibration of the following words:
  1. *Love*
  2. *Compassion*
  3. *Education*
  4. *Joy*
  5. *Striving*
  6. *Encouragement*
  7. *Helping*
  8. *Accomplishment*

   9. Giving
   10. Working

With each of the above words, you can feel the energy. Realize that when you speak these words, you are sending this energy out. The speaking can be done alone, or directly to a person. In either case, the energy is sent. For instance, if you want to send the word compassion, say out loud, "I feel compassion for so and so." Naturally, the words must come from the heart. Otherwise, the energy is diluted.

   Sending a word just as a thought gives it a different energy. Thought energy is more subtle and, depending on the sender, can be more or less powerful than speaking the words out loud.

   In either case, the words need to be carefully formed to convey the strongest impact. The reason why chants and mantras are so powerful is because they are simply formed and the energy is repeated until it becomes a very strong vibration. If someone is working with words in this manner, it is important that the words be not only positive but also clear in meaning.

   Any meaning other than the one intended would become part of the word, so I suggest looking up the word to be certain that you are not using a word with a meaning that is not appropriate to your message. This is especially true if you are developing an affirmation or chant.

Exercise Three:
Ask your Higher Self: Give me a particular chant or affirmation that would be helpful to me at this time.
   • *Then ask: Tell me about the vibration and what its effect on me will be.*

When you speak, remember your words are vibrations. Keep those words in your heart and add your heart's energy to them. Even if the words are mundane, the heart's energy will affect the receiver in a positive manner.

   It is important to remember the effect of words, not just on others but also on yourself. You think about yourself in words. You may even think out loud. You might criticize yourself and call yourself names. You send negative vibrations to yourself when you do this.

Instead, try speaking positive words to yourself. Try telling yourself nice things. Say how well you are doing, how happy you are, how glad and grateful you are, and how wonderful life is. Feel how such words affect your moods. When you are feeling sad or angry or negative, try using words of encouragement that make you feel better about yourself. You will notice your mood changing as you do this.

If you are afraid to do something, tell yourself that it's okay, you can do it and do it successfully. Be optimistic, not unrealistically, but based on observation and truth. Every situation has positive and negative aspects. Know the negative ones, but also know and concentrate on the positive. This does not mean ignoring negative characteristics. Be aware of them, and question how you can overcome them.

Words can change whole courses of events. They can change relationships. They can cause destruction or construction. They hold the key to higher worlds. They contain knowledge and wisdom. They can bring you to a different level of awareness. They are essential in the learning process of a yogi.

Words contain energies that can carry you upward toward the divine or downward into your lower nature. Words can destroy or build, can give love or take love away. Words are both negative and positive and can change your life and the lives of those around you. Words cause karma. Remember to listen to your words before you speak them.

When a respected person speaks, his words are listened to, mainly because of who he is, so realize that if you are regarded by others as someone who doesn't think or is scattered, your words—even if your words are words of wisdom—will not have the full impact on others. If you want to be respected, you need to act in a way that others will respect. Only then do your words take on great meaning.

Unfortunately, in the East, there are many yogis who live in dirt and poverty and are not respected by Westerners because of this. To live a life as a hermit doesn't always mean you have wisdom. In fact, often the opposite is true; the hermit can be frenetic and unbalanced.

A person who is truly wise will act according to the people he is to teach. If he wants to get through to a Western person, he can dress simply but he should be clean. Many Western people have passed by a yogi of great wisdom because the yogi has looked unkempt. In the East, they blame the Westerner for a lack of discrimination.

It is the teacher's fault for not being sensitive to the needs of the students. Such conditioned needs certainly are superficial, but it is important to respect them in order to have time to bring awareness to the student. Once the student understands that the teacher has great wisdom, then the outer appearance does not matter. In most teachings, the teacher expects the student to become like a child and follow blindly. In Higher Self Yoga, the teachers want students who are willing to work with their own inner wisdom and become leaders.

How does one start the process of knowing the right words to use in a conversation? First, it is important to use words that the listener is familiar with. If you are talking to a child or someone who has little education, do not use words that they may not understand. Choose words according to the consciousness of the individual.

Once, when I was a very young child, I told my parents that I wanted to learn the proper words to use in conversation. My father told me that there are no "proper words" and that it was important to hear the word in my head and determine the effect it would have on the listener. I responded, "How would I know the effect?" He replied, "If the word would offend you, do not use it, and if you still are unsure, pick another word."

All of this sounds boring and even tiring. To screen every word is tedious, but you certainly can screen some words, such as words that are condemning or accusatory, words that are unkind, words that have very strong connotations, words that are best used only when special circumstances demand them. Remember, words are energy, and if the word is okay but the thought behind the word is condemning, that word will come off in a condemning way. This is what is meant by the tone of your words.

Often, people feel offended by something someone said, even if that person's words, when analyzed, are not offensive. This is because the words are colored by anger or contempt. Interestingly enough, when someone reviews a conversation and questions what was said to upset the other person, it is more often than not the tone of voice, not the words. If you have anger toward someone, do not talk to that person until your anger is mostly gone. Only then can you express yourself in a way that won't make the person defensive.

Exercise Four:
Take some time to think about the way in which you express yourself. If you are not certain about this, ask others how they feel when you talk to them. Ask them to be specific. For example, ask:
- *When I'm upset, how do I sound?*
- *When I'm trying to explain something to you, how do I sound?*
- *When I'm revealing something about myself, how do I sound?*
- *If I act emotionally, how do my words sound?*
- *If I'm calm, how do I sound?*
- *If I am trying to convey an idea of mine, how do I sound?*

Ask these questions of several people, because each person may perceive you differently and you may, in fact, talk differently to each. Some people bring out the best in you and others bring out the worst. The differences can be due to childhood conditioning or a past-life connection.

Some people are overly sensitive to words. You will need to take special care when you talk to them. Realize that every word will have special meaning to them. Again, screening every word is impossible, but if you see that someone is having an adverse reaction to what you are saying, simply ask, "Have I said something that bothers you?" Try to always be in your heart when you are dealing with this type of person.

Exercise Five:
List the people in your life you know are difficult to talk to. They are either overly sensitive or respond negatively to your words. Then take each name and ask your Higher Self:
- *Is there something I do that makes this person react to me in this way?*
- *Do others have the same problem with this person?*
- *What is the best way in which to deal with this person?*

Now, if everyone else has difficulty in communicating with the same person, then you know that the problem is highly unlikely to be coming from you. But if most people have no difficulty in communicating with the person in question, then it would be wise to look at past connections. If you are operating from experiences in past lives, for example, it's best to try to heal that karma. If you simply have diverse styles of thinking, see this person only when necessary. It may be that your personalities are too different and will always clash.

Of course, if this person is permanently in your life, you can best deal with him with clear statements that can't be misunderstood. Sometimes it's essential to say nothing, even if you disagree, and realize that saying as little as possible makes for a better relationship. There are many people who love an argument. This type of person is to be avoided or not responded to. Otherwise, you can become entangled in a long karmic web.

Clearly, in communication of any type, it is important to not expect a certain outcome, particularly if the relationship is full of karma. Do not project your desires on the outcome. This is difficult to do, but being open is by far the best way to proceed. You may decide that you really have nothing in common with someone. Yet your karmic connection can cause you to want to stay connected. Unfortunately, this may be a big mistake that can only take you down an old road of unhappiness. Be aware of any unspoken or hidden needs that you may have around this relationship. See it clearly as it is today.

Exercise Six:
Ask yourself the following questions:
1. *How is this relationship benefiting me?*
2. *Is this relationship making me happy?*
3. *Do I need to remain in this relationship?*
4. *What does it do for me?*
5. *How would I feel if I ended it?*
6. *Do I know if there is old karma here that is being repeated?*
7. *Do I feel I can change the relationship?*
8. *If so, why would I want to?*
9. *What would the relationship bring me if it changed?*
10. *What changes do I have to make in order for the relationship to be better?*
11. *Am I willing to make these changes?*
12. *Are they realistic?*

After answering all the above questions, you should have a better idea whether you want to stay in the relationship. If you do, then you need to look at the hidden dynamics and decide how to continue the relationship without being hurt by the person. It's best to keep a relationship like this more impersonal; otherwise, it continues old patterns. If there is negative karma, it's best to end the relationship once and for all.

When you look closely at how you communicate, you will discover that there are many ways to get your words across. The simplest is to just express the words, plainly, without any emphasis on any one phrase. Too often the real meaning is conveyed by the tone or inflection of your voice rather than by your words. You can make a derogatory remark in a way that expresses how you feel simply by the tone of voice. No matter how much has been expressed in a clear manner, when there is any aspect that is unclear, that can alter the meaning.

Depending on whom you are with, there can be a different way of speaking. Notice this. Notice the various ways you speak to a loved one, a friend, a child, a person whom you don't like, someone who is working for you, a peer, etc. It is amazing how the voice changes, and you can be completely oblivious of this.

Notice also how your voice changes when you are happy or unhappy, tired or energetic. At times your voice might sound artificial. People who are proud, haughty, or sophisticated make their voices sound aloof, thinking this sets them apart from ordinary people. So often people who want to make an impression ruin that impression by adopting such a manner and tone of voice. And, just the opposite; there are people who slur their words and don't want to be articulate. As a result, any mistakes they make can be blamed on misunderstanding rather than on content.

You use your voice for everything, yet you may be unconscious of how you sound. Pretend for a minute that you are meeting the president of the United States. How do you think your voice will sound? Now pretend you are talking to a bum on the street. Again, how do you think your voice would sound? Ultimately, your voice should sound the same. It should be articulate, warm, friendly, thoughtful, and direct. Anything other than this is using the voice in a manipulative manner.

Look carefully at how you use your voice. Can you honestly say you use it with love, with compassion, with clear thinking?

Sound is very important in the growth of a yogi. As you grow spiritually, sound can be directed into the other worlds. If you are unclear in your speaking, if you use your words for self-gain, if you are scattered in your thinking and your words are confused, then you are causing chaos in the subtle worlds. If, instead, you direct your words so they are bursts of kindness, loving in content and direct in thought, then you are leaving clear, focused impressions in the subtle planes.

It is difficult to always be conscious of how you sound, but the path of a yogi is full of challenges, and the use of sound is a major one. It is better not to speak if you have only unpleasant words to say. Even in an argument, the right words said in the right tone will keep the disagreement from becoming heated and unfocused.

Remember, there are many ways to express yourself. Choosing the right words in a specific situation will guarantee a better reception from the other person. Be intelligent, be conscious of how your words can hurt or help others. Once your thoughts are expressed, they can't be taken back. Many a relationship has been broken because of the misuse of words. Even "making up" and resuming the relationship cannot take back hurtful words. They cause a hidden wound to fester. A continuation of such behavior will deepen the wound until the relationship is either broken or so altered that the initial love cannot be regained.

If you are angry with someone, wait to talk to him. It is important to be in a place of calm and clarity before approaching anyone. Confrontation is important, but only when it can be done with no anger and with words that simply state one's own feelings but do not in any way cause pain or anger in the other person. It is best to write down the points you want to discuss and have them in front of you.

Such care and patience on your part gives you time to consider just what you wish to say, so that you can express all that you are feeling without blaming the other person in any way. Remember to be in your heart and to consciously link with your Higher Self. In so doing, you can be guaranteed an open reception.

Exercise Seven:
The following is a useful exercise to do:
- *Make a list of all the people you have difficulty talking to.*
- *After each name, write the manner in which you speak to the person. For example, your spouse: You may notice that sometimes you speak to him in a loving manner, and often you become irritated and speak in an accusatory manner, etc.*
- *Next, identify the behavior in the other person or the conditions that cause you to respond in either a positive or a negative manner.*
- *Write down what you observe.*
- *Notice if the person's behavior triggers something in you that causes you to respond in a certain way.*

- *Notice also if this response occurs when you encounter similar behavior from someone else.*

Start to analyze what causes your responses.

Naturally, this is work and takes time, but the more conscious you are of how your relationships and surroundings affect the way you speak, the more you are able to change your responses.

Lastly, remember to stay focused while speaking. Everyone knows someone who goes on and on and wanders in his speech, using words to explore thoughts. This type of person is difficult to listen to and usually causes weariness in the listener. He is using speech as a way of thinking, rather than first thinking and then selecting the right words to convey a thought. Directly asking, "What do you mean?" sometimes helps such a person to become more focused.

Ask yourself, "Do I ever do this? Am I clear in my manner of expression, or do I wander around and express myself in an unclear manner?" If this is a habit of yours, ask yourself, "What do I achieve by doing this? And how is this type of speaking affecting my relationships?"

People are generally kind and will put up with someone who talks too much, yet they unconsciously avoid talking to this type of person and only do so if necessary.

Start hearing yourself from the point of view of someone you admire. Ask such people how you sound to them. Be specific. For example:

- Does my tone of voice sound firm and warm?
- Do my words convey exactly what I mean to say, or are they unclear?
- Do I articulate my words so that you can understand them?
- Do I have any words that I use all the time? (For example, do you say "I mean," "such as," "uh," or constantly clear your throat? These are words or sounds that people can use to fill a pause, and they can be distracting if they are used fre-quently.)

- Can you tell by my tone if I am feeling emotional?
- Do I sound angry, even when my words are not meant to convey that feeling? Do I sound sad when I am not expressing something I am sad about? Is there any discrepancy between the tone of my voice and the words I say?
- Do I convey words with conviction? Or do I try to sound too soft and weak when using words that are confrontational?
- Then, ask yourself, Do I believe in what I am saying? If not, why do I say it?

Analyzing speech is important if you are to be in any leadership role. It is also important in establishing loving relationships.

Lastly, ask yourself, after a conversation with someone, "Do I in any way regret what I said?" If you have regrets about what you said, this means you have spoken words that you cannot take back, words that may be hurtful, or even words that are misinformed.

When you begin to analyze your words, you will find yourself speaking less. This is fine; just don't become afraid to express yourself. Awareness is always a good thing. Listen to yourself, your patterns of speech and, most of all, to your tone of voice. The voice can always be changed; spoken words cannot. If you speak words that you regret later, be conscious of the need to apologize to the person. You cannot take back the words but you can apologize for them. Words can be weapons that can ruin relationships. Know that words should never be used to harm, but, rather, to help someone. If you genuinely want to help someone, ask for guidance in choosing the proper words.

Consider the following example of how words can lead to misunderstanding and loss.

One day an elderly woman, Sarah, went to visit Helen, a good friend of hers. Sarah's purpose for the visit was to tell Helen about a new friendship she was forming with a woman named Anna. Sarah wanted Helen to meet Anna, feeling that they could also become good friends.

When Sarah sat down with Helen, she said, "There is a wonderful woman I want you to meet. Her name is Anna. She is quickly becoming a close friend of mine because of her wonderful wit. I really love people who have a great sense of humor, and she has one of the best I've ever known."

Now Helen was a woman who had no facility with wit at all, so when Sarah said this about Anna, Helen felt judged and also jealous. Her response to Sarah was, "Wit is nice to have, but most people who have it are very superficial and not genuine."

Sarah then felt that Helen was judging Anna and also judging her, for being so taken in by someone like that. So Sarah answered, "Well, I disagree with you, and if that is the way you feel, I certainly won't bring Anna to meet you. I was going to ask you to join us on a picnic on Saturday, but now I won't."

Certainly Sarah should have chosen her words more carefully, realizing that not only was she setting up a comparison between Helen and Anna, but also was causing Helen to become defensive. Helen, in her defensiveness, said words that not only put Sarah off but caused Sarah to no longer want to make the introduction.

When there seems to be a misunderstanding like the one above, it can be helped by clarifying what is being said. If Helen had said to Sarah, "Your friend sounds very nice, but when you talk about the importance of a good wit it makes me feel you are criticizing me, because, as you know, I am lacking in what you call wit, though I enjoy it in others." Sarah, who hadn't meant to hurt her friend, could have then replied, "Helen, I'm sorry. I was in no way criticizing you. You have other wonderful qualities that are why I love your friendship."

So often hard feelings arise from words that are misdirected or misused. Look at all the conflicts in families that happen as a result of nasty words and arguments. Parents don't speak to children, children don't speak to each other. Many disputes and arguments that cause negative karma are the result of already existing negative karma brought in from past lifetimes.

If you find yourself in the middle of a family quarrel, try to stay impartial. Don't take sides or be pulled into it. It is far better to remove yourself from the scene. It's also best to try not to intervene. Listen to both parties and if there is a need, try to carefully mediate. Since you are a family member, the ones entangled may see you taking sides even if you aren't. Unfortunately, being impartial will also be viewed negatively, but it's the best action and the one that keeps you free of the karma that is being created.

In some families the karma is very difficult. If you are part of such a family it is even more important to be careful of the words you use in your interactions. Keeping your words warm even when attacked is the best course, though a difficult one.

When you are being attacked, it's important to not respond in a similar manner. I would suggest asking someone that you can both agree on to come and mediate the problem. Some issues keep coming up over and over again. It's best to say as little as possible, to stay clear and focused, and to avoid being pulled into repeated arguments. Some people cannot let go of their viewpoint. If this is the case, stop trying to make them see how you feel. Just let it go.

It's important to clearly see your karmic family ties. Know the karma and let go of it if it is mainly negative. Try to not repeat the patterns and stay tied to this karma. You can help release the karma by using loving and kind words, and by showing forgiveness and acting ethically. If defending yourself is necessary, do so, but in a positive manner. How often does a person stay hooked into a negative situation because of things done and not done? Know the pattern, and even if the other members of your family are caught in it, you can separate yourself from it and avoid repeating it.

Sometimes family karma causes strong conditioning that is carried over into other relationships. By knowing the patterns, you can see when you are continuing those patterns even when you are not with your family. Again, the words and tone of voice you use come from your family conditioning and often are carry overs from other lives.

Exercise Eight:
Make a list of the patterns (words and tones of words) that come from your family.

- *With each pattern, ask yourself, Do I play out this pattern with other people?*

Then, ask your Higher Self:
- *How can I change this pattern? What is my first step?*
- *Does this pattern come from past lives?*
- *If so, is it important for me to know the past life?*

With each pattern, you will be able to determine from where it originally came. For example, a person has a pattern of speaking in a bossy manner. This comes from a family that acts like this, but it also comes from several lifetimes of being an authority. The authoritarian manner has been brought over from those lives, and living in a family full of such types causes the person to become aware of how it feels to be on the receiving end. When this person sees this pattern in the family and in himself, he can begin to change the pattern.

Often a spiritual person is born into a family that has patterns similar to his own, patterns that are important for him to recognize in order to grow spiritually.

When members of your family speak in ways you dislike, look at yourself to see if you also have those mannerisms. What you dislike the most can be part of your makeup. For instance, if you dislike a person speaking too loudly, notice if the members of your family speak loudly. Sometimes you may find that you do the same, or you may do the opposite, speak too softly in order to compensate.

Watch discussions among family members. Are they happy or argumentative? In either case notice if you continue that pattern in your relationships. If you have children, do you talk to them in a similar manner? All of these are questions you need to ask yourself to learn how you sound to others.

With each breath there is sound, with each movement there is sound, with all that is around you there is sound. Listen to nature, listen to others, and listen to your sounds.

Chapter 2

First There Was the Word, Then There Was Vibration

In the beginning there was sound and then came vibration. We speak about energy throughout this teaching, yet energy is an abstract term denoting various states of vibration. To understand the meaning of vibration will require opening your mind to new possibilities, letting go of old concepts, and literally allowing for new definitions.

A false definition is that vibration is motion. Motion contains vibrations, but vibrations do not contain motion. Think about a bell. When a bell rings, the striker hits a surface, causing it to vibrate, which results in the sound. The motion of the striker begins the action that causes the ringing. Very specifically, motion causes the striker to hit the bell, and the vibration of the bell causes the sound to occur. Therefore, motion can cause vibration, but the vibrating bell cannot cause the striker to move.

Where there is vibration, there must be sound. Where sound exists, there must be vibration. Without either one, there is no life. Since life, which is spirit and matter, consists of sound and energy, one cannot exist without the other.

This is an important concept when you look at energy. Energy is the result of vibration. But for the vibration to occur, there must be a source. It is the source that causes the vibration that results in energy. On a microscopic level, the vibration of the atom causes fusion, which occurs as a result of the motion of millions of molecules. In an atom, motion causes vibration, which causes energy.

Why is this important to know in this teaching? Just as you must learn to listen to your words, you also need to be aware of vibrations—how they affect everything around you, how they affect you personally.

People send out vibrations all the time. These vibrations cause reactions, and these reactions cause new reactions, and so on. Clearly, the most important thing is to be in control of the source of the vibrations. If, for example, you are feeling upset or angry, the vibrations you are sending out will be very negative ones. These vibrations, in turn, can affect your house and the objects in it, certainly the people around you, as well as any plant life in the vicinity. It is important to be conscious of how your behavior affects everything around you.

If you walk into a home where there has been fighting and yelling, you can feel the heaviness of the atmosphere. This, in turn, can make you feel depressed and irritable. You can then go home and take those vibrations into your house, and so on.

It is wise to choose friends you know live in harmony, love, and peace. If they do not live harmoniously, then it is best not to be around them, unless, of course, you must because they are relatives. Even then it is important to protect yourself so that you do not bring negative vibrations home with you.

There are many ways to protect yourself from outside vibrations. Depending on your sensitivity, you can do some of the following:

1. Prepare yourself before you enter a room that may contain negativity. To prepare yourself means to cleanse your aura and make it pure. The best way to do this is by spending at least five minutes meditating. When you meditate, picture your auric field full of light. Ask that the light be enhanced so that it may become a thick shield that will keep any negative vibrations away. Anything negative will dissolve in it.

2. Use your intuition to check the room when you enter it.

3. If you feel an area is not clear or pure, then send positive thoughts toward that place. Such thoughts are vibrations that cause positive energy. This positive energy will dissolve the negative vibrations. The only exception to this is if the area has developed strong negative elementals, then it is necessary to command them to leave.

4. If there is a person or several people in the room who have negative vibrations, ask your Higher Self to build a wall between you and them so that these vibrations cannot reach you. This wall can be of mirrors or it can be a wall of steel. Ask your Higher Self to create the wall specifically for each situation.

5. If you have to work with someone with negative vibrations, it may be necessary to continually purify your space. Keep a flower in the space, and also have a bottle of rose water and spray it in the air at the end of the day. Ask the person if she is going through some difficulties. Try to help. If she simply has a negative personality, then you must put your shield up and keep it up while you are in her presence.

6. It is also wise to put your shield up when you are in a crowded place. Even if you are not very sensitive, scattered vibrations are still affecting you. Being in such an environment will make you feel very tired. Try to be aware of individuals who are sending out negative thoughts. If you are certain that someone is doing this, consciously send positive thoughts to counteract the negative ones.

With each vibration comes a counter-vibration. If the vibration is positive, then the counter-vibration will be positive; the same is true for negative vibrations. You attract like vibrations. This is why I stress learning to moderate your thoughts and words.

Now, it is important to understand what kind of vibrations you yourself are sending out. Sometimes you have no idea how much you are affecting those around you. You may think you are being silent, not doing anything, when in fact you are causing many vibrations that are literally affecting everyone in your presence. Ask yourself the following questions:

Exercise One:
1. *What kind of mood am I usually in?*
2. *If I feel tired or irritable, how do I act?*

3. *When someone bothers me, what do I think and how do I act?*

4. *If I have to do something I don't want to do, what kind of vibrations do I send out?*

5. *When I am alone, do I surround myself with nurturing thoughts and love, or do I criticize myself?*

6. *Under pressure, how do I act?*

7. *If I have to meet someone I dislike, how do I prepare myself?*

8. *With others, am I always helpful, or do I resent having to help?*

9. *When I am in a crowd, how do I respond?*

10. *When I am with my spiritual friends, do I try to love all of them?*

11. *If I am sick, do I think positively?*

12. *In spite of difficulties that I may be in, do I respond positively when confronted with even more difficulties?*

13. *With each new relationship, do I take time to understand my vibrations and also the other person's vibrations and how they interact?*

After you have answered the above questions, take time to look at how you can change any responses that you feel you need to change. Ask your Higher Self for help in this.

When working with vibrations, we often lose touch with how our reactions are affecting others. For example, you are meeting with someone who has negative vibrations. Your reaction is to protect yourself and distance yourself from the person. When you are doing this, the other person may feel your reaction and this in turn would cause a hostile response. Therefore, it is important to act in a manner that is not causing you to send out defensive vibrations.

How can you do this? First, make certain that your intuition is true, not based on your own feelings about the person. Then, when you enhance your aura, do so with the command, "May my aura be filled with light and surround and protect me from outside vibrations, and while this is happening, I send love and light to the other person so she feels only positive vibrations from me."

Whenever you encounter this person, ask yourself if she is still sending negative vibrations; you may be making a mistake in still protecting yourself. A person will sometimes be negative and, at other times, positive. This is also true of people to whom you are close. You may not be protecting yourself and suddenly feel a surge of enervating energy and not realize it is coming from your friend.

Just as a friend may be sending negative energy, remember you may also be doing the same. If, for example, you are feeling negative, make certain you protect your friends. Imagine you are dressed in a coat of armor, which none of your negative vibrations can go through. This is particularly important if you haven't had time to work through your feelings.

You are always responsible for your own vibrations. It is your karmic responsibility to always be positive. If you are feeling very negative, which also happens sometimes, it is best to avoid seeing others. When you have worked through those negative feelings, cleanse your house by burning incense or sage.

You are not perfect, and, naturally, as you deal with your lower nature, you will encounter negativity. When this happens, it is important to stay away from making important decisions and to keep clear of appointments with people toward whom you feel any animosity. Releasing negativity sometimes can be done quickly, but often it takes a few days. Keep your attitude toward the process positive. See it all as a process and don't be attached to feelings that keep you a prisoner of the lower nature. Such feelings include self-criticism, self-doubt, and feelings of being worthless.

When you encounter negative vibrations in a specific place such as a friend's house or apartment, a restaurant, a meeting hall, or even a church, remember to protect your aura and send light vibrations to the place. Light vibrations affect elementals in any surrounding. If the elementals are negative ones, they will be changed into positive ones. Consciously sending light vibrations to all the areas of a room is as effective as cleansing it with sage, a positive herb.

On occasion, you may find yourself in a situation where even

sending light will not help the emanations of a place. This is particularly true if you are in an old place where centuries of negative
vibrations have built up. For example, some of the old prisons in
Europe are full of dark elementals that are so laden with sorrow
and evil that light cannot penetrate them. The Coliseum in Rome
is such a place.

If you find yourself in such surroundings, try to leave, as the
vibrations can make you feel ill. This is also true if you are in a
home where the people are constantly fighting. The elementals
there will be very chaotic and difficult to change, particularly if the
fighting takes place all the time. If you are part of such a situation,
make certain you cleanse the place with incense or sage.

If you move into such a dwelling, you will need to paint it.
Sometimes, the vibrations are not negative, but simply those of the
previous owners. You can then cleanse the walls with solutions of
camphor and eucalyptus. If something terrible has taken place in
the dwelling, such as a murder or physical abuse, then it is best to
repaint the place. Chant mantras as you stir the paint and as you
paint the walls. Again, many old houses are full of a history of such
atrocities. If there are any dead spirits still lingering, meditate and
ask them to leave.

Follow this process when you send forth a vibration.

1. First, remember to link with your heart and your Higher
   Self.
2. Ask your Higher Self to send light vibrations through
   your heart to the receiver, whether that is a person or a
   place.
3. Then, consciously use your thoughts to direct the light
   energy.
4. Last, thank your Higher Self for doing this.

If you have a spiritual teacher, link instead with your teacher
and ask the teacher to send light vibrations through your heart.

Vibrations are comprised of many different types of forms. Just
as the molecules within different structures differ, so do the forms
within vibrations differ according to the ability of the sender and
the type of vibration needed in a given situation. The reason you

have the Higher Self or teacher do the sending is because they are tuned into the situation and know what is best needed. Discovering the various types of vibrations is part of a person's spiritual training.

Such experimentation helps to determine what constitutes the makeup of vibration. For example, if you have a small child who is acting upset, you naturally will pick up the child and hold her, soothing her and trying to find out what is the matter. The love and nurturing you are sending has a particular vibration that the child will respond to. That type of vibration is warm, gentle, and full of caring. In contrast, if you encounter a negative vibration in a room and you send light vibrations to change it, those vibrations are strong, direct, and have a penetrating quality.

Now, you may ask how you can feel the difference. It is good to ask to feel the vibration when it is happening. Ask your Higher Self during the process to help you tell the difference.

Walk in nature and ask a tree to let you feel its vibration. Place you hands in water and ask the water to let you experience its vibrations. Do the same with a flower. Everything has vibration and each is unique. You will discover that the same type of flower will have vibrations that will vary, as will the same type of tree. This is often due to their age and how they have experienced nature around them. If, for instance, one flower has grown in a sunnier place than another flower, its vibrations will be different. This is true of all plants and minerals. Animals also have specific vibrations that can be positive or negative depending on their conditioning.

Working with vibrations of any kind makes you more sensitive. As you grow more sensitive you will experience heightened awareness of your surroundings. If you feel overwhelmed in certain situations, it is important to turn off your sensitivity to the vibrations. This is not easy. It requires strong concentration. Since the key is concentration, before you begin working with vibrations, do some exercises that will help your concentration.

The following are exercises that you can try. Some may work better for you than others. Choose those that you wish to continue working with. These also will help you in your spiritual work as well as your mundane work. The first exercise should take five minutes; the others can take as long as you want.

Exercise Two:

1. *Sit in front of a flame. It can be from a candle or a fireplace. Focus your eyes on the flame and try to see the movement, the colors, and the energy of the flame. Do this for at least five minutes. As you do this, stay focused on the flame, trying to keep your mind empty of thoughts.*

2. *Take a shower. While you are in the shower, just stand and concentrate on the feeling of the water striking your skin. Imagine you are standing in a waterfall, and ask the elementals of the water to let you experience their energy.*

3. *While you are taking a bath, imagine you are sitting in a pool of water surrounded by tall trees. Try to experience the stillness of the water and, again, try to experience the water elementals.*

4. *If you are a swimmer, as you swim, try to feel your body as the body of a fish. You are moving through the water naturally, following the elementals of the water, being guided by them. Try to become one with the movement of the water and let the density and heaviness of your body disappear, making your swimming effortless.*

5. *Walk down a dirt road. Concentrate on the road just in front of your feet. As you walk and concentrate, notice the impact of your feet on the dirt. Stop and try to experience the vibrations of the impact*

6. *Sit and look at a scene. Observe the impression of the scene. Is it peaceful? Is it full of energy? Whatever the impression, try to experience it in your body.*

Some of these exercises are difficult to do. Do not be discouraged if you have no results at first. Give it time. The more you do them, the easier they become. Go through them all, and then choose a couple that you respond to most. If you don't respond to any, then keep going through them all until you begin to experience some response.

The first chapter described the meaning of sound and how it affects you in relation to others. The same is true of vibration. It affects not only you but also the people around you, even if they are unaware of the vibration. Most people are totally out of touch with vibrations, and they react to them in ways that often surprise themselves.

For example, if you play music in a room with animals, the music will affect them not so much in the way it sounds but in its vibrations. Some animals respond in a very positive way to music, whereas others respond very negatively to sound vibrations. Some animals will literally become sick when they hear high vibrations. A way of getting rid of certain animals is to simply play high-frequency instruments. They will leave the area. This is particularly true of small rodents. If you have an animal, test it for sound vibration and notice what types of music make it feel happy.

Once in a while it is good to simply sit silently and try to pick up the vibrations around you. If you are still, you can feel vibrations in the air and even in the ground. Listen, and ask your Higher Self to help you be more conscious of what type of vibration is there.

Try this at different times of the day. You will find that there are differences. This is why some people work better early in the morning or late at night. The vibrations during those times are more peaceful. This is particularly true if you live in a city. In the country, the vibrations are free of the impact of multitudes of people living in cities.

When you are aware of the vibrations around you, remember to give thanks to the elementals and ask them to keep the vibrations clear. The elementals are very much involved in vibratory work and can, in a moment, change the atmosphere. If you find yourself in very negative surroundings, ask the elementals to make the vibrations positive and creative.

When you ask the elementals to heal the vibrations, do so with great respect, letting them feel that you are grateful and interested in their methods. Ask them to keep away negative elementals and, again, always thank them. With each weather change, there will be different vibrations in the atmosphere. Always before and during a storm there are strong vibrations that can cause mood changes. Try not to allow these mood changes to happen. If you feel moody or tired, try to call on the elementals to clear up the vibrations and notice if your mood changes.

In conclusion, remember that all of life has vibrations and that it is through these vibrations that we can actually help others. Here is a hypothetical example.

Suppose a friend of yours is feeling very depressed. She lives in a small, crowded apartment and is beginning to feel that life is not worth living. If you visit this woman and experience the atmosphere as dull and somewhat off, try contacting the elementals and command them to change the vibrations. This can help your friend more than listening to her negativity. If she feels the difference in atmosphere, it will help her—maybe not at first, but in time. Sometimes it takes a few hours for the transformation to take place, so please be patient.

We each have a special vibration that is part of our essence. This is why some people feel easy to be with and others do not. The vibration you emit has a lot to do with your spiritual advancement. If you are a yogi, your vibration should be calm and soothing to those around you, unless, of course, you are in a bad mood. Then, because you are a yogi, your negative vibrations will have a very strong impact, causing people around you to feel very agitated. The reason for such a reaction from others is because your vibrations are intensified and affect the elementals far more greatly than do the vibrations of the average person.

Again, this is a responsibility of which you need to be aware. You not only affect those around you, but you develop an atmosphere in your home that is highly charged.

How can you be aware of your vibration? Simply ask your Higher Self to help you understand the kinds of vibrations you are emitting at a given time. If they are too strong or too negative or even too charged, it would be best to avoid seeing anyone until you can consciously change your vibrations to positive calm ones. Be a barometer for yourself. Determine how you affect others and carefully change your vibrations to positive ones. In time you will intuitively know and will be able to change your vibrations automatically. This should become a daily practice.

When you work with vibrations, remember to be certain you are feeling healthy and strong. If you have a particularly sensitive system, it is best to proceed slowly and cautiously. When you follow the proper precautions, you are more apt to have success. If you are not certain about your physical condition, try letting go of any portions of this work that you sense are too demanding, until you are certain you can handle them.

When there electric storms, do not do any of this work. The elementals are very involved in the chaos of the atmosphere and therefore cannot deal with you. You can work with elementals before and after an electric storm, but not during.

Also let go of any preconceived ideas about the work. If you are totally open to doing this work you need to also be very flexible. Things can transform in an instant, so be prepared for sudden changes.

Chapter 3

After the Word and Vibration Came the Light

Every time you look at the sun, you not only experience the brightness of its rays but you also bring the energy of its light into your essence. Light is the strongest component of your body. The body is comprised of matter, which is encased in light. Science has not discerned this aspect of your physical makeup. Every molecule and every cell contains light energy, and this light energy comes directly from the sun.

How does this happen? How is it possible that the sun's energy is part of your cells and is instrumental in your physical well-being? The occult law states, "You are made up of all the elements: water, air, earth, and fire, and these elements are, in turn, composed of energy that is from light." Remember, energy comes from the Higher Sources and contains all the properties that are the basis of human life. When the life force leaves the body, the body dies and decays. The elements then return to their Source and the light energy returns to the sun.

The ancient religions worshiped the sun as the greatest of the gods. In many ways they were correct in their belief in the sun's great powers. As a ball of fiery energy, the sun truly directs the life of nature on this planet. Its light power is the source of the life force of the mineral, plant, and animal evolutions.

Whether we are aware of it or not, the sun's energy affects our daily moods, our emotions, our bodily functions, and those elements in our system that need balancing.

Ill people often want to lie in the sun, and when they do so, they feel better. Elderly people prefer living in sunny places because the sun revivifies them. In countries with little sunlight in winter months, there is more depression, more suicides, and more drug and alcohol abuse than in countries that have sunlight at least seven hours a day.

At this time, science has little understanding of the real properties of the sun. The sun's light rays contain energy that differs from the psychic energy of the body, which is composed of the fire elements. Light energy from the sun is more connected to the spirit and is the force that, on a subtle level, constitutes the properties of the subtle body. It is refined energy that is rarely detected; yet it provides a sense of inner vitality that, again, differs from the type of vitality that psychic energy produces.

For example, if you are walking in the sun, you feel warmth that is physical, and you also feel warmth that comes into your heart. Notice this, and notice the difference between the two.

The physical warmth is coming from the penetrating rays from the sun and, of course, it is important to protect yourself from too much exposure; but the warmth in your heart comes from the light energy that both penetrates the body and enhances the spirit. When you begin to work with the light energy, the process is very subtle, but the more you work with it, the more intense it can become.

Exercise One:
1. *Take a walk and, during the walk, stand in a place that is full of sunlight. As you stand in the light, experience how this feels.*
2. *Ask your Higher Self to let you experience the sun's light energy and ask to feel it within your body.*
3. *Next, go to a place where there is no sunlight and try to experience how this place feels. Again ask your Higher Self to help you discern the difference between the two.*

Try this several times and each time ask to experience the feelings even more. After several tries, you should begin to have some very profound experiences. These experiences are all related to taking in the light energy. When you feel you have achieved this, do the following exercise.

Exercise Two:
When you meditate, ask your Higher Self to let you experience the
light energy again. This time try using the energy in the following
manner:

1. *Feel the energy in your heart and ask to be able to send*
   it to your left arm, then to your right arm, and then to
   other parts of your body. Experience this, and notice if
   the energy feels different in different areas.

2. *Ask your Higher Self how you can begin to utilize the*
   light energy in your daily life. Take the answer and try
   to do what you were given. If the answer is too abstract,
   go back to your Higher Self and ask for more details and
   some steps. Keep working with this. If you are in a group,
   share what you received and experiment with each oth-
   er's processes after you have worked on your own.

3. *As you work with the light energy, with each exercise you*
   should find that the energy becomes more discernible.
   It should differ from person to person, but each person
   should notice that it is becoming stronger. Do not be dis-
   couraged if at first you feel nothing. This energy is very
   refined and not the obvious energy you experience in
   your body and in meditation. It has its own properties
   that are different from what you might expect.

Let's look now at the meaning behind light, what it represents, and what it offers humanity. First, in the ancient traditions, light was a positive force opposed to darkness, which was considered a negative force. With each century, the meaning of light and dark has changed, yet the basic ingredients have remained the same. When you think about light, you think about beauty, you think about Higher Beings, you think about all the abundance of nature, of joy in life. When you think about darkness, you think about slumber, rest, solitude, illness, sadness, and all the negative beings and forces. Essentially, all of this is true, but there are also other areas to be explored that contain these opposites—areas that are not associated with positive and negative forces.

With the advent of civilization as we know it, there came into being a dividing line between good and evil. Light represented the good; dark, the evil. Religion codified this concept of good and evil, and this codification, even today, exists in certain religions. In the higher worlds there is no good or evil, yet there is light and darkness, and both are essential to evolution. Light in the higher worlds contains the spiritual principle. Darkness in the higher worlds relates to the principle of a constantly expanding and retracting universe.

They both also relate to the Manvantara and the Pralaya (eons-long periods of activity and inactivity). During the former, light illuminates the planet as it evolves. During the latter, darkness prevails during the planet's periods of rest and regeneration. In the higher worlds, there are no negative forces; they can only operate in the physical and astral worlds. Therefore, light and darkness in the higher planes are complementary and are important in the evolution of the planet. Do not mistake darkness as always representing negative forces.

When you begin to work with light in meditation, you will also encounter darkness, and, depending on where you are in your spiritual development, the darkness can be an interesting passageway to explore.

The qualifications are that you must understand your level of consciousness and know that you must always ask to see light if some being speaks or appears to you.

Many times a person will ask to see light, but, instead, will see a color. Since light must be present for a color to glow, a brilliant color is usually an indication that you are listening to a positive force. Be assured that you will encounter negative beings when you meditate. That is normal for any striving spiritual person. Therefore, it is very important to demand to see light, and if you see color instead, to make certain that the color is luminous. Even having seen this, it is also very important to put the information that you were given into your heart and ask your Higher Self if this information is truth.

Light in the subtle world contains magnetic properties coming from the sun and is full of the sun's true essence. When the light is perceived as color, it is always luminous and brilliant, strikingly beautiful and full of vitality. When you have this experience in meditation, simply allow yourself to float in it and through it. Often the color will change. Just allow that to happen. When you can do this without distraction or thoughts coming in, you will experience the tranquil beauty of light. It gives you a deep sense of inner peace. Your soul rests in the light like a baby in the arms of a loving mother.

Don't be afraid to go further in exploring the light and, if the light leaves, to explore the darkness. Often there will be darkness and then brilliant color and then darkness again. Don't give up if you see darkness again. Keep going and, usually, more light will come.

In meditation, light comes from the sun, not the physical sun as you see it during the day, but the hidden sun, the sun of the subtle world, or what is called "the Sun behind the sun." It is basically the subtle body of the physical sun and produces light in a similar way, except this light will never burn you. It is the light of the higher worlds, the light of the Eternal Flame of Hierarchy, of the Guardians of humanity, of the Forces that shine Their essence onto humanity with love and benevolence

In recent times, more people are actively meditating. This has caused a change on the subtle plane and has made the higher worlds more accessible. There are several ways you can access these worlds.

First, you must be in good condition and not have aches and pains or other distractions that will affect your concentration. When you start to meditate, check throughout your body to see if there is some disturbance. If there is, simply breathe into it and let it go. See it as a cloud leaving your body and disappearing into the sky. If you have a permanent condition that causes distress in the body, spend more time on the above procedure, and also if you have a teacher, ask your teacher to take the pain away during your meditation.

Next, when you feel free of any disturbance and can be really focused, try to meditate and go into the subtle plane. Concentrate on your third eye and actively try to see with it. If you begin to see color, focus on it and imagine you are going through it and up. Continue this process even if you encounter darkness again. This is the beginning phase of trying to reach the Higher Planes of the subtle world. Be aware that it won't happen at once. It takes constant practice.

When you find you are in a realm of brilliant color, just feel that color expanding upward and outward and continue going with it.

The next stage is to begin to see images or hear voices. If there is darkness again, always ask to see light, and, if you don't see light, tell the images or voices to leave. If you see light, then carefully record what you have received. Put the information in your heart and feel if it is true. The feeling in the heart should be an instant knowing. If you have any questions at all about the truth of the experience, then simply write down the information so that you can check on its accuracy. If you have a teacher, you should check all of this information with him or her.

Exercise Three:
- *Draw for yourself an illustration of a symbol and color it. For instance, it can be a six-pointed star or a triangle or even a rose. Pick something that has meaning for you.*
- *Look at the illustration. Really focus on it. Now, close your eyes and ask to see the color in your mind's eye. Then open your eyes and again look at the color in the illustration. Keep doing this until you can see the color internally.*

When color from the subtle world can been seen physically, then you know you have developed a particular ability that is associated with clairvoyance. It is the ability to see into the subtle world with your eyes open. This is a particular type of clairvoyance that is related to the colors of the subtle world.

Working with symbols can help develop this ability, as symbols are always associated with color. Frequently, you may see a color on the subtle plane that you cannot identify. It is so extraordinary in hue that it is unlike any color you have seen on the physical plane. It is all relative. Humans have a prism of colors that is part of their ocular perception. Animals have an even more limited perception of color, so naturally, as you evolve, your ability to see other colors also becomes more refined.

When you see colors from the higher worlds, you are opening the door to developing this ability.

In working with color, always take the time to allow it to slowly materialize. It will not happen if you are not concentrating or if you are distracted in any way. It is necessary to use your will and your heart's desire in order to succeed in this work. These two qualities are essential for working with colors or any other process that requires focus.

Too often, people think they should be achieving a certain stage of development without realizing that it's not about being given something, but that it's about striving to the place where it can be easily accessible. Usually, people give up the practice if they are not "given" something right away. Try to remember it's important to constantly strive upward; only then can Higher Beings contact you and help you go further.

When a student gives up too soon, teachers feel it shows a lack of desire to grow spiritually. It's sad when this happens. Even students who have achieved a great deal will often give up or take long breaks because of mundane activities. Lack of responsibility is the cause of this behavior. Responsibility to oneself is the key to spiritual striving. When the work is stopped, or given up temporarily, it is usually because the individual has encountered parts of his lower nature and that influence has prevailed. It is important to stay vigilant to prevent this from happening. Sometimes a student will say, "If I don't make it in this life, I have other lives ahead which will give me that opportunity."

This is a wrong assumption. Such an attitude would, instead, cause the soul to have a much more difficult time achieving spiritual growth in a future life, particularly if his dharma were to attain spiritual initiations in the present life. The karmic consequences would add to those feelings of lack of striving. Every life that is added to the progression of a soul only takes away from the evolutionary ascent. So often someone has the potential to achieve the highest and, instead, chooses to fall behind. Teachers can help anyone who is willing to strive, but they can no longer help those who have given up.

Light is the essence of striving. When you are striving, the light of your aura becomes luminous. It shines forth and not only reaches you but is also felt by others. If the others are friends, then they benefit from the energy. If the others are enemies who want to kill the light, then the battle to achieve more spiritually takes place. Remember to be aware that lack of striving brings negative thoughts: self-criticism, criticism of others, lack of concentration, and, most often, a lassitude about life.

You can resist this downward spiral by remembering that you have the source of light within your heart. When you feel a lack of striving, simply link with your heart and call on your Higher Self to help you come back to your true Self and bring back light energy.

Try to visualize the energy as a rainbow of colors. Feel the light, feel the colors coming from your heart. Hold fast to them and keep them active. If the light and colors leave and you feel heaviness set in, battle that with your will. Use your will energy to refuse to listen to any negative thoughts. Keep vigilant when you are feeling drawn away from your light. The source of light is constant, but you must activate it with your will.

Again, remember that the light is always there. It is within your spirit. It is within your heart. It is correct to want it flowing through you all the time. Light is our source of creativity, the inspiration to create, and the means to manifest the creative work. It is closely aligned to God Consciousness and it brings you happiness, joy, love, all the beauty of the subtle world, and all the beauty of the physical world.

The following are some exercises that will help you develop your ability to maintain a state of striving

Exercise Four:
  1. Take time every day to look at nature. Even if it is for

only fifteen minutes, simply take the time to be aware and see the beauty of nature with your heart. If you live in a city and have very little nature around you, then buy flowers or a plant and sit and look at it without thoughts. Appreciate the beauty of its form.

2. *Begin each day by setting one or two goals that you know you can complete. Make certain that the goal or goals are not too much or too complicated for you to do. Your goal may simply be to clean your house or start a project. If you are working on a project, give yourself a reasonable goal in the continuation of the project. At the end of the day, check to see if you completed your goal. If you have, feel happy about it and praise yourself and let yourself feel good that you completed the goal. If you didn't fulfill it, look at what happened without self-criticism. Perhaps you set yourself too large a goal to finish. The next day, do the same and adjust the amount you need to do. If you completed the goal, you may want to see if you could add to it the next day, but only do so if you know you will still be able to do the work.*

3. *If you need to do spiritual work, such as meditation, reading, etc., make certain that those tasks are part of your daily goals. If you miss a morning meditation, be certain you make it up later in the day, even if it's for five minutes. Plan the spiritual tasks as part of your routine, to be done at specific times of the day.*

4. *When you sit down to do your work, try dedicating the work to your teacher or Master, if you have one, or any of the teachers and Masters you feel close to. Their light will help you in your work.*

5. *Finally, at the end of the week, look back and assess what you have accomplished. Did you complete your daily work? If so, how has that affected the outcome of the week? If you didn't complete the daily goals, how did that affect the outcome of the week? Look at what obstacles came up to stop you. Check with your Higher Self about*

what the obstacles are and the steps you need to take to overcome them, so that they don't impede you in the week ahead.

6. *Remember to be positive about yourself, send positive thoughts to others, and ask for the help you need to stay on track.*

When you work with these exercises, be aware of your Higher Self. Always keep pulling It down into your heart, bringing It into your consciousness. Remember, you are striving to be one with your Higher Self. It is imperative that you have this goal in mind at all times. Create a symbol or a saying that you keep near you to remind you that this is your goal. The more you use the Higher Self in all parts of your life, the sooner you will succeed. You will experience a definite difference between when you work with the Higher Self and when you fail to do so.

In the beginning there was light. I have described various characteristics of its energy, but there is another aspect of light that needs clarification. Light is spirit energy, but it also relates to the subtle body. Spirit light governs the auric field and is affected by the subtle body that receives and reflects back the energy of light. I will explore the concept of the subtle body in another chapter, but for now it is important to realize that all the higher forms of existence are governed by light energy.

Where there is light, there is color and sound. All three are the bases for existence on this planet, all three are needed for spiritual growth, all three constitute the pure essence of the Higher Self, and all three reveal God.

Chapter 4

When Humans Were Formed

The existence and makeup of humans have yet to be delineated properly. *The Secret Doctrine* by Blavatsky talks about the Origins in concepts closer to the truth. Even this present book has omitted information about the Origins that the planet is not yet ready to understand. The makeup of human beings is one of the concepts to be explained.

Most people see physical men and women in a definite form that differs only with age, skin color, and physical features. Yet, how many of us see man and woman in their true form?

With each generation, there are physical changes. For example, in the Middle Ages men and women were much smaller in size. Also, there was a race of giants living on the planet thousands of years ago. If you start wondering about physical humans of today, realize that the current form is the result of a minute period of time in the longevity of humankind's existence on the planet. If you ask people what they think men and women will look like a thousand years from now, most would say they will look the same, possibly taller, that's all. However, the shape of the primitive person's head is very different from a modern person's, so why wouldn't you believe that at a future time we will not only be different looking, but may have radically changed in our physical shape and form?

Why is it important to understand that thousands of years in the future we will look radically different? How can this knowledge in any way help you spiritually? What good does any of this accomplish?

These are questions that many of you will be asking, questions that obviously come from a lack of understanding of man and woman and the concept of evolution. For example, some good questions would be: Why must humans go through physical changes? Why does evolution produce species of any kind that transform from one shape into another? Does the new shape relate in any way to the evolution of the planet? If so, how does it relate, and again, why must the evolution of the planet involve going through physical changes?

To begin, let's look at the planet itself. Originally, it was composed of huge areas of water surrounding much smaller land areas. As the planet evolved, the land shifted and formed continents, which in turn submerged and shifted into new formations. Our present formation will also change and shift in the future due to volcanic eruptions, earthquakes, and climate change. To see what this planet will look like five thousand years in the future would be shocking to most of you. Continents will no longer look the same, islands will have sunk back into the oceans, new islands will emerge, and some land that has never been connected will have land bridges to other land. Some of this future, although not all of it, is known by the Masters, and what they can see is fascinating.

Again, why does this happen? Why do planets change? We know that nature is constantly changing, but why does change need to happen? If we look at anything in nature, whether it is a plant formation, an insect, or an animal, we see that some species die off and others remain and go through some physical transformation.

The basic idea underlying the evolutionary theory of "the survival of the fittest" is mostly true, but rather than being based on what is known to be the best or "fittest" of the species, it is based on another, unknown element. This element is spoken of in esoteric schools as "the evolution of a seed strain." When a species seems to die out, it, in fact, does not die, but transfers its seed to another species that it can relate to. The seed is similar to the DNA in humans in that it contains specific life forms of energy.

When an animal species becomes extinct, it too transfers its seed to another animal species, different in appearance but similar in characteristics. This latent seed in an animal will produce, over time, a new type of animal that has characteristics of both the transferred seed and the new animal form. For example, a dinosaur seed is part of an animal that, unknown to scientists, eventually produced the antelope.

When the large mammals existed, their cohabitants on the planet were the giant races. Since the population was sparse, these larger species could exist. As the planet became more populated, members of species became smaller, primarily so they would take up less space.

Humans now occupy most of the land formations. The animal kingdom, as well as nature itself, is taking up less and less space and also decreasing in types and in numbers. This, too, is part of the planet's evolution, and thousands of years in the future much of the animal kingdom as we know it will no longer exist. Most people consider this a decline of our civilization whereas it is part of destined evolution.

If the animal kingdom is meant to decline, then humans must also be subject to the same outcome. Humanity, as we know it, will not exist in the future. This does not mean the consciousness of a person will die. It, similar to the animal seed, will be transferred to another, emerging form where it will continue its evolutionary path.

The seed of a human being I am referring to here is called the Monad. The Monad contains the higher principles and has attached to it the skandhas (attributes from previous lives), which carry the individual characteristics of the evolving human. The seed of the spirit, which is within the Monad, is the fiery energy that propels the soul or individuality to evolve.

These changes must take place, as they are part of the Cosmic Principles. All of nature, from the glaciers to the lowest insect, goes through metamorphosis. It is a universal principle that spirit/matter is constantly in motion, is constantly taking on new forms, and is constantly evolving as it returns to its Source.

In the centuries to come, there will be distinct changes in the human form. As it continues to undergo physical changes, there will be a definite change in its connection to the subtle body. Most of humanity will begin to experience the subtle world and become familiar with nature spirits. Many of the so-called New Agers will become part of society and influence the political scene. In general, the world will be comprised of nations that are fully developed and are bringing their influence to bear on those nations that are lagging behind. Democracy will be the primary system within these nations, yet even democracy will take on new meaning and change its form.

The major physical changes on the planet in the coming period will not be as drastic as has been predicted.

Along with the above changes, there will be new scientific developments that will have the potential to cure some major illnesses. These cures will raise human longevity to much higher numbers.

Unfortunately, war will continue well into the middle of this century. The prediction that we will be in an age of peace that will last for two thousand years is still correct, but the full beginning of that age will not take place until the year 2055. At that time, those nations still at war with each other will go through radical transformations.

People will continue to grow spiritually. Some will be open about it, others will not, and of course there will still be an esoteric branch in most religions.

Looking at humanity in all its aspects, it's important to realize how humans have changed and evolved throughout the centuries. From a materialistic viewpoint, humans have developed the means to live well, receive an education, and plan for a family. Much has happened in the past five hundred years. Humans have come through the changes ignorant of why these changes took place at all.

If you look at the animal kingdom, you will find very little change in the past five hundred years. This is because most of the animal kingdom belongs to group souls. The exceptions are domesticated animals such as cats, dogs, and horses. These have individualized and have a separate monad, but even domesticated animals contain aspects of their group of origin. In the beginning of evolution, humans were not physical in the sense of having a touchable physical form. When humans began their evolution, they were simply forms composed of changing matter. Changing matter can best be described as form in which light moves and breathes. Because the light source is in constant motion, the form itself is also in constant change.

Think of matter that is luminous with the light contained inside radiating through. The next stage of evolution consisted of such luminous forms. Subsequently, in the next evolutionary period, form was no longer luminous but instead held the light within a dense blanket of matter. This form resembled a being with very white skin that had a luster or glow. From this form, the physical went through many changes, resulting in a gross body form covered with hair, like the animals. Then, over the centuries, the body changed to what we have today.

As we move forward in time, we will begin to experience a reversal of the process. Slowly, we will evolve from the present body to a more luminous one until we finally reach the original body of pure spirit and light. We will no longer have to descend into the gross body, as we are evolving upward. The gross body is at the lowest physical stage, which need not be repeated.

During the entire process of human evolution, one thing remains constant: the ability to change. This ability distinguishes us from the animal kingdom. Change in humans is constant and proceeds in many different ways.

One way, of course, is through the physical body. Another is in our psychological makeup, and a third, in our capacity to grow spiritually. There are stages of evolution in all three areas, and all are involved in the conditioning that produces change.

If, for example, you have had many years of experience laying tiles, then you will be able to do this work very quickly and efficiently. If, on the other hand, you have limited experience doing this work, you will of course be less productive and efficient. Experience causes change, and change enriches experience.

After laying tiles for many years, if you begin to install wooden floors, although it may be a new task, your work ethic and knowledge will help you learn to do the new work more quickly than someone without your experience.

In general, people learn through experience and change.

The advent of technology has provided new experiences that are altering how people do things. A child today has skills that many adults do not have, and those children will, in turn, have children who will learn even more advanced methods of working.

During these changes, it is important to keep the striving soul stable. Stability comes from self-knowledge, and self-knowledge comes from looking within to learn and understand how change is affecting your spiritual being. If you are always aware of the right goal, then it is easier to accept the changes that will most definitely occur around you and within your own field of work.

The journey is difficult, and there are many roads that can take you off the path. Remember, it is always possible to travel the path focused and open to change if you can simply keep your Higher Self constantly at your side. Otherwise, the temptations will pull you in many directions that keep you from growing. You need to be vigilant, to be aware of how these changes are affecting your everyday life. See them as positive and see them as the only way you can move forward.

Keep the past, the person that you were, in a place of observation. Learn from the past, but do not go backward. See the goal in front of you, and that the only way to achieve it is to go through changes, good ones and difficult ones. Within each change is the seed of karma, and you must recognize the karma and pass through it.

When you can do this, you will no longer dwell on past mistakes and hurts but instead will see them simply as experiences you needed in order to end old karma and go forward. It would be helpful to do the following exercise.

Exercise One:
1. *Ask your Higher Self: Is there anything in the past of this life that I am still hanging onto?*
   - *If the answer is yes, ask: What is it? How do I let it go?*
2. *Look at your present life and ask your Higher Self: What are the changes I need to go through to grow spiritually?*

- *Then ask: When will these changes begin, and how do I accept them happening?*

3. *Ask your Higher Self: What blocks do I have that will keep me from being open to the changes that will be happening to me?*
   - *Then ask: How do I overcome these blocks?*
4. *Ask your Higher Self: When I go through change, how can I receive the most benefit from it happening, even when the change seems negative?*

When changes take place in your life, write them down and try to understand how they are affecting you on the three levels, the physical, the psychological, and the spiritual. If the changes are negative ones, such as a loss of a loved one or a friend, ask how to let go of the feelings connected to the loss. Be aware that even when there is a loss, there can be spiritual growth, and of course, spiritual growth is the most powerful and the most rewarding change of all.

If a change is going to take you away from spiritual growth, it is important to question if it is necessary. Every change should have spiritual growth connected to it. If it doesn't, then it's important to question and try to prevent this change from happening. For example, you may be involved in a relationship that is psychologically painful. This could be either a positive growth experience or, if you are in a victim relationship, a negative one. In the latter case, the positive growth would be to leave the relationship, or to stop being the victim by creating change with the person involved. Mostly, it is important to remember humanity has potentials, but it is up to each individual to work with those potentials and make them realities.

With each change, there comes a definite direction in which to move. The direction is determined by your free will. Free will is the ability to take the change and use it positively in order to enhance your spiritual growth. If you use free will to avoid the changes and to go in a different direction, you unfortunately lose the opportunity that will carry you toward more changes that will help you grow further. For example, if a person is destined to develop spiritually and instead chooses to live a life of excesses, then the karma created by the excesses will keep her from growing spiritually, not only in this lifetime, but in future ones.

When you use free will to follow your destiny, that will help you achieve more. For instance, going back to the example of a negative relationship in which you are being victimized, you need your free will to say no to the karma and leave. Your destiny may be that you must be in the relationship to pay off karma, but your free will can break the karma and you need not remain in a karmic pattern with the victimizer. Free will allows you to make choices, some good and some bad or difficult. You may be destined to be with someone for a time, but remaining in an abusive relationship only produces new karma that keeps the wheel going around.

Exercise Two:
Ask your Higher Self: Do I use my free will correctly?
  • *If not, how do I change this?*

When a person follows her destiny and uses free will to augment this process, then that person is truly following the path toward God Consciousness. If you can be aware at all times of how often you use free will adversely, then you can begin to develop discrimination.

Using discrimination on the path is a major method of growth. To use it correctly is to have the wisdom to understand how the lower nature can play with your free will to take you off the path. It is always important to ask yourself, "What have I done today to use my free will?" And then ask, "Have I used my free will to help me grow spiritually?"

These are the kind of questions that will make you actively aware of when you are being influenced by your lower nature or the negative forces.

With discrimination, you can look at the changes in your life and determine whether or not they will help you grow spiritually. Remember, these changes can have consequences that result in karma. Make certain those consequences will bring you positive karma or eliminate some old negative karma.

In other words, welcome the changes, but always question if they are necessary and what you need to learn in the process. Make any change a positive one that results in furthering your understanding of yourself, helping you to learn something new.

Knowledge is part of change. Let knowledge accompany your desire to grow. Many people embark on a spiritual path only to go off in another direction because they lacked the ability to see change as positive. Often, when a person's life is disturbed by change, she cannot accept the change and decides to remain the same, letting the opportunity pass by. How many opportunities have you missed because it would require change in your life?

Exercise Three:
Ask your Higher Self: Have I been aware of the opportunities that have been given to me in the past year?
- *If not, what were the opportunities?*
- *Did they relate to my making changes that would have been hard for me to accept?*

Continue to see life as a series of changes happening on the three levels, physical, psychological, and spiritual. Evolution requires that you go through many changes in every lifetime. Accept them with an open awareness. See them as part of your spiritual growth. Ask that you be given the changes that can help you the most. Recognize it is never too late to change, never too late to grow, never too late to transform. To be a yogi is about accepting change.

Change is opportunity. How can you use change, even a negative one, as an opportunity? Obviously, any change will cause you to go through emotional disturbances, but can you disidentify from the emotions and be clear-sighted?

With the advent of telecommunication, there is ample opportunity to reach out to thousands of resources that can help you research places that are new to you.

For instance, if you have to move to another location, one you are not familiar with, you can discover through specific computer searches exactly how many people live in the area, where the shopping centers are, what companies exist there, and even how many schools there are and the specific courses those schools offer. In a very short time you can become familiar with your new location, even before you make the actual move.

With so many resources right at your fingertips, how is it possible to feel isolated in any way? Being alone is a very important part of spiritual growth. When loneliness becomes a fear, then you lose the opportunity to benefit from what being alone can offer. Many times people will allow such fear to drive them into relationships that are incompatible with who they are, especially if they are spiritually striving.

Our society looks upon living alone as terrible, antisocial, and, in the extreme, a situation of absolute rejection, whereas being alone can be a very important opportunity to discover the inner you.

Usually, all of us must be alone during some portion of our life. Those who see this as an opportunity will enjoy the experience; those who hold it as a fear will spend countless hours busying themselves with outside resources. These people will not even try to use the opportunity to expand their consciousness.

There are many causes for this fear. The primary one is the fear of facing yourself, of truly seeing who you are. This particular fear goes back many lifetimes to a fear that is part of the evolutionary path. Always at some juncture on the spiritual journey, it is necessary to face yourself, with no outside forces interfering in the process. If you have fears around this, then you will lose the opportunity that such facing of self offers for freedom and moving forward on the path.

Human nature has many different twists and turns. Some can cause suffering and pain, others can be full of joy and fulfillment. How can a person use these trials as an opportunity? Each person must define this for herself.

The one process that helps in personal growth is to step back from what is happening, even if you are full of emotion, and observe the circumstances as if you are a third person. To see anything from afar is to see truth. Truth only becomes cloudy when you are ensnared in emotions. Realize that it is far wiser to observe than to jump into any given situation.

Observation helps you to be open to change, to see new solutions, and to benefit from what is happening.

Usually when an opportunity appears, it is important to take advantage of it right away; otherwise it is lost. In rare instances, the same opportunity will present itself to you again, and it is important to recognize what is happening and act on it.   Unfortunately, most people go through life missing opportunity after opportunity without ever realizing what they have lost.

Exercise Four:
1. *Ask your Higher Self: When an opportunity is given to me, do I see it and act on it?*
   - *If the answer is yes, ask for a recent example of that happening.*
2. *Then ask: How can I always be aware of opportunities?*
   - *If the answer is no, ask: How can I improve my awareness when an opportunity is presented to me?*
3. *Also ask: What are my blocks around this?*
4. *Finally ask: How do I overcome my blocks?*
   - *What are the first steps to do this?*

When you see how often you have missed an opportunity, you will begin to realize how much the human condition has interfered with evolution. Humanity still has a long way to develop, and if you neglect to see change as opportunity for growth, then the evolutionary path will take much longer than needed.

Chapter 5
Letting Go of Old Concepts

If I tell you a story that is very important for your spiritual growth, will you listen to it and take from the story the real meaning and then make that meaning part of your life? Similarly, if I ask you to do a mission that would be of service to others, will you do it without question? In both instances, your answer might be "maybe."

There are no "maybes" in a spiritual teaching. Maybe is a watered-down "no." Maybe keeps you in a place where you don't have to make a decision. Making final decisions can seem very difficult. It requires letting go of the other existing possibilities and committing to the decision. Of course, you can then change your mind, but to do so is unacceptable in a spiritual teaching. Changing your mind can be likened to the maybes. It evades the responsibility of dealing with the choice you have made.

Unfortunately, the human condition looks upon decision making as a difficult task when, in actuality, it can be the easiest thing to do. If, for example, you are asked to run an errand, you can easily answer yes or no. If instead you think about it and can't decide whether or not to do it, then you are spending excessive time thinking about it, time that could have been spent running the errand.

How easy it would be to devote five or ten minutes to making a decision and then to follow through. If you have made the wrong decision, you learn from it; if it is the right one, you have quickly advanced.

Life is about making decisions, some wrong, some right. It's the thinking about a decision that is the waste of time. It's the ruminating about it, pro and con, that is the waste of time. Naturally, it is wise to spend a given amount of time linking with the heart and using your intuition, but then act upon what you decide. When you do this, you are using the feminine and masculine principles in a balanced way.

In our daily work life, we are forced to make decisions, but how rarely we apply this principle to our personal life, particularly if these decisions revolve around relationships. What causes this type of scattered behavior? Why can't we function in the same way with our loved ones as we do in our work life? What is it that weakens our inner resolve? What keeps us from behaving in a precise and concentrated manner?

Women will say, "Well, that's part of being feminine; women always have a hard time making up their minds." Men will say, "It's rare when I can't make a decision," yet they will overanalyze and procrastinate to almost the same extreme as women. Generally, men will think it out, and women will feel it out. Of course, these roles are often reversed and you will find a woman who is overly analytical and a man dominated by emotions. In both cases, when decisions must be made, time is wasted.

Let's experiment some more with this issue. If I ask you to pick a color, can you do so without thinking about three colors? If I ask you to not think about a person, can you do this? Probably not. If this is the case, then we must realize that something happens to the mind when we direct it to perform a given task. It doesn't do what we ask it to do. It also keeps us from decision making. Why do our minds sabotage us?

In looking at these questions, we can see there is an underlying lack of commitment. The human condition is very alienated from commitment. Why is commitment so frightening to people?

If you view your life as a procession of events and see that each event comes about as a result of outer circumstances and inner decision making, then you can begin to understand how your old patterns affect the way you move through life.

By going to the source of these patterns, you can discover the root cause of the way you cope with the events in your life. Unfortunately, most people go through their lives living out their patterns with no awareness. This is why it is so difficult to change patterns of any kind. They are like habits that have been repeated so many times that they become part of the response mechanism.

The following exercises should help you become more aware of these patterns.

Exercise One:
1. *Ask your Higher Self:*
   - *When I decide to do something, does it take me longer than necessary to reach that decision?*
   - *If the answer is yes, ask: Is there a reason for me to take longer than necessary to make up my mind?*
   - *If the answer is no, ask: Is there anything I need to do that I am not doing in my decision making?*
2. *If you were given a yes answer in the above exercise, continue with the following:*
   - *Taking the reason given, look at it carefully and try to analyze whether you do this all the time, some of the time, etc. Then, notice if there is a pattern that occurs in your decision making.*
3. *If there is a pattern, ask your Higher Self:*
   - *Is there a root cause or a core belief that is activating this pattern? If so, what is it?*
4. *Again, if this is a yes and you have the root cause, ask your Higher Self:*
   - *Does this root cause come from childhood conditioning or does it come from past lives?*

When you have achieved full awareness of your pattern, you then need to begin the process of overcoming this pattern. Start with:

Exercise Two:
Ask your Higher Self:
   - *Give me a process that will help me change this pattern.*
   - *Ask for a first step, and follow it.*

It is also important to do a nightly review to determine if you are catching yourself in the pattern and changing it.

Doing the above is not going to be easy. Remember, any conditioned pattern takes time to change, so do not be discouraged if you are still not aware of the pattern until after you have acted it out.

When you feel you have mastered the pattern of how you respond to making decisions, then it is time to look at the many areas in your life where you need to make decisions.

Everyone has cloudy issues, issues that are gnawing away at emotions that have never been resolved. The importance of making decisions around these issues is primary in any spiritual teaching. To grow spiritually requires discipline, and an unresolved issue breaks down discipline. Remember, it is very important to make a choice, whether it is right or wrong.

If it turns out to be wrong, look at your decision-making process. Did you really think it out correctly? Did you take the time to list all the pros and cons of the given situation, work with the lists using both your mind and heart, and then decide? Or, did you quickly come to a decision without going through this process? Was your resolution coming out of your desire body instead of your heart? These are major ways in which decision making can have negative consequences.

Often you will make a choice based on karma. Again, it is important to understand if this was a factor in the decision-making process. All of the above can still be accomplished quickly in one sitting. It does not require days or weeks of contemplation. This is also true of major decisions you make in life. If you proceed with precision and discipline you can take the most difficult circumstances and make the correct determination without a lot of effort.

Often a person will avoid making a decision that he thinks will harm or hurt another person. Rather than avoid acting, it is important to decide the best and kindest way to carry out your decision. Naturally, karma is involved in this to a large extent. If your decision is going to cause negative karma, then you probably have made the wrong determination. It might be necessary to plan things in a way that will negate the karmic ramifications.

For example, if you are in a negative relationship and you want to end it while the other person wants to continue, then you may have to make concessions that allow the separation to occur more gently. A couples therapist can clarify issues and help both people realize that separation may be the best solution. If both people agree and can part as friends, then, of course, no negative karma will result.

Always, when your decision making involves someone else, you must consult with the person and bring him in as part of the process. If the other person has trouble making decisions, then you must be firm in planning deadlines, always giving the person a little more time. You can also help the person by asking questions that will help clarify some of the more nebulous issues that cause indecision.

One of the main causes of a pattern of procrastination comes from old feelings embedded in your skandhas. These feelings can come from past lives and have no real significance in this life, yet you may still be conducting your life based on these old concepts.

For example, if you were a military man in a past life and were very rigid in your daily routine, you may have the tendency to be overly rigid and fanatical in situations that require a more relaxed approach. Your need for a disciplined routine could very well interfere with your ability to be open to change and to creative ideas coming into your consciousness. You could also fail to respond spontaneously to meaningful events that occur.

To be open to change is very important in any spiritual teaching. Self-discipline is also important, but it can easily become rigidity when taken to the extreme. In such a case, it may appear to be discipline, but it is really fanaticism, which blocks creative movement. Obviously, balance is necessary on the spiritual path.

One of the causes of indecisiveness could be that you made a decision in a past life that caused suffering and destruction. Thus, you would likely have a very difficult time making important decisions that could affect others. Unfortunately, this can cause stagnation and lead to a loss of opportunity to fulfill your dharma.

A failure in a past life always causes karma. The fear of making new karma is a primary factor in the difficulty of letting go of old concepts and keeps a student from developing leadership.

If you have difficulty making decisions, it is important to understand if there is some old karma that is causing this. Try the following exercise:

Exercise Three:
Ask your Higher Self:
- *Do I have a past life that directly interferes with my decision making?*
- *If the answer is yes, then ask, Am I ready to see the life?*
- *If the answer is yes, try to meditate on the life or go to a counselor who does past-life work.*

If your Higher Self tells you that you are not ready to see the life, try asking questions that may help you to understand how this past life relates to your decision making in this life. For instance, you can ask, "Did I make a decision in this past life that caused suffering? Did my decision concern more than one hundred people?" Continue in this fashion until you have received the information that will help you understand your blocks. Then at a later time, go back and again ask your Higher Self if you can see the past life.

Then, when you again encounter the feeling of wanting to avoid making an important decision, tell yourself that this is a new life and that your decision will not have the negative outcome that occurred previously. Naturally you will be careful to avoid hurting another person and be conscious to make the decision a kind one.

Many times you will be faced with having to make a determination that turns out to have a negative outcome. You always learn from such decisions, but people often abort the learning process by becoming self-critical and self-condemning. If you fall into such negative thoughts about yourself, it is very important to disidentify from the thoughts and stop them. Then you will have the clarity to calmly ask yourself, "What really happened here? What is the learning from this? What caused me to make the wrong decision?"

Learning from your mistakes is one of the most important processes on the spiritual path. The more you learn, the more quickly you overcome the obstacles and come to a clearer understanding of your true nature. If every decision you make is perfect and correct, you most probably are not taking any risks in life and you are being very conservative in your decision making.

This usually is a cover-up of old karmic patterns. Fear keeps you from acting and experimenting with life, and such a fear will keep you grounded in old ways of thinking. Let go of these by probing into your behavior patterns. Remember, negative karma can be the result of failure to make a decision as well as from making a wrong decision.

If a decision you make hurts someone, then of course you need to apologize to that person and ask for forgiveness.

There once was a king named Alberto who lived in a country very similar to America. This king wanted his people to have a wonderful life, so he set about making the kingdom wealthy and prosperous. He distributed most of his wealth to the people, so they all were equal in their material processions. He himself lived simply, with not many more possessions than his subjects. Naturally, all the people adored their king and believed themselves to be very fortunate in having him as their ruler.

Since their country was surrounded by seas, they lived in peace, with no outside interference except for traders who came from afar with foreign goods. Most of the wealth of this kingdom came from gold and silver mines and it was this wealth that was given in exchange for goods.

King Alberto lived to be very old, and he had many children from several wives. Unfortunately, his children were not as wise as he. He knew this, and had to decide which son or daughter should rule when he died. Not only was the king worried about this decision, but also all his statesmen and ministers feared their prosperity would end when he died.

King Alberto, when asked about his decision, could not make up his mind. His advisers suggested he test his children to find the right one. He had difficulty doing so, as this would make the children aware that he was going to pick one of them over the others. Being kindhearted, he did not want to hurt any of them, as he loved them all equally.

Finally, when he became crippled with age, King Alberto decided to follow the advice of his ministers. His children were also older by then, most in their thirties and forties. Their behavior and temperaments were well established. Some were obviously not capable of real leadership, so they were quickly eliminated from consideration, leaving him with three choices, two men and a woman. They were all intelligent and capable, but when he really looked at their personal lives, he saw that they lacked compassion and understanding of people. He had been so busy ruling benevolently that he had had very little influence over how his children were being raised. Even though their wealth was not a great deal more than that of the populace, they had been treated differently because they were royalty and, unfortunately, had been spoiled and glorified because of their heritage.

King Alberto was unique because his inner spirit was far more advanced than that of others. He now saw that his great mistake was in not realizing that his children were different; they did not have his spiritual background. He had neglected to train and teach them his ethics so that the kingdom could continue to prosper as a true democracy. He had waited too long to determine his heir. All he could do now was to make all three the succeeding rulers, and he tried in vain to teach them his beliefs.

When he died, the three children split the kingdom into three parts, taking control of the gold and silver, and soon there was war between them for full control of the kingdom.

This is a true story of a time and a kingdom long forgotten. This king, in the subtle world, saw the consequences of his indecisiveness and suffered great remorse for his mistake. In the lives that followed, he became a great leader and never made that mistake again. He is now one of the older Masters of Hierarchy.

Chapter 6

Choosing the Right Path

In this teaching there are many different paths to walk. Although these paths resemble each other, each one is unique and demanding. To follow a path means to propose a specific goal and adhere to the path that leads to that goal. Even if many people have the same goal, there will still be many different approaches to it.

The right approach must be carefully determined; otherwise you may begin one path or approach and encounter obstacles along the way that could be too difficult for you to tackle at a particular time. Another path might be better and easier, even if it takes a little longer to arrive at the goal.

Determining which path is the best for you to achieve your goal is a very important decision in your life. Obviously, if you choose the wrong path, you could be stuck for many years, or you could lose the enthusiasm that is so necessary to continue onward. All the paths have their difficulties, so it is important to choose the right one for you. Let's explore the many paths that you might choose as your personal approach if your goal is becoming one with your Higher Self.

First you need to determine if your goal really is to become one with your Higher Self. Instead, your goal may be to achieve God Consciousness, and even though both goals are similar, they are different in approach. For instance, if your goal is to become one with the Higher Self, your concentration and practice will be around strengthening your link to the Higher Self and consciously bringing it into your everyday life. Obviously, if you achieve this goal you also will achieve God Consciousness.

If your goal is to achieve God Consciousness, your practice will be very different. You might pursue another spiritual path with specific disciplines, or you may become a Buddhist, or a monk in any of the recognized religions. Again, when you achieve God Consciousness, you will also become one with your Higher Self, but the focus will not necessarily be on utilizing the Higher Self in most of your interactions with others and in the world.

If you decide to pursue this particular Yoga to become one with the Higher Self, then, again, you'll choose the appropriate path for you to achieve this goal.

This chapter outlines each path. The outline is flexible. For example, at any given time, you may begin one path and later realize that another would be more appropriate for you at that particular time in your life. You might then change your direction and start at another level on the other path. The first path may be too much work, so you might choose to change to a lighter path and then later discover that you are in a better place to return to the more rigorous path. It is important to realize that the path can be changed as long as your movement is always forward.

The paths can change and your pace can change, but if you stop completely and rest too long, you will lose the momentum needed to continue. Remember, it is not how much you do, but how you do it. If you are moving forward but feel stressed and unhappy, that will also affect your achieving your goal.

Often you do not understand the ups and downs that are part of every path. You see a hill as too difficult when it could be easily climbed, and you think it is much too long when actually, it is short. At times a path will have clouds that are so dense you cannot see where you are going. At other times the clouds may be obscuring something very minor and you are fooled by their darkness.

The tendency to give up on a path is often the inability to pace yourself properly, to judge just how much you are capable of doing. Sometimes a person will take on too much and become too tired to continue. The reverse is also true: Sometimes a person will take on too little when capable of doing much more, and as a result, the movement is too slow. This is why choosing the right path is so important.

It is also important to not, in any way, compare your path to someone else's. Each person is unique and has many skandhas that she must work through, develop, or let go. Because of this, you will find two people on the same path moving at different rates and encountering different obstacles. One person might climb the hill quickly; another must do it slowly and stop to rest along the way. Then, that person may jump over a chasm, leaving behind the quick climber who is too afraid to jump.

People always talk and compare themselves to others in a group. In the past, these teachings were given one-to-one and the person was told to not discuss what was given with anyone else. This kept the path a secret one, but as we move into the New Age, the emphasis is on developing community, and in any community secrets are difficult to keep.

I suggest that you be guarded about your path and do not discuss it with others at length. It does not have to be a secret, but it should be kept sacred to you. Some people are able to tackle the more difficult paths and succeed, and others will still succeed, but it may take them much longer. All paths reach the same goal in this teaching. Remember this always, and do not compare your journey with anyone else's.

Again, some people will change paths. Do not wonder why, or judge them. Changing a path may be the correct decision at a given time.

When you choose a path, do so carefully. Read about the paths once, twice, many times before meditating on them. Take time to answer the questions I will give you. Look at everything that is happening around you and decide only when you definitely know which path is right for you.

Use your Higher Self as much as possible and be aware when you could be listening to your desire body instead. Keep questioning your decision until you are completely sure about it. When you are certain you have made the right choice, put it on a shelf for at least a month. Then, take it down and test it again with your heart.

Finally, take your decision to your teacher if you are working with one, and check it out. If you have chosen wrongly, go back and meditate about why that happened. How did you misjudge yourself? What has caused this? Look at core beliefs about your-self. Most of all, do not be judgmental. Be careful to stay open and flexible.

Let's begin to look at the paths in relation to different per-sonalities. If you are an extrovert and must spend a lot of your time in the world interacting with different types of people, you will find certain paths more desirable, as they would fit better into your mundane life. If you are more of a loner, spending less time with others, you will find several paths that will best fit your soli-tary needs. You may also be a mixture, needing to be active in the world and sometimes desiring solitude. Of course, there are those who would like more solitude but cannot find the time to be alone. Others may wish to be more active in the world but due to circum-stances must be more of a hermit.

Exercise One:
Look at your life. Which one of these descriptions is closest?
1. *You work full time in an office and have family com-mitments in your home life or are active socially in the evenings with little time for solitude. If this is the case, do you like your life? Would you want more time alone?*
2. *You work full time and spend your free time primarily alone. If this is the case, do you like your life? Would you like to socialize more and have more friends, or would you want a lover or family?*
3. *You long to live alone and not see people, yet you're stuck in a relationship or with people for whom you are respon-sible. Or, your work takes you into relationships that you prefer to not be in.*
4. *You work at home, long to be working with people, but you must continue as you're doing because you love the work. When you are not working, you spend as much time as possible with others.*
5. *You work independently, love being alone to work, and spend your free time socializing.*
6. *You work independently and love to be alone both when*

you work and also during your free time. If you live with
someone, it must be someone like yourself: You would see
very little of each other.

The above are just guidelines to go by. Assess your life and your
preferences and needs carefully. For example, you may be living
in a situation that causes you to be in relationships that make you
want to be alone, but do you really want to be alone?

Look at your life and, first, write down the work aspect that is
mandatory, and then write down the social aspect you prefer. After
you have determined this, take time to meditate on the ideal situation you would like for yourself. What is missing in your life? Do
you really want more free time to be alone? Would you prefer to
be in a relationship instead of living alone? What is the ideal living
situation for you in both work and social areas?

Exercise Two:
Step back from your feelings and thoughts about your situation and
ask yourself the following questions:
1. *If I could have more time alone, would I want to spend it*
   developing myself spiritually?
2. *Would I prefer to have more time in my life to develop*
   relationships with others?
3. *Are my spiritual needs being met?*
4. *Is there something I have not done that is hanging over*
   me?
5. *Do I feel fulfilled in my vocation, or do I need to change*
   it?
6. *Are there relationships that I neglect?*
7. *Do my relationships fit into my spiritual life?*
8. *Is my spiritual life always separated from my everyday*
   life?
9. *When I am alone, do I feel happy?*
10. *Does being alone make me feel uneasy or unfulfilled?*
11. *If I love someone, do I want to be with the person all the*
    time?

12. *Can I have freedom in a love relationship?*
13. *Am I in a relationship that limits me spiritually?*
14. *When I am alone, how do I entertain myself? With TV or reading, Internet, etc.?*
15. *Can I sit quietly and contemplate without feeling that I need to be doing something else?*
16. *Is my life too full of outside activities?*
17. *When I find myself with others, can I enjoy myself?*
18. *Do I sleep a lot?*
19. *Do I prefer being alone and exclude people as much as possible?*
20. *When I work with others, do I enjoy the interaction?*
21. *Do I enjoy being in a group?*
22. *Am I silent in a group or do I take an active role?*

These questions are to help you determine your lifestyle and your personal needs. What makes you happy? What make you feel love? Perhaps when you meditate about someone, you feel more loving than when you are with the person, or vice versa. Or, you may have to be with the person you love or you don't feel loved.

After you have determined the ideal lifestyle that makes you happy, you can determine the best spiritual path to pursue. Obviously, if you have a great need to be with others and if you choose a path that will demand you spend a lot of time alone, you will feel unhappy and it will affect your spiritual progress. The opposite is also true; if you prefer to be alone and you choose a path that is too easy, you will feel unfulfilled and want to do more.

It is important to also realize that you may gravitate to a certain lifestyle because it is what you know and are used to. For example, you may spend a lot of time alone, but, when you analyze your needs, you discover that actually you would prefer to be more social than you are.

The missing aspect, whether it be to become more active socially or less active socially, is important in your spiritual practice. If you feel there is a part that is lacking, this will interfere with your progress on the path at some time, and you will need to fulfill it; otherwise you will become unhappy and perhaps project your unhappiness onto your spiritual practice. Even if the missing piece remains unfulfilled, placing it in its proper perspective is important or else you can become mired in the emotions around it.

Choosing a spiritual teaching as a replacement for unfulfilled relationships always backfires. The proper motivation is not there, and the student uses the teaching as a substitute for the unfulfilled desires. Eventually, the student will become unhappy, as the teaching can never be a substitute for personal needs. That's why when you look at these issues, be certain you are aware of unfulfilled desires, as they need to be worked out or let go of if you are going to progress on the path.

All of the above is not as difficult as it sounds. Most people, when they take the time, can easily determine what makes them feel the happiest. The hard part is to determine if your lifestyle is coming from your true self and fulfills you, or if it is the result of circumstances based on karma. Is it the lifestyle you really want? If it is not fulfilling your true self, then you must come to terms with it if for some reason you cannot change it.

If you have a karmic bond with someone who is making you unhappy, you must either change your feelings or change the relationship. In other words, you need to face yourself and accept a lifestyle you cannot change or, dramatically change your situation. If, for example, you have a child, placing you with a lifestyle that is not suited to your true self, you obviously must take on the responsibility and raise the child in a loving environment. Later, you can adjust your life to fulfill more of your personal needs. As long as you are aware of your needs, you will not necessarily project them onto your spiritual life and can therefore continue to progress on the path.

After you have taken the time to evaluate the kind of lifestyle that will make you feel the happiest, then you can begin to look at the different paths that can lead you to oneness with your Higher Self.

The paths are going to be described in detail. If some of the details seem to not fit your needs, it is because the descriptions are meant to include more than one personality. At least 80 percent of the detail should appeal to you, or it is not the right path. If you find that none of these paths appeal to you, then you should ask your Higher Self if you are ready to pursue a spiritual path at this time. Perhaps you need to wait for a while or to choose another teaching.

PATH OF ILLUMINATION

This path is the most difficult. Are you ready to spend at least three to four hours a day in study and contemplation? Are you willing to sacrifice yourself and let go of all earthly pleasures? Are you ready to give up your attachments, whether they are physical or mental? Are you interested in developing your abilities in subtle planes of existence? Do you feel ready to face your lower nature and walk through the temptations of the dark forces? Are you in a place surrounded by nature so that you are not inundated by outside vibrations of underdeveloped humans? Do you have the courage to battle and confront all the unseen forces that will try to dissuade you and make you turn back?

The most important quality you will need is a powerful will, a will that is developed enough to withstand any obstacle and any delay. Only if you have developed such a will should you consider choosing this path; otherwise you will not be able to move forward.

And most of all, do you feel you are fulfilling your dharma, including the work you were destined to do in this life? If you work full time, you will still need to devote at least two hours a day to devotional practice and study, and, on free days, at least three hours. The time spent in this way should be divided between meditation and study.

You must also have a strict, disciplined routine, a living situation that is clean and uncluttered, and an environment free from irritation. In other words, if you live with someone, you must live in harmony and be surrounded by positive vibrations. A partner should feel supportive of the time you devote to this work. If this is not the case, it is better to choose a less strict path.

When you walk this path, you will encounter all your past

demons and will need to overcome all your negative skandhas. It is a path of letting go and forming new habits, new ways of thinking and new disciplined methods of working and acting. Your friendships will be limited. Your family will be part of your life, but not the most important part. You will spend more hours alone than with others, and you will often need to overcome enormous obstacles that will require all your heart energy and your entirely focused mind.

You must always be open to change. Flexibility is a requirement. You will have to work closely with a teacher and Master; otherwise you can be seduced by the temptations that will come your way.

If you do not have a teacher, you need to ask to be led to one. This path requires guidance. The struggle sometimes will seem difficult, but never too much for you to handle.

It is a path to the Higher Self. You will need to work every day, every hour with the Higher Self and listen to its suggestions, knowing when you are really in contact with the Higher Self or an illusion from your lower nature.

Remember, this is the path that will bring you the most attention from the negative forces. It is the path that requires constant vigilance. Your armor needs to be well tested before you start on this path.

If you choose this path, you will have to begin on a lesser one to see if you have chosen correctly. The lesser path is connected to this one only and will test your strengths and endurance. Most of all, you must be willing to listen to guidance and accept the obstacles without complaint or denial.

Do not expect rewards for your labor. Know that the only reward is spiritual wholeness; the only gain is achieving the goal of your journey. You will never be destitute on this path, but expect to be tested for right motivation, right thinking and the right use of occult powers.

If you fall off this path, you fall hard, and it will take some time to regain your footing on another path. This path is far more difficult than the others and far more difficult than this description.

PATH OF LOVE

This path is also difficult. The main emphasis is on developing the use of the heart. It requires someone who is willing to sacrifice personal needs to expand the heart to include others and to focus on service in the world.

This is the path of the humanitarian. It will lead you in active pursuit of ways to help others. It is the path of the compassionate Buddha. It requires a disciplined mind and heart, with an emphasis on using the heart at all times as an instrument of the Higher Self. With the constant use of the heart, there will be many challenges to be met on this path. These challenges affect the personal ego, personal love needs, and personal desires.

The person who attempts this path must be psychologically sound and able to disidentify from outer circumstances, to be very much in the world, but not of it. This person will be much more active in the world and will be required to deal with many more relationships. Times of solitude will be needed to regain focus, but, primarily, the time of this individual will be spent interacting with others. Much of the teaching will be put into practice with this path. There will be less concentration on studies and meditation and more concentration on relationships. The person on this path will need to meditate at least twice a day and study for at least one hour a day and two hours on free days. The studies will vary, and focus first on developing the ability to disidentify and developing the qualities needed to use the heart at all times.

At a certain time on this path, when the heart is more developed, a stricter routine will begin that is more like the first path. At that time, readjustments in work and surroundings will be necessary. At the beginning, the person can live anywhere. She will need to have an organized home and beauty of some kind within the home.

The people who are part of this person's life must also be open to this teaching and not interfere with the daily practices of the student. Obstacles will also accompany this path, but not in the same manner as on the first path.

This path will never be the first path, but there will be many of the same struggles and obstacles as the student achieves higher initiations.

In the meantime, the student on this path can take much longer and concentrate more on developing the relationship skills that will be needed for the outside world. If you want solitude, do not choose this path. It definitely is for the person who must be in the world and needs to work closely with others. This person is going to be far more capable of becoming a spiritual teacher who must deal with many kinds of students. But, eventually, even this person will have to give up friendships and spend more time concentrating on the disciplines needed to reach the goal.

The Path of Love is also one that requires courage, strength of will, and sacrifice of one's time and energies to do service. Later on, it will be necessary to accomplish the work of the third path to achieve balance.

PATH OF HIGHER MIND

This path is for the person who is more inclined to Raja Yoga. She derives the most inspiration and joy from learning about the higher principles and actively training the mind to focus. The path is extreme in the discipline of the body, and employs strong methods to curtail any desire coming from the lower nature and any personal desires.

This student must be a vegetarian, have no sexual inclinations, and want more of the solitude of the first path. This path differs from the first path in that it concentrates on achieving shamanism and, in that achievement, attaining access to the Higher Mind. In so doing, the Higher Self will be partly accessed, but later in the practice, even this student will have to work more with the heart to become one with the Higher Self.

The amount of time spent studying far exceeds that required in the others. The student must devote at least three hours a day to studying and, at the beginning, one hour in meditation. Later, this will change to more meditation time, putting into practice some of the methodology that has been studied. This person will need to do this even if she is working full time. Much of the study can be done throughout the day, and relationships should not interfere. This path is difficult because of the time spent studying.

If the student is in a relationship, the partner needs to accept the need for discipline and not be too demanding of the student's time. Relationships, therefore, can be difficult to maintain. For this reason, a person can begin this practice more slowly, spending less time at it and gradually increasing the time for meditation and study.

The mind needs to be very focused, and a certain amount of intelligence is required to do the work, but even that is not essential if the person moves slowly in this direction. The mind will develop as a consequence of the work.

It is important to remember to use the heart, as the Higher Mind practices can most definitely lead a person to become one-sided. There is also a tendency to become too intellectual and believe that knowledge is the only way to achieve God Consciousness. As a result, the lower nature can use this belief to make the person feel superior to others. This path is a far more difficult one because of these temptations. Those wanting to pursue this path must work every day on using the heart and look at how their lower nature can trick them. One of the fallacies of this path is the belief that achieving the Higher Mind brings God Consciousness.

This is not true. It is the balance between the heart and mind and the awakened spirit that develops into the Higher Self and God Consciousness.

People on this path also need to do service in the world. Their dharma takes them into fields that can benefit humanity. They may want to live in solitude but generally they can't. They are also the teachers who need to help others. Their methods of teaching will differ from those of someone on the second path, and they gener-ally will be much stricter with their students.

It is a path that can take them far before they must join the second path, the Path of Love, for the sake of wholeness.

The above three paths are the ones that should be chosen if you seriously want to develop your consciousness. There are other paths that can be taken, but all of the others are worldlier and less concentrated on study and meditation. If you are serious about achieving God Consciousness then, undoubtedly, you should choose one of the above. If you are on the edge and, at this time in your life, prefer to walk more slowly, then you can select one of the following.

PATH OF DEVOTION

This path is one of devotional service. It requires less time in study and even less time in meditation. The neophyte often chooses this path and, usually, is in an ashram, working to serve the guru. The ritual of devotional practice is very important for this student, and much time is spent in chanting, dancing, and ceremonies of all kinds.

The focus is the work of the ashram that is usually simple and mundane. After years, many of these students will move more into one of the first three paths. People on this path are often good-hearted "New Agers." They rarely express their own ideas but are totally dependent on the teacher and "higher-ups."

They may spend their entire lives in devotional practices, especially in Indian ashrams. The essence of devotion is needed in all spiritual practices, but in this practice, the devotion is more mundane and ritualistic. If a person pursues this path and must work in the world, she will spend other hours in devotional practice, whether it be in the home at her personal shrine or at a nearby ashram. It is good groundwork for the first three paths, but not essential.

The Higher Self is a concept people on the Path of Devotion believe in, but rarely are they in contact with It. This path is the most religious of any of the paths in that there are set beliefs and practices that are followed. The disciplines are also rigid in these practices and need to be followed if the student wishes to remain in the teaching. Many of the Indian gurus are proponents of this path. The true teacher of such an ashram will have an inner group following the first three paths, but generally most of the other disciples are on the Path of Devotion.

PATH OF SPIRITUAL LABOR

This student spends most of the time working. If the work is a job, people on this path will often work long hours and offer their spare time to outside causes. They believe that life should be focused on service of any kind and that such service will help spiritual growth. Even though this is true, and students are accruing positive karma, they lack the spiritual discipline of meditation and study. Little time is spent on meditation, and even though spiritual books are read, the student doesn't actively pursue the practices.

These people are the "do-gooders," rarely going forward in their practice. They also rarely seek a teacher to guide them. They believe they can do it on their own and, because of this, can become egotistical and self-centered.

If they experience inner guidance, they accept this as being true knowledge and seldom question the inner voices.

Even if they find a teacher, they have difficulty asking for advice and continue working with the same sources that have led them before. These individuals feel spiritually superior to others and develop a false identity based on this belief.

Seldom can they pursue the first three paths until they acknowledge this false identity and let go of their spiritual pride. This is difficult to do. The only way it can be accomplished is if they trust the teacher to guide them.

This path can lead to higher guidance only if the person lets go of the lower guidance. Because people on this path often have psychic abilities, they may mistakenly believe that their higher centers are open and that they are clairvoyant and clairaudient. Letting go of these psychic abilities is very difficult, because the person's identity is tied up in them.

This path is the hardest to leave for the higher ones. It requires more devotion toward the teacher in order to trust the teacher's direction.

PATH OF SERVICE

This path is a combination of some of the above. People on this path work to help others and will often choose a career in a service-oriented field. Much of their labor is spent in working for humanity. Their purpose in life is more orientated in this direction, and the spiritual aspect is minor. They feel if they help others, their spiritual life will grow as a consequence, and so their spiritual practice takes a back seat.

If they have a teacher, they more likely will attend the classes or retreats, but overlook the daily practice. Their lives are too busy. Relationships with others are of primary importance. They work toward becoming leaders and develop people skills for that purpose.

Their goals, although humanitarian, can become self-centered as they enjoy the gratitude they receive from those they help. Their spiritual abilities are minimal compared to those on the Path of Spiritual Labor.

People on this path can move into the higher paths because of the good karma they usually earn; yet they need to develop the discipline to meditate and study. If they have a teacher, they will be the ones to help the teacher the most in worldly matters.

If they work in jobs other than humanitarian ones, they try to be the "good" managers, often giving their staffs too much leeway. They are kindhearted and always try to please others, sometimes too much so.

Generally, they have the necessary qualities to be on any of the top three paths but because of feelings of unworthiness, they tend to not try harder, but give up on themselves. If they overcome their insecurities, they will move forward.

PATH OF DETERMINATION

This path usually comes into people's lives when they first encounter spirituality. They are novices and must learn more before moving into the higher paths. Often their knowledge is more fantastical. They may have seen or experienced something that makes them wish to move into a spiritual teaching. Even though they feel a sudden determination to start a path, they are very cautious. Some will continue, and others will decide a spiritual journey is not for them at this time. They will question any spiritual experience and their caution often can become a major obstacle, preventing any forward movement. If they can surmount this obstacle, they will be able to move forward on any of the above paths.

Sometimes, spiritual indications will frighten them, holding them back. Other times, they simply want to be certain that a teaching is right for them. The latter will generally move forward into one of the esoteric teachings.

These people will have difficulty accepting and trusting a teacher. One reason is the fear of losing identity. They have a strong sense of self and need to keep that intact. Any type of surrender, whether it is to their own Higher Self or to a teacher, is too frightening for them.

These people need time to study and meditate more and learn to be in touch with the Higher Self that will lead them. If they move onto a higher path, it will be with a strong sense of knowing it is right. They can therefore become strong disciples.

When you take a look at these paths, you may discover that you began one path and are now on another. This is important, as there will be crossover even on the lesser paths. To determine where you are takes time. Look at your responses to the questions that were given to you earlier in this chapter.

Exercise Three:
When you have determined which path you are primarily traveling,
then ask your Higher Self:
- *Is my determination correct?*
- *Is this the right path for me at this time?*
- *If not, which one should I try to walk on?*

If your Higher Self is indicating that you need to be on another path, read the description of the path and evaluate what you must do in order to walk it correctly.

Exercise Four:
Consult your Higher Self for help by asking:

- *What is the main thing I need to start working on in order to walk this path correctly?*

When you have an answer, schedule it into your daily life and begin the work. It may take time to fully be on the new path. Don't rush it. Know in your heart it is right for you. If you have blocks around the path, ask your Higher Self for guidance on how to resolve them. If you have a teacher, ask the teacher if you are ready to work on the path. Otherwise, make certain your Higher Self is giving you the indications rather than some other part of you that wants you to attempt something for which you are not prepared.

It is most important to walk the right path. If you try another path and it doesn't feel right for you, check it again. Go slowly. These paths have many twists and turns, which reveal new hurdles that can slow you down. Do not be discouraged. You are still walking forward even when it seems the going is more difficult. Always see your path as the way to God Consciousness. Keep that goal forever in sight.

Chapter 7

Finding Your Teacher

When you enter a spiritual path, at some point you must find a true teacher to guide you. This is an esoteric law. Many New Agers feel they can grow spiritually without a teacher. Sometimes, teachers prove to be false, which adds to the confusion around having a teacher.

First you need to understand why you need a teacher to grow spiritually, even though some teachings claim you do not need one.

When you reach a certain stage on the path, you will be subject to different types of energies that will affect you. There are negative forces that will also begin to notice you and want to block you from continuing, or even to misguide you.

A teacher is one who has developed spiritually and can work on the subtle plane. It is this work that you need the most, as the teacher literally watches over you and keeps the energies balanced. Without the teacher's help, the student may inadvertently open up chakras and misuse the energies, resulting in damage to the centers and causing chaos in the subtle world. Many misguided students travel, lost, in other worlds, looking for a way back.

Unfortunately, the people who feel the strongest about working alone are often the ones who can be the most easily influenced by negative forces. Their ego is key to their feeling that they don't need help, and this type of person can more easily go off the path and misuse the energies.

"When the student is ready, the teacher will appear." This is an old saying originating with the Vedas. In essence, this is true, although sometimes the student is ready and, for many different reasons, chooses not to seek a teacher.

When this happens, the student will often sit on the fence too long and lose the opportunity that is awaiting him.

Many conditions must be addressed before a teacher will appear. Some of these conditions are the need to deal with psychological issues and fears around commitment and responsibility. Often a student will enter a path and be confronted by psychological issues and need to go into therapy before continuing. In any case, it is important to be psychologically fit; otherwise, your unconscious desires will erupt and block your spiritual growth.

How do you know if you are ready for a teacher? What are the indications and the right conditions? Usually, you will meet someone who is in a teaching and you will be curious and ask questions that lead you to meeting the teacher and attending some classes.

Sometimes the circumstances around meeting a teacher are profound, as if some invisible force guides you. When you experience meeting the teacher this way, it leaves you with little doubt that you are on the right path and have found your true teacher.

When you meet the teacher because you have been told about him or her from a friend or acquaintance, it makes it less miraculous, and you are more apt to question if this particular teacher is your teacher. Yet, even in those circumstances, when you meet for the first time, you know in your heart that you have found your teacher.

Some people, even though they meet their destined teacher, do not know it or recognize this truth. Why is this? Usually this happens because they are not ready to commit themselves to anyone's guidance. There may be a strong ego that sees teachers as being no different from themselves, or they may even feel superior to the teacher, focusing on worldly accomplishments rather than spiritual ones.

There could also be some psychological problem that blocks the knowing. If, for example, the teacher reminds the student of a parent the student has difficulty with, then the student may project some of those feelings on the teacher and not accept the relationship.

Some people have a deep resistance to any type of teacher, which could be a result of poor relationships with teachers during their school years. This type of student may study a teaching and love the teaching but not allow himself to love the teacher. Usually this goes on for a while, and then the heart of the student will open up to the teacher and there will be that recognition. If this doesn't happen after a period of time, then it's very possible that the student hasn't met his teacher and needs to look further.

Exercise One:
If you haven't met your teacher yet, ask your Higher Self the following question:
1. *Am I ready to meet my teacher?*
2. *If the answer is yes, ask: What do I need to do to make that happen?*
3. *If the answer is no, ask: What do I need to do to become ready?*
4. *If you have met a teacher and are not certain whether this person is your destined teacher, ask your Higher Self:*
5. *Is _____ my destined teacher?*
6. *If the answer is yes, ask: What is keeping me from opening my heart to him and accepting him as my teacher?*
7. *If the answer is no, ask: Is there another teacher that I am meant to have? How can I find him?*

Sometimes, you can't receive a clear answer because you have some fears around having a teacher. If this is the case, ask your Higher Self:
8. *Am I afraid to have a teacher?*
9. *If the answer is yes, ask: What is causing this fear? How do I overcome it?*
10. *If the answer is no, ask: What is causing my fears?*

A fear may have something to do with the spiritual community around the teacher. There may be some old karma holding you back.

Most of these issues can be resolved so that you can come to a closer understanding of the importance of having a teacher.

There is a saying in the East: "Each student is a seed that needs to be planted and nurtured into a blossom. The teacher can water and fertilize it, but if there is no sun, it will not survive, and will die." This means that the teacher can help the student grow spiritually, but the student must have the energy of the sun to grow, which is the energy of striving. Otherwise, there will be only a small plant that can quickly die.

When you have met the right teacher, it is important to have a good relationship with him or her. You must feel trust, love, and the ability to tell your teacher everything about yourself. Some people believe the teacher should know everything about the student without information being offered. This is a wrong assumption. The teacher is not allowed to clairvoyantly find out about a student unless the student has given permission to do so. It is wise on the teacher's part to want the student to volunteer information about himself. Through conversation, the bond grows closer, allowing deeper trust to grow.

Those students who spend the most time with the teacher have more opportunity to learn. But this depends on whether the time spent is more on a mundane level or whether they come to the teacher with spiritual questions that will help their growth. Having fun times with the teacher is also important; otherwise the relationship becomes too serious and lacks humanness.

It is wrong to place the teacher on a pedestal. When you do this, the implication is that the teacher is perfect, and even the Masters are not perfect. It is impossible to achieve perfection in a physical body. Wanting and expecting the teacher to be perfect can cause difficulty for students because either they will idealize the teacher and not see the imperfections, or they will criticize the teacher if they do see some. Let the teacher be human, and know that this is the way to grow closer. At the same time, realize that the teacher is more advanced than you, has traveled the path, and has a deeper understanding of himself.

The path is a long and difficult one, so respect the teacher's achievements, emulate the qualities you admire, and let go of the need to be exactly like him. Each teacher is different, even when teaching the same text. Some will be stricter, others less strict.

Some will be more disciplined, others will be more lax.

If a teacher has been with you before, you will generally know it. There will be recognition, sometimes immediately. Most often, you are with the same teacher for many lifetimes, with a few variations. Sometimes you will be attracted to two teachers and not know which one is your teacher in this life. It's important to ask your Higher Self which teacher is the one with whom you are meant to study. People will choose a teacher because of the feeling of having been with him before. Most often, this feeling is correct, but on occasion another teacher, perhaps in the same teaching, will appear later and be the right one. Therefore, always check with your Higher Self. Ask for verification. Ask to know the nature of the relationship. It could be a mundane relationship rather than a spiritual one. Your heart always knows the truth. Trust it.

When you work with the teacher, be aware that you are not the only student. Even if you have a close relationship, be careful to respect the teacher's time and energy. There are not only physical demands but also subtle world demands made on him. Only when you have become a teacher yourself will you understand these demands.

Whether the teacher is consciously aware of it or not, he is working all the time, the subtle body always in contact with the students and disciples and the Masters. The teacher may have a job, work on projects, teach, and do many mundane things, but there is not a moment of rest for his subtle body. It is always working in the subtle world, during waking hours as well as when the teacher sleeps. Such activity often makes the teacher physically tired. If you see the teacher overworking in the physical world, it's important to help him.

Traditionally, the teacher lived in an ashram and the students took care of everything, leaving the teacher to simply meditate and teach. Many teachers continue this tradition, but there are others who do not have ashrams, live normal lives in the world, and continue to do the same spiritual work. These are the teachers emerging in the New Age. These are the teachers who have chosen to be in the world in order to grow further on the path. Service in the world is part of the karmic requirements for achieving adept-ship in the New Age.

The path for the disciple has also changed in this age. The disciple now must live an ordinary existence, being in the world but not of it, achieving adeptship in the midst of distractions, mundane obstacles, family life, and so on. It is no easy task, but a far more liberating one. As the student develops in the mundane world, he has more opportunity to face the inner challenges that make growth possible. This type of path is now seen as the true path to adeptship.

The teacher is your spiritual guide on the path. Be sure you go to the teacher with a genuine desire to learn, with an open heart, and with the feeling of devotion. If you are in any way not feeling this, but are instead more in your lower nature, it is best to not visit the teacher, as you will be bringing negative vibrations into the teacher's environment. A teacher can dispel negative vibrations but it should not be necessary for him to do so. These vibrations are of your own making and should be dealt with by yourself, unless you simply do not know they are there or cannot handle them.

If, for instance, you are in a bad mood because of a job situa-tion, you should work through those problems and change your mood. If you are feeling depressed, it is fine to ask for help from the teacher, but it is not acceptable when you are feeling negative. The difference is that depression is contained within oneself, whereas a negative mood projects outward toward others. The teacher can lift the depression but cannot change a person's mood unless the person works on doing so. When you are in a negative mood, look at it in a disidentified manner and try to understand where the mood has come from and what could be causing it to continue. When the mood has passed, then it's all right to talk to the teacher about it.

The following is an exercise you should do when you meet with your teacher.

Exercise Two:
Ask your Higher Self:

1. *Am I in any way afraid to talk to my teacher about personal habits and personal relationships?*
2. *If the answer is yes, ask: Why? And how do I overcome this?*
3. *If the answer is no, ask to meet with the teacher, and notice when you talk to him if any fears or constrictions come up. Are you approaching the teacher with confidence and looking forward his observations, or do you find yourself not expressing yourself clearly or explaining how you feel?*

It takes time to find the right way to have a conversation with the teacher. Remember he is human. You can talk about mundane things. You can ask the teacher questions that are not offensive. Look at your teacher as a friend, but do not abuse the friendship.

If the teacher gives you specific directions, it is very important that you follow them. If the directions are not specific, but more general, then you can interpret them, but be certain to check with the teacher to see if your interpretation is correct. Always check everything with the teacher that you receive psychically. Many students go off the path because they listen to outside influences and believe the information they are receiving is coming psychically from the teacher, when it's not.

When you select your teacher, you are acknowledging the path and your fellow travelers. Your teacher will most certainly have other students who are studying the teaching. These students are part of your spiritual family. Generally, you will feel close connections that come from other lifetimes together. You will have good karma with some of these students and bond with them immediately. With others, you will have negative karma and have instant feelings of dislike. Part of your journey together is to work out the difficult karma and benefit from the good karma.

This process requires patience and discrimination. You need patience to take time to uncover the hidden feelings and how they manifest. You need discrimination to see the new personality and recognize how your karma together plays out today. This is important for both the good and bad karmic relationships. Sometimes you will see positive qualities in a person you dislike and not understand your feelings. Similarly, you will recognize some negative aspects of someone you feel love for and fail to understand why you feel the way you do. In both instances, it is important to understand your old relationship and realize how it can affect the new one.

Exercise Three:
A good exercise is to ask the Higher Self:
　　1. *Do I have karma with _____?*
　　2. *If the answer is yes, ask: Is it more positive than negative?*
　　3. *If the answer is yes, ask: Can I know more about the life?*
　　4. *If the answer is no, ask: Can I know more about the life and what is the best way to begin to let go of the negative karma?*
　　5. *Then ask, how can I best work with this person today?*

With each relationship, you will come to a deeper understanding of yourself. Isolating yourself does not help you to grow spiritually. Sitting in a cave has never been the way to God Consciousness. You may have done this in a lifetime or two, and that certainly helped to develop your spiritual nature, but to really achieve the highest initiations, it is important to serve in the world and mingle with all types of humanity. It is through these interactions that a student finds a sense of his true Being.

When you find a teacher, it is also important to give that teacher a spiritual history. The history tells the teacher what to expect in terms of your striving. For example, if you are a person that has been interested in spiritual matters most of your life, then you will acclimate to some of the rules and structure of a spiritual community. If, instead, you have never practiced a spiritual discipline, you will find it more difficult to begin one.

Usually, the best students have a long history of religious practice, no matter what specific religion they embraced. If you have had little spiritual practice, it is important to take your time and not make too many demands on yourself. Give yourself the time to adjust to the rhythm of such a practice, and certainly do not compare yourself with the other students. Others may find spiritual practice easier, and this may cause you to feel insecure. Even though you may not have had religious discipline in your youth, it does not mean you can't develop it and be on the same level as those who did.

Also, do not compare yourself to the older disciples. Obviously, there will be students who have been with the teacher for a long time. Their relationship has developed. Again, it is up to you to develop your own relationship, based on karma that may be equally old. Ask your teacher how you can best develop your relationship with him, and write down the answer to refer to on a regular basis.

The following is an exercise to help you work with your heart in relation to the teacher.

Exercise Four:
Ask your Higher Self:
   Is there anything else I can do to develop my relationship with my teacher? Give me a first step in doing this.

Try to follow your Higher Self's guidance. After you have completed the first step, ask the Higher Self for a second step, and so on.

Everyone's relationship with the teacher is different. Do not compare your steps with those of any other student. Your relationship is very special and comes from previous lifetimes with your teacher

In the end, only one thing is important: your link to your spiritual teacher. For it is only through that link that you grow spiritually. The spiritual path has been forged by your teacher. Walk that path in gratitude. It is through the teacher's efforts that you can move along it more easily.

Chapter 8

Looking at Obstacles

When a person enters a spiritual practice, it is important to understand that the practice itself will force obstacles to arise that may not have been there if the person lived just an ordinary life. This is true of any spiritual practice. The saying "Through the obstacles you grow" is true wisdom that people rarely understand.

Why must a person suffer in order to become spiritual? This is a common question.

In reality, no one has to suffer at all. The suffering is caused by the student's inability to disidentify from the problem, becoming emotionally involved instead. All suffering is created by the individual. A high adept never feels personally involved in the most charged situation. The adept simply steps back and sees the whole picture, feeling compassion for those who are less enlightened.

But how does one come to the place of disidentification? Obviously, much inner work is required to be able to do this. So let's start by analyzing what it means to be disidentified.

For example, a man is walking down the street and is struck by a car. He falls and is injured, suffering a broken back. The pain the man feels is genuine, part of the physical mechanism that indicates something is wrong, which is why this kind of physical suffering is important. Once he is aware of his condition, even this suffering can change. After he is put into a cast to heal the broken bones, he can let go of the pain with the following concentration exercises.

- See the pain as a black ball and hand the ball to your teacher or Master.
- Focus on the pain without any other thoughts, and the pain will move. Follow its movement and you will discover that the pain will begin to fade.

- Believe the pain will leave, and if it tries to return, simply tell it to go away.

Obviously, to be able to control physical pain, you must be very focused and use your strong will to control it. If you cannot control it mentally, then it is best to take pain medication temporarily.

EMOTIONAL SUFFERING

I have been speaking about physical suffering, but emotional suffering is the most difficult to control. If the man who broke his back were also suffering emotionally from the loss of time and the loss of mobility, he would have more physical pain, because emotional suffering causes physical pain.

For example, a person feels emotional stress because a loved one is ill and nothing can be done to cure the illness. If this person holds these feelings within and doesn't truly acknowledge them, or express them in an appropriate setting, the tendency is for those feelings to begin to appear in the person's body and cause physical illness. A person who is a caretaker often becomes ill and even sicker than the person being cared for.

Emotional suffering can degenerate into depression, which is a sign of a deep inner disturbance. Obviously, this refers to a person who has a normal physiology and not someone who has a chemical imbalance. When depression is not cured, it can cause physical ailments and sometimes, in the extreme, can lead to suicide.

Childhood conditioning causes many emotional states that, on a deeper level, can be the result of old karma from past lives. Healing this conditioning will change the emotional state of an individual. Most often, a person will choose the quickest way to cure these states by taking antidepressants. Long-term use of these drugs dulls feelings and keeps a person in a state of euphoria. The easiest way is not always a cure-all. Delving into past conditioning and healing the wounds of childhood are a far better method of overcoming emotions.

Let's define some of these emotions:
- Emotions related to fear

- Emotions around loss
- Emotions causing self-pity
- Emotions of anger
- Emotions from inner wounds
- Emotions forming core beliefs
- Emotions that attract mental and physical abuse
- Emotions that attract mental and physical dysfunction
- Emotions that cause addictive behavior
- Emotions of stubbornness
- Emotions that cause an imbalance of needs
- Emotions that make a person immobile
- Emotions that cause physical illness
- Emotions that cause death

The following are examples of the emotions listed above. These may help you clarify how the emotions can function in a person.

• **Fear:** Fear is a difficult emotion. Sometimes the fear is so prevalent that a person can't understand what it is about. It is difficult to step back from it when you are in it.

For example, Juanita felt afraid to change her job even though she was unhappy there. Such fear could come from fear of the unknown, fear of loss of security, and fear that a new job will be worse. A first step might be for Juanita to look at her fear around security and plan for a strong financial base before leaving. Also, as she looks for another job, she should really investigate the company and, if possible, talk to the employees. Just walking around an office can give her a sense of whether or not the workers are happy.

It's also important to take risks in life, and if Juanita is fearful of taking risks, it could be her psychological conditioning that needs to be examined.

• **Loss:** Losing someone you love, whether in death, divorce, or simply a broken friendship, can be very devastating. Loss also covers losing a job, or a home, or something that has great sentimental value. It can be an opportunity that you missed or loss of anything that is meaningful to you.

For example, Abdul's heart was broken because Malika left him. Besides the feelings of abandonment, feelings from his childhood arose around not being good enough. A first step might be for Abdul to give himself some loving care. He needs to see friends and try to do fun things. Loss always takes time to heal, especially if a person genuinely loves someone. Abdul needs to spend time doing things that make him feel good.

• **Self-Pity:** This emotion is very difficult to deal with. A person succumbs to inner depths of despair where the spirit is overshadowed by heaviness. Usually, self-pity comes from not having what you think you deserve or from suffering an illness that is very painful. It's looking at life through a dark lens and projecting those negative images onto others.

Taking the example in section on loss, Abdul, with the broken heart, could also go into a phase of self-pity. Woe is me! He gave everything to Malika and look what happened. He wasn't even appreciated, and so on. This emotion usually comes from past conditioning and having strong expectations that cannot be fulfilled. A first step may be for Abdul to watch his thoughts, and when a thought loaded with self-pity arises, try to stop it at once and change it to a positive thought. For instance, if he thinks, "Malika never loved me. I'm stupid to have gotten involved with her." He can change the thought to, "It was nice while it lasted. I know there is someone else I will meet who will really love me."

• **Anger:** Anger triggers negative feelings that return to you. Before confronting someone with your feelings, it's always better to wait until the anger is under control. If your anger triggers anger in the other person, you will both say hurtful things. In this way, relationships are either destroyed or worn down.

An example: Jean was livid with fury at her husband for making vacation plans without consulting her. Anger usually comes from childhood conditioning. Jean had a controlling mother who wouldn't allow her to express herself. If you come into life with repressed anger from another life, you may also have extreme reactions. A first step for Jean may be to get some old phone books and rip them up, or go to a secluded place and scream, or hit a pillow with her fists. Then, when she feels calm, she needs to talk to her husband about how she feels.

- **Emotions from Inner Wounds:** This refers to the feelings that usually come from childhood conditioning and also past lives. These are the wounds of the inner child as well as the wounds that come from the inner critic.

An example: Tony felt very sad when he saw a mother nursing a baby and displaying warmth and love. He was the fifth child in a family of seven children, and all his mother had time for was taking care of his basic needs. Tony never remembered being held by her. To heal this wound, he was told to visualize himself as a small child and then to visualize picking the child up and giving him lots of attention and love. Doing this alleviated the pain and allowed the child within him to feel more accepted and cared for.

Tony also suffered from much insecurity and was very self-critical. Criticizing himself made his inner child feel less confident. By saying "no" to his inner critic and trying to not listen to that part, he put a stop to further wounding his inner child.

- **Core Belief Emotions:** These are subtle emotions coming from false beliefs usually formed in childhood. These beliefs can cause people to go through life holding on to emotions that no longer apply to them as adults.

For example, Sasha was very bright. She had a master's degree in business but lacked the assertiveness to go after the higher-ranking jobs she was capable of doing. When she started working on this issue, she realized that she believed she didn't deserve to be successful in life.

Like Tony, these feelings came from childhood, when she felt unloved by her parents. This conditioning produced beliefs that she was unworthy and didn't deserve to be happy. A first step would be to change the core belief with an affirmation: "I deserve to be successful in life." Also, Sasha needs to work with her inner child by building up the child's sense of worth and self-esteem.

- **Attracting Abuse Emotions:** This refers to the victim pattern. When a person has experienced abuse, whether it is physical or emotional, this can often cause passivity and an expectation of abuse from everyone the person encounters. In fact, this type of victim pattern usually attracts people who will continue to victimize the person.

For example, Maryanne is married to a man who constantly abuses her emotionally, calling her denigrating names and saying terrible things about her in front of others. She had a father who abused her physically and emotionally. A first step for her is to confront her husband (most victims have a difficult time confronting) and demand a change in behavior or insist that they go into couple's therapy to change the abusive patterns. If he physically abuses her, then she needs to go to a special clinic that deals with such issues.

• **Attracting Emotions that Cause Dysfunction:** This refers to the hidden cause of some physical and mental illnesses. Obviously, if abuse is extreme, it can cause physical reactions. Mental illness can certainly come about if a child is tortured or beaten. When such abuse happens, a child can become incapable of speaking out and can appear retarded. This is the extreme, but abuse can affect people in different ways, particularly if the person is highly sensitive.

For example, Ingmar suffered from asthma from early childhood and sometimes was afraid that he wouldn't have enough air to breathe. Such a condition can come from a childhood fear of any kind. He could have been traumatized by a parent or sibling, or even have brought these fears over from a past life. Extreme fear can cause many physical ailments. A first step would be to determine if trauma caused the asthma, and then work with healing the frightened inner child.

• **Emotions Causing Addiction:** There are many types of addiction on the planet. The obvious ones are substance abuse of some kind. But there also are addictions to money, possessions, and other material things as well as the opposite, addictions to being poor or to having no possessions, even those of beauty. There are also psychological addictions, such as obsessive-compulsive behavior. Addiction represents anything in excess. It does not apply to basic needs and moderate desires.

For example, when Madison feels upset, she eats chocolate, the result of an intense craving. She remembers that when she was two, she was crying, and her mother, who was busy, would give her a piece of chocolate instead of picking her up. The chocolate became the comforter. A first step is to realize the source of the addiction and, if it started in childhood, work with the inner child. There are also many programs for drug and alcohol abuse and programs for those who are overweight as well as for other addictions.

- **Stubbornness Coming from Emotions:** Stubbornness is a difficult problem. It's locked into the need to be right. Usually the emotion that triggers it is the feeling of not being listened to, which causes a need to take a strong stand and not budge. This emotion is often accompanied by a fear of rejection, and, of course, being stubborn often causes this fear to be validated.

For example, when Jacob's wife repeatedly asks him to mow the lawn, he feels she is nagging him. Every time she does this, he decides not to mow the lawn that day, which of course causes a fight. The first time she asks him, he says, "I'll do it later," but she doesn't seem to hear the "later." That's when the nagging begins.

His response can come from childhood conditioning, being told what to do by a demanding parent, or the opposite, not being given any direction at all and having to decide everything for himself. A first step is for Jacob to make a lawn plan he can follow and to give a copy to his wife with the stipulation that she not remind him about it unless three days have passed beyond the date on the plan. In general, nagging causes stubbornness and vice versa.

- **Emotional Needs Causing Imbalance:** When someone has emotions that are extreme, sometimes the person will flip to the other side of the spectrum and take on the opposite emotion, also an extreme.

For example, Helena felt furious at her ten-year-old son for not coming home on time. When he did come home an hour late, she screamed at him and sent him to his room for the evening, no TV, no dinner. The next morning Helena felt remorse and took him a big breakfast in bed and hugged and kissed him over and over again, telling him how much she loved him.

This of course was very confusing and not helpful to her son. Helena felt guilty and responded from feelings of unworthiness. She is divorced and, basically, feels inadequate as the sole parent. Often she flips from strictness to nurturing behavior and is unable to balance the two. A first step is to calm down her feelings and only then talk to her son about setting up more careful boundaries.

- **Emotions Causing Immobility:** Any of the emotions listed, if developed in the extreme, can cause a person to become immobile. The person then sleeps around the clock, can't work, and in general is incapacitated.

For example, when Stephanie broke up with her boyfriend, she couldn't cope with life. She called in sick to her job and just slept all day long. It felt too difficult for her even to cry. She had no energy to get up and eat. Such a state can come from severe depression as a result of a chemical imbalance or by abandonment issues. A first step would be to obtain medical help. Medication could bring Stephanie to the next level, a place where she is able to work on some of the psychological problems causing the depression.

- **Emotions Causing Illness:** This state relates to becoming physically ill as a result of deep-seated emotions. Many illnesses arise from long periods of stress-laden emotions.

For example, Marco was a sickly child and has been sick most of his life with various diseases, primarily in the stomach and bowels. He finally came down with bleeding ulcers, a condition his father had suffered from. Marco's family environment had been highly volatile, which caused his susceptibility to manifest.

At the time Marco's ulcers flared up, he was working in a chaotic atmosphere. A first step in any illness is to follow all medical recommendations, but it is also important for Marco to be living and working in a stress-free environment.

- **Life-Threatening Emotion:** When one is extremely emotional, beyond the normal reactions to life, it's possible the person will try to end her life. The karma of suicide leads to a future life that will have an even greater psychological impact. One who commits suicide must suffer the length of her destined life on a plane in the subtle world best described as purgatory. Suicide also has a major psychological impact on the lives of the family the person has left behind. This type of karma is most difficult to change in future lives. That is why suicide is so condemned in most religions. This does not include the martyrs who sacrifice their lives for a cause; these people are clearly not acting out of emotion and are in a special category.

For example, Fujiko was forty years old and felt her life was a total failure. She had nothing to live for. She was in a spiritual practice, but even that seemed fruitless to her. She had no energy to strive to change anything in her life. Feeling hopeless, she began to have thoughts about ending it all.

She had a history of mental illness in her family and severe depression brought about by feelings of unworthiness. Her first step was to ask for help, which fortunately she did. A friend took charge and took her to the hospital, where she received medical and psychological help.

The above emotions constitute the major obstacles on a spiritual path. Freedom comes only to those who have learned to control and transform negative emotions.

The positive emotions are not listed. They relate to the higher feelings of love, joy, and contentment and, of course, spiritual ecstasy. To achieve these feelings, you must be free of those that keep you in the mundane world.

To identify your personal emotions, try the following exercise.

Exercise One:
Ask your Higher Self:
   1. *Taken the first emotion listed, fear, and ask, Do I have any emotions that relate to fear,?*
      - *If you receive a yes answer, ask: What are they? And where do they come from?*
      - *And then ask: How can I overcome this state? What is my first step?*
   2. *The next day, ask your Higher Self about the second item*

on the emotions list:
- *Do I have any emotions around loss?*
- *If you receive a yes answer, ask: What are they? Then continue with the same process you did for the first emotion.*

Keep doing this, taking a new question each day. You will end up with a list, methods, and first steps related to those items on the emotions list to which you receive a yes answer.

Obviously, you cannot work on the whole list, so I suggest you prioritize your list; then taking the emotion that is the strongest, begin to work on changing it. If you find you have many inner wounds that need to be healed, you may want to consult a therapist who does inner child work. In the case of anger, often those feelings can come from a wounded inner child, even when they are directed toward someone not connected with your childhood.

It is also important to do a nightly review, looking back over the day and noticing if you felt emotional. If you did, identify the emotion from those listed above.

If you find a particular emotion keeps coming up for you, then choose that one to work on. Also, notice if there is someone in your life that triggers you to feel that emotion, or if a certain kind of situation brings it up. For example: If you always feel anger when you are in the presence of a certain person, notice what causes this anger. Maybe you simply need to express how you feel to the person and talk things out. By not expressing feelings, you can cause other feelings to arise.

When you look at your list, try not to feel overwhelmed. Work on one thing at a time, but if you notice another emotion coming up, try to take the first step given to you. If you find it is too much to do, then just make a note of the feeling to be worked on at another time and continue working with the main one you chose.

KARMIC RELATIONSHIPS

Another major obstacle on the spiritual journey relates to past lives. When a person reacts to a situation of any kind, the reaction often comes from the unconscious realm, without any understanding about it. This happens often when two people meet for the first time. If they have a karmic past together, that causes the reaction. You may know someone whom everyone loves, and you simply can't stand to be around that person. Or, you may be enamored of someone who is obviously not at all interested in you. Karma can play tricky games with the mind and heart. Those games are part of the karmic pull, which draws a person into even stronger karma.

If you are in a negative karmic relationship, it can keep you from growing spiritually. Since everything is karma, it is very important to clarify all your relationships to be certain they are not in any way causing you to act in a manner that will incur more karma. If you realize you do have a strong negative karmic relationship, it would then be important to either change the relationship or end it in a manner such that the karma does not continue.

How can you do this? First, do the following exercise.

Exercise Two:
Place the name of a person you have a relationship with in your heart and ask your Higher Self:
1. *Give me an indication whether the karma with this person is good. If your heart responds when you ask if the karma is good, then you can be assured that the karma is mainly positive.*
2. *If your heart doesn't respond, you can then ask your Higher Self: Is my karma with this person more negative?*
3. *Again, if the answer is yes, your heart will respond; otherwise it will remain the same. If it remains the same, ask the question: Is my karma with this person equally good and bad?*
4. *Again, a response is a yes. If you have no response, it may be that you are feeling some fear around asking the question. If this is the case, imagine the fear as a huge black ball and pull it out of your heart and hand it to your Higher Self. After you have done this, try the questioning again.*

If your answers were more in the negative or equal category, it would be good to try to understand what the karma is about. If the person you are asking about is also spiritual and believes in reincarnation, you can ask her to sit down with you to discover more about the karma. This can be done in the following way, with both people sitting and looking at each other.

Exercise Three:

Try looking in each other's eyes, focusing only on the eyes. If a thought or vision comes to mind, close your eyes for further clarification. Ask for an image from the lifetime involved. If something comes, put it in your heart and ask to see more.

Keep doing this. You may just get a sense of something such as, for instance, you were married to each other. Compare notes with each other. Then, again, both of you meditate on the information and ask to know more.

Bringing up the negative karma gives both people a better understanding of the hidden barriers affecting the connection. You can then talk about the dynamics that presently are controlling the relationship.

For example, a married couple was coming to an impasse in their marriage. The marriage had started off well but, after a few years, hostility arose that couldn't be resolved with a couple's counselor. Steve was feeling controlled by his wife, Lillian, and she was convinced that he was controlling her.

The lifetime that emerged for them was one in which Steve was the son of Lillian who, in that life, was his father. The father was very controlling and dominated the son most of his life. In the present, anytime Lillian insisted on doing something her way, Steve responded with anger, wanting it done his way. He still carried feelings of anger at being controlled by her in the past life, and Lillian still had a need to control him and others.

To make the marriage work, they had to look at the past life and understand how it was interfering with who they are today. When they realized that each had an unconscious desire to control the other, they had to come to a resolution on how to change this desire so as to develop a more sharing relationship.

If the marriage ended in divorce because of these unconscious dynamics, then they were bound to return together until they worked their issues out. Instead, knowing the karma, they both decided it would be better to divorce and remain friends, because, at this stage in their relationship, it would be too difficult to stay married. Now they are free of their karma and needn't return together again. Of course, the karmic patterns they are carrying individually still need to be healed if each is to grow spiritually.

FEARS STEMMING FROM PAST LIVES

A major obstacle that everyone on a spiritual path must confront is fear coming from past lives. We have all done many things in the past. Everyone has been a murderer, a thief, a destroyer, a tyrant and has developed all the negative characteristics that make up the shadow side of our psyche. You also have a chalice of the beautiful good lives, but in the lower depths lie the negative ones that must be transmuted as you strive toward the heights.

These negative lives impact you in ways you don't realize. They are the negative seeds that make you feel unworthy, unlovable, and unable to be successful in relationships and in your vocation.

How do these negative seeds work? First, they attract the soul to a family environment that will be karmic and cause those negative characteristics to mature. If you killed your mother in a past life, be assured she is not going to give you the love and nurturing you long for. Her lack of love will make you feel unworthy, and, of course, the hidden knowledge of having killed her will add to these feelings and cause you to feel you are truly bad and unworthy of love. You may then become a pleaser, doing everything to please your mother so she will give you love. This interplay goes on and on, forming your identity and attracting you to similar situations as an adult.

This is just one scenario. There are many more that affect a person's personality and are directly related to past lives. If, for instance, you died feeling you failed in your vocation or in a relationship, you will carry that fear of failure with you into new, similar situations. You may have been tortured and even killed for your religious beliefs, and as a result you may feel very frightened to be part of a spiritual group. You may have lived in a country whose politics kept you from expressing yourself. In this life, traveling to that country may affect you negatively. These stories vary from individual to individual, but they indicate blocks, resistances, and hidden fears that inhibit a person's growth.

Exercise Four:
Ask your Higher Self: Do I have any hidden fears related to past lives that are affecting me at this time?
- *If the answer is a yes, ask: What are these fears?*
- *List them, and then take the first fear and ask your Higher Self: Does the fear of _____ come from one past life or from several?*
- *When you have the answer, ask: Am I ready to see the past life (lives)?*

If the answer is yes, try to then find someone who does past-life regression and ask the therapist to work with you on the life or lives related to this fear.

If, for some reason, you can't go to a therapist, then ask your Higher Self to show you some scenes of the life, either in meditation or in your dreams.

If you can't see a past life, then try to look at your fear and understand how it is blocking you from moving forward. Take the fear and break it down, analyze it, work with ways to overcome it, but, mainly, try to release it with positive affirmations and positive thinking. Know that it can be dissolved.

If you do see a past life that is negative, forgive yourself, and through understanding, let it go. Be careful to keep the past life private, particularly if it involves others whom you know at this time. Only talk to others about it if you plan to sit down with them and work out your differences.

Most of all, realize it is the past. You have had many lives, and one lifetime is just a drop of water in the sea. Give yourself time. Hidden fears take time to be understood and overcome. Be patient and, most of all, be kind to yourself.

In conclusion, the obstacles are hard tasks on the path. Remember to take one at a time and really analyze it, seeing it fully. You may work on an obstacle and find that it comes up again in a different form. Keep a journal of the work you are doing. Realize that every obstacle you succeed in overcoming is a step upward toward your spiritual goal.

Chapter 9

Letting Your Intuition Decide

When you are born, several senses are already developed. These senses are part of your skandhas and have been with you for many lifetimes.

One of the senses is your ability to know things intuitively. Some people have a strong intuitive nature; others need to develop this very important sense. It is also essential to understand that the intuition resides not only in women, but also in men. It is a force in nature that is directly connected to the Feminine Principle.

If someone has a strong intuition, that person will generally make the right decisions in life. If not, the opposite is true; decisions will be based solely on the rational mind and therefore can be incorrect.

With each decision, whether it is right or wrong, a definite shift in direction results. Therefore every decision, even a minor one, should be decided upon carefully.

Let's look at what can happen when a decision is made using only the rational mind. Here is a true example.

Leslie had to decide whether on not to take a trip at a time when travel was dangerous. When she thought about the danger and she decided not to go, but when she used her intuition, there was a decided positive response. Leslie had the feeling that something beneficial was going to happen. She released her fears and went on the trip. Her intuition was correct. She met a man on the plane who became an important influence in her future work.

Timing can be very crucial. When you listen to your intuition and fail to act on it immediately, a shift occurs that can change the circumstances and outcome of a situation. When you listen and act, then you are in a definite flow that can result in a very positive outcome. Often this fails to happen because you wait, and the action is delayed. You blame the intuition when, in fact, it was your free will that was responsible for the outcome.

With each completed action that fulfills the intuition, you become more confident in your intuitive sense. Following the intuition also strengthens it. With each success there ensues a deeper connection to the Source, the Feminine Principle.

Exercise One:
Let's do an exercise to determine how intuitive you are:
Sit quietly in a chair, close your eyes, and link with your heart. Ask the following question and place it in your heart:
- *When I have an intuitive understanding of something, do I listen to it?*
- *Then ask: When I don't listen to it, how do I make decisions?*

If you only use your rational mind to make decisions, then you lack the ability to gain access to your intuition. If you have an intuitive understanding, but still follow your thinking, then you simply don't trust your intuition and feel safer with the mind.

With each decision you make in life, it is important to follow the intuition and use it in conjunction with the mind, particularly if the decision has many levels.

For example, Ivan was offered a new job as a project manager and had to decide whether to take the offer or not. It was a good company and the job met most of his requirements, but his intuition told him that to work with the director of the project would be very difficult. When Ivan thought about the job, he felt a lot of excitement, but when he considered his future supervisor, he experienced feelings of dread.

What would you do? The rational person would take the job and hope the relationship with the boss could be worked out. The intuitive person would not take the job.

Before making such a decision, it is better to combine the rational mind with the intuition. For instance, someone in Ivan's position could find out more about the director, then take the information, put it in his heart, and ask about the source of his feelings. Is it a general feeling or does it come from something much deeper? Is there personal karma with this person? If so, what is the karma? And can it be worked out?

These are the kinds of questions that must be asked first. If the karma is very difficult, it would be best that Ivan not take the job. If it is possible to work out the karma, then it would be all right to accept. It's important for Ivan to be certain that his feelings aren't based on the director's personality in another life. There may be old karma, and the director, having gone through additional lives, may have changed, and would therefore be much easier to work with than the first impression suggests. The opposite could also be true. The director hasn't changed and it could be a terrible work situation. It's also possible there is no direct karma; rather, Ivan is picking up that the director is someone with a difficult personality who could cause him to become entangled in new karma.

Working with the intuition is very important in any potential karmic situation. When you meet someone with whom you have bad karma, often the first meeting will be deceptive. Karma can strongly pull together those involved in old karmic relationships in a seemingly positive way, and it sometimes takes months for the real karma to emerge. However, your intuition will always tell you the truth about the negative karma, even when the feeling is positive.

With every important decision you make, try to listen to your intuition. It is connected to your Higher Self and sends direct impressions from the Higher Self. Too often, the intuition is thought to be an ancient sense used when we were more primitive. But that primitive sense is entirely different. It is an animal sense that works from instincts, particularly the instinct to survive.

The intuition is much more refined. It is neither part of the animal kingdom nor part of the subtle world. It is an inner sense that is cloaked in mystery. If we were to explore its source, it would become even more mysterious. Without a doubt, the intuition is a wisdom that comes from deep within. It is linked to the Higher Self, and the Higher Self will use it, but it is a sense that is innate in all human beings whether or not they have developed a connection to the Higher Self. When a person has a strong connection to the Higher Self, he is highly intuitive and can use both the intuition and the Higher Self simultaneously.

When the Feminine Principle is active in an individual, the intuition is more developed. Too often the Feminine Principle is repressed, and therefore the intuition is repressed. This is particularly true when someone has a very developed Masculine Principle. To begin to work with the intuition, it is necessary to try awakening it to its full potential. The following are some exercises that will help you do this.

Exercise Two:
1. *When you think about doing something, first place it in your heart and try to sense if it is good for you to do.*
2. *Look at your relationships with others. Place each name into your heart, one each day, and sense if you have any past karma with this person. Then try to get a sense if the karma is positive or negative.*
3. *Find a story in the newspaper, read it, and then put the story in your heart. Sense if the story is complete or if something is missing.*
4. *Write in your journal any intuitive impressions you may have during the day. For example, you notice something in a store. You look at some foods or some remedies and wonder if they are good for you.*
5. *See objects as tools to use the intuition for deeper understanding.*
6. *For example, take an antique piece of jewelry or any other object. Hold it, and get a sense of the previous owner. Try to also sense if the vibration in it is positive or negative.*
7. *In your mind's eye, see an image of a person, and get a sense if everything is all right with that person or not. Or place a location in your mind's eye and sense if the location has positive or negative energies.*
8. *Take time to read a poem, and use your intuition to*

> *interpret the poem. What is the hidden message from the poet?*
>
> 9. *Look at your past relationships and try to intuitively understand your karma in those relationships.*
> 10. *Be more aware of circumstances and how they happen to you. Do things just happen, or do you feel you make them happen? If they just happen, use your intuition to understand the hidden messages.*
> 11. *Try to follow your intuition. If things don't work out the way you thought, don't be discouraged. Often desires can interfere with fulfilling the intuition.*
> 12. *Lastly, come to a deeper understanding that if you really follow your intuition, events will always work out better than if you didn't.*

The above practices will help you discover the wealth of the intuition. Try to work on at least one practice a week. Some of the practices, such as Exercise One, should be ongoing.

INTUITION VS. THE GUIDE

It is important to distinguish the differences between the Guide and the intuition. The Guide is a separate being that is attached to you at birth. It is part of the Devic kingdom and will be with you throughout your life. After you die, it returns to its kingdom to await another person to be born to attach itself to. If the Guide has done a good job in getting through to you and you have listened to it, then the next person it is attached to will also be spiritual and even more advanced than you. This spirit is very ethereal. If you see your Guide, it will appear like an elongated form with sharp, elf-like features. Most Guides are genderless, yet will take on a gender if the person they are guiding prefers a certain sex.

A Guide is truly a great help in everyday life. It will send you specific directions to help you. Generally, these directions relate to the mundane world. For example, if you leave the coffee maker on, as you get into the car, you receive a flash that you left it on. The same is true about any item in your house. If you lose something and can't find it, just meditate and ask your Guide to find it for you. Usually the Guide sends you a sense of something, but sometimes you may even receive a vocal direction.

Imagine the Guide as a figure standing next to you. This figure will tell you if there is something that needs to be done, or something you may have forgotten about. It constantly checks your actions and thinking and tries to help you follow through. For instance, if you need to make out a check to someone and you forget about it, the Guide will try to nudge you into remembering. Sometimes a person listens, sometimes not, but the more you try to listen, the stronger the Guide becomes. As you grow spiritually, so does the Guide, so it is in the Guide's best interests to get through to you.

When you consciously use the Guide, you are strengthening it, so it is important to remember to ask for help on an ongoing basis.

The Guide will always assist you in your daily work. If you need to learn to be more organized, ask your Guide to send you suggestions. If you find you are too scattered, ask the Guide to help you discipline your mind. You can ask the Guide for any kind of help that relates to objects. For example, if you buy an antique, hold it in your hands and ask the Guide to let you feel the vibrations to know if the object has good or negative energy. You can even get a reading on the previous owner this way. Essentially, the Guide is a Geiger counter. It is in tune with your needs and desires and knows the right direction you need to take. It will always be encouraging and helpful. If you receive any criticism from it, then you know it is not your Guide you are listening to.

INTUITION VS. THE HIGHER SELF

There is a major difference between knowledge sent to you by the Higher Self and intuitive knowledge. The intuition is a strong feeling, whereas the Higher Self is a deep knowing. There is always wisdom surrounding a message from the Higher Self, whereas intuition is more a sensation that often isn't understood. To understand the intuitive message, you have to go deeper and ask the Higher Self to explain it. The two often work together. The intuition comes from the Feminine Principle and the Higher Self comes from the Feminine and Masculine Principles working together.

When you wish to deepen or clarify an intuition, you must connect to the Higher Self. The opposite does not happen. The Higher Self doesn't need the intuition for clarity. With each inner knowing comes an opportunity to discover the source of that knowing. The source always lies within the Higher Self. The intuition is an instrument of the Higher Self and is developed when the individual begins to work with his spiritual nature. Often the Higher Self is referred to as separate from the individual, whereas the intuition is always a part of the individual. This is true, but, in reality, the intuition is always connected to the Higher Self and so has access to information that comes from outside.

When you access your intuition, you are also connecting to the Higher Self. It is very much like someone playing the piano. The person's hands make the music happen, and the keys make the sound. The hands would be likened to the Higher Self and the keys to the intuition. The keys communicate the essence of the piano, whereas the hands controlling the keys draw out the sound either beautifully or dreadfully. The same is true of the interplay of the Higher Self with the intuition. If the Higher Self is developed and used by the individual, then the intuition will be clearly heard. But if the Higher Self is seldom used, then the intuition will also be vague and unheard.

The ability to work with the Higher Self is developed with each lifetime. A young soul who has lived only a few lifetimes will obviously have not used the Higher Self, and therefore will not be very intuitive. Men and women who are working solely with the Masculine Principle will also be less in touch with the intuition. Accessing the intuition is an inner process, and the Masculine always reaches outward. These individuals will probably find it difficult to listen to anything other than pure logical thinking. They are imbalanced, and need to learn to meditate and listen to their inner voice.

When you work with the Higher Self, you can ask the following questions.

Exercise Three:

- *How can I develop my intuition more?*
- *Is there anything blocking me from using my intuition?*
- *How can I work with my Higher Self and my intuition so that they are perfectly coordinated?*
- *What signs do I receive that indicate my intuition is fully present?*
- *When I follow my intuition, is there any way of checking if I followed it completely?*

In conclusion, try to remember to check things intuitively, then go to the Higher Self and verify what you receive. In this way, you will learn how your intuition works for you and whether you are truly listening to your intuition or to another part of yourself.

Chapter 10

Inside the Subtle World

Every spiritual aspirant has experiences of the subtle world. Much has been written about it in esoteric literature. Too many opinions have been expressed about what the different planes contain and, of course, this can be very confusing for a beginning student. In order to become a spiritual leader of any kind, it is important to know how to work within the different levels of the subtle world.

First, I shall define the different planes of existence, and then we will go into more detail about them. There are six planes, the first being the Physical Plane. The others that exist in the subtle world are the following:

2. Lower Astral Plane
3. Subtle Plane, sometimes called the Higher Astral Plane
4. Mental Plane
5. Buddhic Plane
6. Nirvanic Plane

The astral plane is broken into two separate planes because it is, by far, the most populated and contains the largest levels to travel through. In reality, it consists of many overlapping levels. The higher planes are more refined and flow from one level to another with only a slight distinction, whereas the Astral Planes are more defined by their inhabitants.

If one could describe the differences between the Astral Planes and the Mental and Buddhic Planes, it would be that the Astral Planes are full of all different types of life forms, from decayed husks of humans in the lower levels to forms of Higher Beings on the higher levels, whereas the higher planes are always full of Higher Beings. None of the distorted forms can leave the Astral Planes and go higher. In general, most people are stuck on the

Astral Planes, lacking the refined energy needed to travel in the upper planes.

If you are studying a spiritual teaching, you can travel to the higher levels of the Astral Plane and, in certain instances, enter the Mental Plane. Usually, however, only high initiates can make that transition.

Ordinarily, a person will travel a long distance at night or in meditation. Generally, your subtle body begins the journey in the Subtle Plane or Higher Astral Plane and then travels upward through that plane. If a person is spiritually advanced, she can then enter the Mental Plane, but must always go through the Higher Astral Plane to arrive at the Mental Plane.

The Mental Plane is also divided into many levels. The levels in the Mental Plane do not overlap, but flow from one to another, making it difficult to tell when one has gone into a higher level. On the Astral Planes, the inhabitants define the overlaps. For example, you may see one level inhabited by certain types of life forms and, when you go into the next level, you will still see some of the same life forms, but much fewer, and as you continue through that new level, the previous life forms will disappear and new forms will appear.

Your subtle body determines how high you can travel. The more refined it is the higher it can go.

Each person's subtle body relates to accumulations in previous lives. If, for instance, you have in the past lived a life dedicated to spiritual pursuits, you would bring a developed subtle body into the present life. This is true even if your last life was not spiritual. Actually, you never lose any development, although there may be lifetimes in which it will lie dormant, and then the subtle body would have to be reawakened to its full potential in each spiritual life.

In order to understand the different levels of each plane, we will start with one plane and analyze its contents and conditions.

THE PHYSICAL PLANE

The physical plane is very obvious and the one with which you are most familiar. It is the physical world you inhabit with all the physical objects around you. You live mostly in this world, and most people know of no other world other than this one. You function in this world in a physical body that stays alive as long as your bodily functions continue working.

When you travel into the other planes, you do so in what is called the astral or subtle body. Most people have an astral body but haven't developed it enough to reach the higher levels of the Astral Plane.

THE LOWER ASTRAL PLANE

This plane consists of several levels. Some of these levels are so full of distorted entities that they are not passable to most people.

The entities that inhabit these regions vary in nature. Some are discarded shells that clung to the physical plane and, therefore, were not destroyed. These shells are nebulous and can be seen as dark vapors. There is no consciousness in them, but they clearly impress negative energy on any soul in their realm. The Higher Beings call these shells "entities" and try to destroy them whenever possible. Most of them stay close to the physical plane and try to affect humans. When an entity is near, you will feel depressed and, often, low in energy without an obvious reason.

The best way to be rid of their negativity is to purify your room or house with sage and camphor oil in water. Roses are also a deterrent to entities, but the water must always be fresh. Negative forces influence these negative entities. They use them to cast negative energy over their enemies. If you have an argument with someone, that energy will draw these entities in quickly to fuel the fire. They will stay around you unless you cleanse your surroundings.

When you feel any negativity at all, be certain to check if it is coming from your lower nature or if it is an outside energy. Your lower nature will attract these entities when you are immersed in it. If you have negative thoughts, these thoughts will affect your surroundings and attract these entities. Be vigilant about your thinking; otherwise you can pollute your living area, and such pollution will affect your meditations.

In contrast, pure thoughts will cause the entities to leave. Each day, you should light incense, which also cleanses vibrations as long as you haven't polluted your home with major negative thought patterns.

A dirty and cluttered home will also attract these negative entities. The most important thing you should do is to have a home that is clean and organized. If you have an office, either at home or elsewhere, it is also important to have it in good order. Papers can be in neat stacks if you can't file them right away. The main thing is to create beauty around you, with paintings on the walls, and plants, and even flowers, as long as they are fresh and in clean water.

An entity can never harm you, but it can frighten you and be very menacing. If you don't have a teacher or Master then call on Lord Jesus or the Lord Buddha. They may not personally come, but they will send you a high initiate who can help you. Only use these names when you feel you are in danger or are really frightened. Some people have a very strong imagination, so make certain your frightened inner child is not producing the experience.

Entities of any kind can also produce sounds and smells that will be distorted and unpleasant. They differ from what is called ghosts. Ghosts are generally not in the Lower Astral Plane but in a level that is a little higher. They can resemble an entity in that they can be negative and have strong vibrations. When a ghost is negative, it will try to frighten a person. It will throw objects, emit sounds, and produce odors. Again, do not be afraid of these ghosts. It is best to address them directly, and, again, to not be frightened.

Often, ghosts are benevolent and are waiting for a loved one to die and be with them. This type of ghost needs to be helped to go on to another level. If you have a teacher, ask her to take the ghost away.

Often a ghost simply doesn't know it is dead and is living an illusionary life, believing its loved ones surround it. It is difficult to prove to it that it is really dead. When the ghost understands this, it will leave and go onward. Sudden death can cause this condition, so if you experience a ghost, simply tell it that it is dead and needs to go on. If it won't listen, then bring in your teacher, if you have one, to take it away.

When you feel under attack by any of the creatures in the Lower Astral Plane, be aware that you are being targeted because they see you are spiritual and that you can become a force that will destroy them. They recognize who you are, so never let them think that you, in any way, can be reached and influenced. The more you strike back, the less persistent they become. As you grow spiritually, the most obvious creatures will not even try to reach you.

THE HIGHER ASTRAL PLANE

This plane is the one that most spiritual people enter at night and in meditation. Your subtle body will quickly go through the lower levels, which will not be revealed to you.

On this higher plane, you will encounter Higher Beings. There will be adepts and other more advanced initiates who are there to teach and help you. If you are studying something in the mundane world, you will have a helper at night to continue your studies and reinforce your knowledge. Most of the work on these higher levels is geared to teaching and studying, preparing you to accomplish your personal goals in your physical life.

If you are an initiate you may have a Master give you an assignment; you then will always be taught on the higher planes. Even if you are not now aware of the work you need to do, you will still be guided to your helper, who will prepare you for the future work. If you are having difficulty in any of the areas you need to study, you can ask for help on the Subtle Plane, and you will always receive that help. In order to do the work, you must be prepared on the physical plane as well. For example, if your work is to do scientific research, you will need to take the right courses to learn the skills, but the work on the Subtle Plane will be to give you ideas for your research and help you plan the correct way to proceed.

Another aspect dealt with on these planes is the concept of community. You are often in classes with other students, some from your spiritual community and some from other communities. There, you are taught sound methods on how to build community.

It is also there that you encounter others who are part of your spiritual family who may not have arrived on the physical plane yet. Sometimes, when you meet these students in the future you will feel you know them and, often, this knowing comes from working with them in these communities and not necessarily from past lives. This is even true when you meet people in other spiritual practices or in spiritually based organizations.

One day, you may be in a class and remember the lessons you were taught. A high initiate often has full recollection.

You will often see brilliant colors and brilliant scenes on these higher levels. Some people will be given auditory messages or have flashes of insight.

The vibrations and sounds of the higher planes are very beautiful, much purer than in the lower planes. The colors are luminous and full of light. Even everyday objects, such as furniture, are more pronounced and usually larger than life.

Another thing to notice on these planes is the natural environment. There are large levels full of beautiful flowers and trees, and, at times, even huge, friendly animals. When you are in one of these levels, try to see as much as possible and bring back that knowledge. Most of the time, you will be inside buildings and won't notice the natural surroundings, but it's important to try to remember and bring that memory back with you.

These higher planes of existence are endless. There are places for every type of learning, as well as places that bring beauty to the soul. These are the gifts you are given. You strive and face obstacles because you know, consciously or unconsciously, that you long to return to these worlds. The physical plane cannot, in any way, compare to these higher planes.

One last thing to remember about these planes: When we speak about the higher worlds, we are referring to these planes and those that are even higher. Never do we refer to the Lower Astral Planes as Worlds. These Worlds contain order, and the people in them have developed their higher principles. The lower levels are just chaos and darkness. The creatures there do not contain the higher principles except for those ghosts who can still move upward. Living humans who have not opened the seed of the spirit cannot go to the higher worlds. Their dreams are just psychological, as they cannot travel far beyond the physical plane.

When you travel on these higher planes, always ask to remember the experiences. Even beginning students can have recall. Every time you meditate or go to sleep, link with your Higher Self and ask the Higher Self to take you to the higher planes. Make this part of your prayer, and thank the Higher Self for helping you.

With each journey, take some notes; just a line or two is fine. This way, in the future, you can determine if your travels become clearer and more refined. Travel in the Higher Astral Plane is a direct indication of spiritual development.

Lastly, try to give yourself enough time to meditate. To be able to go to the higher planes takes practice when you are a beginning student. Meditate for at least half an hour, and try to meditate two to three times a day. The more you do this, the easier it will become to leave the physical body and to fully experience your subtle body.

With each journey, you must try to observe everything. Keep your attention focused, with no extraneous thoughts. It will certainly take time to have full recall and, usually, you must be a higher initiate to have this ability. There are a few who have this gift right away, but they generally have studied a spiritual teaching many times and open up that old faculty quickly. The same holds true with the higher skandhas. Those initiates who were clairvoyant and clairaudient will develop and open these skandhas right away. Sometimes someone will develop too rapidly, and has to be closed down a little for the person to be more in balance.

THE MENTAL PLANE

This is the plane where the Masters reside. It is a plane that cannot be described to you. The energy is very different from the Astral Plane, and the atmosphere is full of beauty and love. To be on this plane is a goal of all striving initiates.

Generally, the higher levels of the Astral Plane and the lower levels of the Mental Plane are where the Masters sometimes work with students. Primarily, the Higher Astral Plane is used, but, on occasion, the Master will take the student to the lower levels of the Mental Plane. Depending on the refinement of the subtle body, a more advanced disciple can sometimes reach the lower Mental Plane by herself.

The inhabitants on the Mental Plane vary. Some are high initiates awaiting rebirth. Others are alive in a physical body, but perform special work on this plane. All types of energy are there and they can be used in various ways and take on various forms.

The Masters can gain access to all kinds of beings and bring them to this plane for specialized work. These beings are from other worlds, separate from ours, such as the Devic kingdom. Some of these beings are life forms coming from other planets. They are in their own subtle bodies, which are specific for their world.

Some students may see these other beings and become bewildered about what they are, but if you could travel to their planets, you would see them in their present life cycle. The Masters visit them in their worlds and they visit the Masters in ours by contacting them on the Mental Plane.

THE BUDDHIC PLANE

This plane is still higher and completely inaccessible to any disciple. Even some of the Masters cannot go there; only very high Masters and those above them can enter it. It will become more accessible in future cycles.

THE NIRVANIC PLANE

Still higher, this plane is beyond even the Masters' knowledge. Only a few High Beings have entered it. Buddha is one of these Beings, and even He could not remain there for long.

This is just a brief description of these planes. As you travel to the higher planes, you will see many wondrous things. These worlds are full of beauty, energy, and forms beyond earthly knowledge, and, most of all, there are many loving souls who abide there. These souls will assist you when you need help. Many are awaiting rebirth, and many are simply there for a long duration. Karmically, they have earned the right to remain on these higher planes, and if they return to the physical world, it is only for a special mission or to work through some karma.

When you meet someone in the subtle world who wants to help you, be careful that the person is from the higher planes and is not an impersonator coming from the Lower Astral Plane. If you ask to see light, these Higher Beings can produce light; the lower beings cannot produce light. Use your Higher Self and your discrimination at all times.

The lower ones can be very tricky. If you are told something, put it in your heart. Does it feel right? You can be clouded by your desire body or be influenced by a negative force. Travel with care and question everything. If you have a teacher, she is your guide and can verify your information.

Now, here are some exercises that may help you to identify some of the things you will experience in the subtle world.

Exercise One:
  1. *In meditation, try to focus your third eye on a point in space. If you see a light, that is even better. Just focus on the light. Ask to see colors, and you will begin to experience brilliant colors. These come from the Higher Astral Plane and are very beautiful.*

Once you experience a color of any kind, do the following exercise.

  2. *Watch the color and, carefully, try to make it form a symbol. For example, you may see the color green. Try to make the green form a ball, and then try to make it form a thick line or an elongated triangle. If another color comes in, take that color and put it around the first color. It is very easy to make colors move into anything you want.*
  3. *Another phenomenon you may experience is waves of light floating toward you. When this happens, try to hold the light still, in one place. If you can do this, then ask to*

*see something in the light. You may see a figure of some
kind. If you do, then ask the figure to identify itself.*

4. *Also, you may experience the beginning of hearing sound.
If this happens, try to hold on to it by focusing your attention on the sound. If it is all around you, simply be still
and try to make it louder. All sound in the astral world
comes from the higher levels, so be aware when you are
in those higher levels.*

5. *When you experience sound, try to identify whether the
sound is music or coming from words being sent to you.
If the sound is words, ask the sender to identity herself.
Sometimes the sender will appear to you visually.*

The more you work with the above exercises, the stronger will be
the messages. Part of your work is to remember everything that
takes place. People fail to write down their images, and then they
forget them. Keep a paper and pencil by your bed and next to your
meditation area. Often, messages are sent during your sleep. You
may want to hold on to these sendings by keeping them in a special
notebook, since loose paper can be lost and forgotten.

Some people have a constant barrage of things happening. If
there seems to be too much, it is more than likely that these images
or sendings are made up in the person's fantasy world. These should
always be checked with a teacher; otherwise you may be living in
an unhealthy world of illusion.

A general rule of thumb is that no one will have every meditation or dream full of images or sounds unless that person is at least
a fourth initiate.

One other thing to keep in mind is about the use of any kind of
drugs, or even alcohol. Never meditate if you take drugs, because
that will generally push you into the Lower Astral Plane. A lot of
alcohol can do the same, so never meditate when drinking. You
need to wait several hours.

In the case of drugs, you need to have been free of them for at
least one year, unless you were a heavy user, and in that case, you
should be free of drugs for two years. The nicotine in cigarettes

also affects the subtle body. If you smoke, it should be on a very limited basis and, certainly, for health reasons, you should never smoke.

Excess food, especially meat, must be curtailed. You should eat wholesome foods and as little meat as possible. Fish and even chicken are better and, of course, lots of fresh vegetables. Remember, anything in excess is not good for meditation. When a person starts to enter the higher planes, she will need to refrain from all meat and alcohol. This applies to someone who is a sixth initiate. In addition, sex of any kind will need to be given up at that stage.

In some teachings, the students are asked to be vegetarians and refrain from sex from the beginning. This is fine if a person lives in an ashram and has little contact with the outside world. In the Higher Self Yoga teaching, we ask the student to live in moderation and not be addicted to any substance, whether it be drugs, alcohol, cigarettes, or food. Obesity is also an addiction and needs to be looked at as such, unless a person has a physical problem that is responsible for the condition.

When the Masters observe a student's subtle body, they can discern her former development. As stated earlier, the subtle body may be very refined, but it still must be awakened to its full potential. If, for example, you have been a high initiate in a past life, and in this life you only have one initiation, you are carrying the subtle body of the high initiate, but to use it, you still must go through the higher initiations to open it fully. It is easier for you to do this than if you had never achieved those higher initiations. In general, the potential can be achieved again, yet many people still can become caught in the mundane world and never achieve the higher levels.

It is important to always strive upward toward the higher planes and open your subtle body to work at its full capability. Striving makes all potential a reality.

Chapter **11**

When You Reach an Impasse that Stops Movement

In every student's journey, there comes a time when the student reaches a plateau that seems impossible to move through. The experience is one of helplessness and a lack of motivation to even try to let go of what is causing the difficulty. If a person is at such an impasse, it's very important to change the energy and try to regroup.

Unfortunately, many students leave a spiritual teaching at this point or they simply remain in the same place and fail to move forward. Then the obstacle becomes a genuine block instead of an imagined one, and even the teacher cannot guide the student through it.

Let's look at what these impasses look like. They can be categorized in the following manner:

1. Stuck in a mundane situation that consumes all of the student's time.
2. Lost in a quest for perfectionism.
3. Caught up in physical desires.
4. Caught up in emotional desires.
5. Wanting worldly recognition.
6. Wanting material things to excess.
7. Lacking a strong enough will to move forward.
8. Lacking a strong enough desire for God Consciousness.
9. Losing sight of reality.
10. Needing more joy and fun.
11. Finding a substitute for the teaching.
12. Putting the teaching on a back burner.
13. Giving power away.
14. Losing oneself in emotion.

15. Lacking desire for more wisdom.

The above are the ways that a person can fail to move off a plateau. Let's start examining them.

1. Stuck in a Mundane Situation That Takes All the Student's Time

This one is probably the cause of most impasses. When a person is too busy to meditate, read, and go to class, then he has clearly stopped moving forward. There are always a million excuses, which will be unacceptable to any teacher in an esoteric teaching. If a student is serious about studying a teaching, excuses are simply not acceptable.

When the student totally gives up, not even trying to study or meditate, the energies slow down and even become atrophied. He will stay in one place, sometimes for months at a time. Only a real shock can move the student off the plateau and provide the energy to desire the teaching again.

Lack of desire is the key. With such a lack, the need for God Consciousness has disappeared and given way to the need to be in the mundane world. Often, the student leaves and never returns in that lifetime. The person may think about returning, but is too ashamed to face the teacher and gives up completely.

Let's look at some of the signs that signal the beginning of this process. The first sign is a lack of enthusiasm. What had been wondrous and exciting is now commonplace. The need to learn more is gone, replaced with a feeling of being overwhelmed if anything else has to be done.

The second sign is the student's feeling of wanting more than the teacher can provide. This is an aspect of the perfectionist sub-personality that can appear at this stage of the process.

The third sign is totally forgetting about meditation or class, putting something else ahead of either one. The student must meditate in order to keep the connection, but even connecting no longer seems important. Usually, when the teacher feels this happening, he will withdrew his energy to see if the student feels the void and wakes up.

In the case of failure to attend class, the student puts social events before class, not simply turning them down, but, instead, thinking that the event is more important. This obviously prevents the student from continuing, and soon the need to see the teacher disappears and all the energy is withdrawn. In some cases, the student will literally break his discipleship through neglect. The teaching is forgotten to the point that, if the student thinks about it again, it is as if he has passed through a phase of life and moved on.

Usually, a student will wake up and realize what he is missing, particularly when the energy is completely withdrawn. Even the least devoted student feels such a loss, but it is usually felt briefly, and because there is little desire to reconnect, the student will not return to the teaching.

This plateau is the most difficult one to be on as it keeps the student from continuing. Stopping at this point is dangerous because the negative forces will try to influence such students and lead them away. If you feel you are in a busy period, without the time or energy to work on the teaching, it would be good for you to notice whether you have any of the following thoughts:

- I'm too tired to meditate.
- I'm too tired to go to class.
- When I get up in the morning, my time is limited and other things take up my time, so meditation is too difficult.
- I have a very difficult job and need to just relax at night.
- Class is located at a place that takes too much time to go to.
- I have more important things I need to do (on a class night).
- My boyfriend or girlfriend or spouse needs my attention tonight.
- Getting a baby sitter is too difficult and expensive.
- Some classes are boring; I would rather read the books.
- My meditation practice is not good. It's too difficult to have a good meditation.

In general, the excuses can become more and more refined, and, before you know it, the time between meditating or going to class becomes longer and longer. When this happens, notice how negative your thoughts become. The more the energy is taken away, the more negative are the messages from the negative forces.

How can you avoid becoming stuck on this plateau? First, meditate and ask your Higher Self to help you move on. Then, ask for a first step to help you conquer the negative feelings that are arising. If you have a teacher, ask for assistance. This will bring back the teacher's energy and protection, which will ward off the negative thoughts.

Try to be more vigilant. Force yourself to go to class and follow a schedule that includes reading and meditation. Even if the enthusiasm isn't there at the beginning, just doing the work will reawaken your interest. Find a good spiritual book to read, even if it doesn't relate to your teaching. Mainly, work with your heart to reconnect to your teacher and feel the love of the teacher toward you. Remember, you are in a particular teaching for a reason, and that reason, fundamentally, is the desire for God Consciousness. Do not lose that desire in the mundane world around you. Remember, it is your right and your heritage.

When you are off the plateau, look back and notice what happened in your life to put you there in the first place. Write down those circumstances and be aware that those patterns can come up again and pull you away.

2. Lost in a Quest for Perfectionism

The next strong plateau is the area of perfectionism. As mentioned earlier, it can come into play, along with the first one, as a result of judging the teacher as imperfect. This is the primary reason a student will break the relationship with the teacher. The student will put the teacher on a pedestal. When, in the eyes of the student, the teacher fails the student's expectations in any way, he falls from grace. Needing the teacher to be perfect comes from the student's own expectations of perfection. If the teacher isn't perfect, how can the student achieve this?

The perfectionist will even criticize other disciples who are more advanced if they fall short of what the perfectionist feels a disciple should be. Many perfectionists leave a teacher for these reasons and continue to look for the perfect teacher and teaching. What really needs to happen is that the student must recognize and let go of this "holier than thou" attitude. Even the Masters say they are not perfect, and if this is so, how can a student expect the teacher to be perfect?

At the other extreme, a student may see the teacher as someone without flaws and never question anything because in the student's eyes, the teacher must be perfect.

A spiritual teaching is very complex. It contains many hidden meanings, and only a teacher has access to those meanings. Sometimes, a teacher may know the answer to something a student asks but can't reveal the truth because the student isn't ready to receive it. Even the teacher isn't given access to certain knowledge from the Masters until the teacher receives higher initiations and has the ability to contain such knowledge. All these factors count in understanding the role of the teacher.

A teacher may have great understanding and spiritual knowledge, but may not necessarily have great knowledge concerning the mundane world. That depends on the teacher's education in worldly matters. If the student expects a teacher to be educated in a scholarly manner, that is a big mistake. The teacher's tasks are far more difficult than that and involve working on many planes of existence. Book knowledge is nice, but not required of an earthly teacher. The teacher can develop this knowledge at a later time. The teacher's main task is helping the student move forward on the spiritual path. A perfectionist will require that the teacher be all knowing about every subject and certainly expect the teacher to be well read in a given area. No matter how much a teacher knows, this type of student will require still more.

Such a student may also expect the teacher to have a wonderful personality. Since personality comes from childhood conditioning, there certainly can be major differences in the personalities of teachers as there are among students. If a student doesn't like the personality of the teacher, this also falls in the category of perfectionist expectations. In general, the personality of the perfectionist is full of flaws, because there is an inner rigidity that can be detected on the outside. Perfectionists want the teacher to have a personality more like their own, which would make them feel more comfortable and also help them avoid seeing any flaws in the teacher. When a teacher has a different personality, such as more casual and relaxed, perfectionists have a harder time relating to the teacher.

When it comes to studying any teaching, perfectionists need to know it all. They can be very demanding, and this type of demand is not for God Consciousness, but for knowing everything in order to be more perfect. Unfortunately, this can cause a student to get stuck on a perfectionist plateau, and moving from that plateau is very difficult.

Perfectionists will also leave a teacher and a teaching if they feel their expectations have not been met. Naturally, to change, these students must let go of such needs. It takes a lot of therapy for this to happen, as the issue is very rooted in the student's psyche and identity. Perfectionism is one of the most difficult traits to have, as it requires much high-energy maintenance to hold on to it. Many a student has given up because he can't achieve the highest spirituality in a short time. There is also a high level of competition with other students, perhaps thinking, "I'm better than that person, so why is he more advanced?" This can be an attitude that sets up failure.

In order to overcome this plateau, first you need to identify the cause of your perfectionism. Usually a person has a perfectionist parent who told the child what he accomplished was not good enough.

The need to be perfect keeps most people from succeeding in life. Even if they are high-level achievers, the feeling they carry is, "I could do better." This keeps the student dwelling in the negative self-critic and, usually, the critic then, in turn, criticizes others. Such people have a difficult time in relationships because they project their needs onto others.

Once you have identified the cause of your perfectionism, then you need to start to change your behavior. This will take a long time because it is so very much a part of your identify, and to change the identity means to undergo careful day-to-day observation. Only when you truly see yourself and realize the extent you are compelled to be in this pattern, can you start to change.

Many people are perfectionists in certain areas of their lives but not in others. For example, a man whose job performance is slow because he anguishes over details can be very sloppy in his home, leaving clothes all over the place and vice versa. A person who is neat to an extreme can have a messy filing system.

Perfectionism, no matter what form it takes, needs to transform into orderliness, which places no demands on others. It's better to be disciplined and organized than to be a perfectionist.

The best way to work with this issue is to do a nightly review looking at the situations that come up for you during the day. Determine if you were in your perfectionist pattern during those situations, and also notice if you used your pattern to judge others. As you work with the nightly review, begin to notice your perfectionism as it occurs during the day and try to change it to something positive.

Let go of the need to change others and try to simply see those you love as human, with good and bad characteristics. If someone has more negative characteristics, question whether you want to continue the relationship, but be careful to see if your evaluation is accurate and not based on your perfectionist needs. Clarity comes from looking at a situation from a disidentified place.

Disidentification is a path to freedom. It means you no longer desire anything from anyone. Letting go of perfectionism is very hard to do. Just say to yourself, "I am not perfect, no one is perfect, and that's okay."

Lastly, when you sit down and speak to someone, carefully check your tone of voice for a superior attitude. Perfectionists often appear and sound as if they were superior.

3. Letting Go of Physical Desires

The third impasse concerns letting go of physical desires. As stated before, normal physical desires are part of being human, but if a desire becomes an addiction, then the student would be at an impasse. Any addiction keeps a student from growing spiritually.

One of the most difficult problems that can arise in any spiritual teaching is the desire for love. The need for love can cross over into the sexual realm, and, since sexual energy is very strong, this particular desire can be harmful. Many initiates have fallen victim to the desire for sex and have strayed off the path because this desire causes them to misuse their energy.

In general, sexual energy is very strong in most spiritual people. This is because it is an energy that can lead to ecstasy. Many people think that ecstasy resembles the state of Samadhi. This is a misunderstanding by some initiates. Without a doubt, excessive sexual practice can keep a student from growing spiritually. Moderation is the key, but moderation can be misunderstood.

Generally, an initiate should not have sexual intercourse more than six times a month. Less is better, but it depends upon the circumstances. If a student is married to someone who is not in a spiritual teaching, and his spouse desires sexual intercourse more frequently, then the student sometimes should fulfill that need.

Other abuses can be in the form of drugs, alcohol, cigarettes, and food. The previous chapter explained these addictions.

Physical desires can also refer to thoughts. If a student is thinking of the sexual act and isn't actually engaged in it, this can also cause him to be out of balance. Thoughts, even though they are not actions, can cloud the student's path. Eventually, the thoughts can become actions, and the excess begins.

Physical desires can cover a variety of subjects. For instance, some students may have the urge to exercise to the extent that they build up the body to disproportionate levels. Such a strong physical body can impede a student's subtle body from moving upward to the subtle world after death.

When I speak of moderation, I also refer to keeping healthy, strong, and fit. Some spiritual people think meditation is all they need to be healthy. This is wrong. Lack of exercise can be very unhealthy. The body is meant to be used in the world. It needs nourishment and activity. Monks in the old days used to flagellate themselves, believing the body was sinful. This type of self-punishment shows a lack of judgment. The body is beautiful when used properly.

It's important for you to examine your life in terms of excess and addiction. A student needs to be in control of all the bodily functions. Excessive physical desires of any kind will keep the student from moving forward.

4. Letting Go of Emotional Desires

The fourth impasse concerns emotional desires. First and foremost is the need for love—not sexual love, but the deep desire to love and be loved. The love from the teacher, the love from a companion or friends, and the love from brothers and sisters in the spiritual as well as the physical family, are all emotional desires that can be played out to excess.

A student's need to be loved usually comes from a lack of love and nurturing as a child. The student will then seek love from the teacher, who does love the student, but not as a parent. Since the student is very needy, unconditional love from the teacher will not suffice, and the student will feel abandoned or unloved as a result.

The same is true if this needy student seeks love from others in the teaching. Since the love isn't what the student really desires, which is parental love, the student will feel not only unloved but also not included. These feelings, which are really projections, can cause negative feelings toward the spiritual family.

This excessive need for love can also extend to outside relationships. Such a student will put love before the teaching and look at outside relationships as being more important if he finds someone to fulfill his need.

This plateau can last for a while until the student realizes the nature of the inner craving and lets go of this need.

Often such a person will have inflated ideas about what he should be given and will feel justified in believing that others are neglecting him. Such a student has narcissistic tendencies and is very difficult to deal with. Usually, this type of student can cause disruption in a spiritual teaching by trying to divide students and cause difficulty for the teacher.

Such an individual has an array of other emotional desires. Most of them come under the category of personal needs. These include the need to be taken care of, the need to be given material support, the need to have a family, the need to become successful, the need for the right type of home and surroundings, the need to become independent, and so on. Again, some of these needs are normal and are very much a part of the individual's life path.

If you have a need to live in beautiful surroundings, this can come from your Higher Self, but if you have a need to isolate yourself in the countryside and be a hermit, then that need is excessive and should be looked at.

If you need to be independent and you take that need to excess by refusing any help if you are sick or destitute, then, again, your need is beyond what is normal.

If you need to have a family and you have so many children that you can't afford to take care of them, then your need is not based on reality but on self-indulgence.

If you look at your life and think about your emotional needs, notice if any of them are not normal. It would be good to list the needs and notice the ones that are excessive and unrealistic. Take these needs and work with them by first determining the cause of the need. Learning to discipline yourself will help in overcoming needs that can take you off the spiritual path.

In most cases, emotional needs originate in childhood, but some can go further back to a past life. Check with your Higher Self about whether or not this is true. To eliminate an excessive need of any kind, it's important to reveal the source and notice how it plays out in your present life.

5. Wanting Worldly Recognition

The fifth impasse is very specific. It relates to the way a person acts in the pursuit of fame. Such a person needs worldly recognition, even when the recognition is not appropriate. For example, a student who is an artist feels he needs to become famous and sell his art for high prices. The student also feels that the spiritual community, the teacher, and the Master should help make this happen.

When this doesn't happen, the student becomes very disillusioned and actually angry that the help was not forthcoming.

The Masters help students fulfill their dharma and may even send specific indications to help a student proceed in the right direction, but the student also needs to be active in developing his profession and to follow the indications given.

In the first example of the artist, he may have been given indications on how to develop his art but did not follow them. Therefore, he didn't achieve the professionalism needed to sell his work. Along the way, the student became enamored by his art and lost sight of its true value. The need to become famous was so strong that he was incapable of seeing what he still needed to develop to become successful.

There is a hidden belief in some students that the Masters will always help them. In some cases that is true, but only when the student is striving and is free of all ego needs. If a student's ego needs fame and fortune, the teacher will not help in any way, as the motivation is self-serving rather than based on the need to serve humanity.

There is always a fine line here, and it is very important to observe your motives and watch your lower nature as you follow your dharma.

6. Wanting Material Things to Excess

The next impasse is not very common in a spiritual teaching. It relates to a student's becoming very greedy for material things, taking that desire into the realm of excess. There is nothing wrong in wanting a nice home, clothes, and money to take care of your needs. A student may be born into wealth or even make a lot of money, and that is also okay.

What is meant by excess is where someone who is comfortable and has enough wants to have much more in the way of possessions and wealth. This person may be generous, but is still caught up in pursuing all that wealth provides, such as a larger home or more money in the bank or a new car every year.

Even though this material greed is rare in spiritual teachings, there are people who base their identity on how much they have, not who they are spiritually. Such a person can reach an impasse when his values need to change and he becomes blocked from moving forward.

One of the most difficult things a student needs to do is to become totally unattached to material things. You can own beautiful objects and create a home full of lovely pieces. As long as you are not attached to any of those things, then you can fill a home with as many objects as you want. The key is to never be attached to any of it.

7. Not Having a Strong Enough Will to Move Forward.

The seventh impasse is one of the most important ones. A strong will is the major factor needed to move forward. Without it a person can remain stuck. If a student has a strong will there is virtually nothing he cannot overcome. If he has a weak will, almost everything holds him back.

What determines a strong will? Many factors come into play. The most important factor comes from past lives. A student is more likely to have a strong will if he has taken on leadership roles in the past. It is more difficult to develop a strong will if a student has lived many subservient lives.

Besides coming from past lives, this difficulty can also come from a childhood of being abused and subjugated to the will of a parent or a sibling.

How does a student develop a strong will when he has such a difficult history? To develop the will takes time and knowledge about the will itself. When I speak of a strong will, I are referring to a determined will, not a stubborn will.

The will can be looked at in a negative or a positive manner. The positive strong will is a beacon of energy that helps a person look at an issue, determine how to overcome any problem, and move through to resolution.

For example, a person cannot overcome an eating problem. A strong-willed person would look into various diets, determine which was best, and proceed to follow the diet and lose the weight.

Once the weight was lost, the person would watch the diet so as to not gain the weight back. He would also work on discovering psychologically why he had gained the weight in the first place and try to change that pattern.

If the person had a weak will, he might lose the weight but have a difficult time keeping the pounds off and would not go into any depth about why the weight gain happened in the first place.

Now, a person may be strong willed in many areas of his life and weak willed in others. This is determined by the person's psychological makeup.

Self-discipline builds a strong will. If someone has a lack of will, taking a project and working on it a step at a time until it is completed is a good method to strengthen the will. Anyone can build a strong will, but the key is self-discipline. Remember to take one step at a time, and not overdo, or you can go on overload and fail to complete the project.

8. Not Having a Strong Enough Desire for God Consciousness

When a student comes to this specific impasse, the lower nature is taking away the desire for God Consciousness. How does this happen? What can cause a yogi to let go of the main impetus that has placed him on a spiritual path in the first place?

Unfortunately, this question is not easy to answer. There are many things that take a student off the path, but the one that is the most difficult to change is the loss of striving for God Consciousness. Somewhere on the path, the student's lower nature has crushed the hope of achieving this, and so the desire for God Consciousness is lessened.

Since each student is different, each requires an individual approach to dealing with this issue. The best way to restore the longing for God Consciousness is to try to regain the original feelings that brought a student onto the path. It means letting go of everything that took place after that.

For example, perhaps a student had a difficult obstacle to overcome and, in the process, lost the feeling of joy about the teaching. Or, maybe a student had difficulties with some other students or even the teacher, and in the process of working through those difficulties, lost the longing. Perhaps, over a long period of time, the student simply gave up feeling he could make the higher initiations that bring one closer to God Consciousness.

Whatever the reason, the loss of the desire can cause a student to remain on a plateau indefinitely. With each new challenge, the course of progress slows down because the impetus is no longer there. Imagine seeing yourself lost in a tunnel with no turning back and with no light ahead to guide you. This is what happens to a student who loses his longing for God Consciousness.

If you are at this impasse, try to surround yourself with beauty and realize that beauty is part of God Consciousness, that beauty brings joy, that beauty restores the longing to return to the Source.

9. Losing Sight of Reality

The ninth impasse concerns reality. Losing sight of reality refers to a student who has become carried away in the world of fantasy and who has lost the ability to determine what is real and what is produced by his imagination.

Many students have experiences that are fanciful but they believe their experiences are real psychic experiences. Some students think they are special because they "see" Masters and High Beings on a regular basis. Some students hear voices and believe they are listening to Masters and even believe they are being given special messages from the Lord Maitreya. Others believe they are given special missions to save humanity.

Channeling has become a major concern for humanity. Many who channel are not in any esoteric teaching and do not even have a physical teacher who can guide them. In most cases, these channelers are listening to beings in the lower levels of the astral world and are being deceived and influenced by the negative forces. Channeling is a new word for the old form of spiritualism.

If a student falls into the above category, it is very important to check all visions and messages with a physical teacher. Only in rare instances does a student receive direct messages from the Masters. Those students are carefully selected for specific work and are trained to use their discrimination at all times. They are very realistic and practical people who do not indulge in fantasy of any kind.

It is obvious that communications are also given to the higher initiates but initiations are always given by the physical teacher when the teacher is alive, and this relationship continues after death. Too many disciples think they are receiving initiations on the subtle plane. If this happens and the teacher is no longer alive, then another high initiate will be told to verify any such initiation. If it is not verified then you need to question it.

It is important to know that the first initiation is always on the physical plane with a physical teacher. There are no exceptions to this cosmic law.

Often, students lose sight of reality because they have an over-developed spiritual subpersonality that wants them to feel special. Unfortunately, this subpersonality can easily be influenced by negative forces that can take a student off the path. For example, a student may believe he is being given special recognition and may even be told by a negative force that he is higher than the teacher. Such belief enhances the ego and can cause the student to leave the teacher and teaching. Often, such a student will give accounts of false visions and messages to others and try to influence them.

It is important to question things and check them with a real teacher. Some people can open up their clairvoyance and clairaudience on their own. If this happens, the person may have this gift but lacks the occult knowledge needed to handle it correctly. If you do not have a teacher, don't believe anything you receive from the subtle world until you can find a teacher to work with. Otherwise, you may lose sight of reality and become lost in a realm you cannot control.

The other area of fantasy is in the mundane world. Some students feel that being in an esoteric teaching makes them special and that, because they are special, they deserve more in life.

Everything is karma. If one student has more worldly things and another doesn't, that is karma. Remember, karma is reality. Expectations are not reality. Reality is very personal and whether you are a yogi or not, you have to deal with life according to your karma. This is a cosmic law.

At the end of your life you need to see, even for a moment, the consequences of the actions you have taken. This is one reason there is a flashback of all the important events of your life. If you have negative karma as a result of those actions, then the karma is impressed on your monad. Positive karma is also impressed on the monad. When you are reborn, you will be attracted to the family that will help you live out your karma.

A student can overcome negative karma with good deeds. He can also make positive karma by being of service in the world. It is important for you to review the reality of your personal karma. Then you may have a better understanding of the different life styles of spiritual people in the world. To question or even judge others around you is losing sight of reality.

10. Needing More Joy and Fun

Seeking joy and happiness on a personal level comes from the desire body. Joy, of course, also relates to a higher state of being. The joy that creates an impasse is personal and is not in any way linked to the higher Joy, which is a particular state of wisdom.

When you need to spend a lot of time engaged in fun things, whether it is watching TV, going out socially, playing a sport, or even filling your life with all kinds of activities that feed the need for fun, then you are indulging in excessive pleasure. This need to be entertained usually comes from a deep core of sadness. Or a difficult childhood can lead to a feeling of inner emptiness that you try to fill by keeping yourself continually entertained. To be still and alone with your thoughts and feelings can be too scary.

Another reason a person indulges in entertainment comes from a sense of "I deserve to have fun, I work too hard." This is why many people work all day and come home and vegetate, and watch TV. This comes from a desire not to have to use the mind anymore. Relaxation represents fun and diversion. Again, some relaxation is good and necessary for the body, but when you are a yogi, too much relaxation makes you neglect your spiritual practice.

Look at your life. Is it filled every day with entertaining activities? Do those activities take up a great deal of time? Watching TV every night is a good example. Do you mix your free time with a variety of things, including household tasks? In general, a yogi needs to keep exercise, socializing, and entertainment in proportion. Doing just one of these activities in excess can be indulgent.

A good plan is to spend three to four evenings, plus one day, doing fun and relaxing activities. Sometimes, an evening spent in meditation and spiritual practice provides a good balance.

In addition to the need for fun and joy sometimes there is the need to become more active in community affairs. Spending an evening doing volunteer work that is of service is a good activity that can bring a person joy.

It is important to recognize the need for balance. Just as some people are stuck in the desire for fun, others are stuck in the need to always work. Though it is more positive for a yogi when work, rather than play, becomes the only focus, it is still excessive and requires balance.

11. Finding a Substitute for the Teaching

This impasse is a subtle block. It relates to the desire to make one's path easier. If, for example, you are studying a teaching such as Higher Self Yoga, and, while you are working in this teaching, you come to one of the other impasses, you may decide to leave this teaching and take up another spiritual practice that doesn't have the challenges that are blocking you in this one.

Generally, this other teaching is a church or faith that makes no demands. Some students have gone back to church and have found that was enough. Some have taken up a meditation practice that is similar to the one they left, but is not a path of initiation, which requires a teacher and has stricter conditions. The meditation practice becomes a substitute and is, in many cases, a way to feel connected. Yet it doesn't entail the struggle with psychological and spiritual obstacles that promote growth.

In some cases, choosing another teaching is fine. The person may have touched upon a teaching like Higher Self Yoga only a few times and is meant to come for a short time and leave.

In other cases, the student is copping out because the impasse he is facing is difficult to overcome. In those cases, the student is meant to work harder, but instead leaves the destined path. The student may then study another teaching, but in time feel the new one isn't right and move from one to another because no other teaching will satisfy the spirit's urge to be on its true path. Such a student loses the opportunity in this life and will have to wait until the next, or the next, to return.

The student can return if he realizes the mistake and comes back without having broken the connection to the teacher. But once a student has made that choice, it is rare that he realizes the error and returns.

12. Putting the Teaching on a Back Burner

This impasse relates to the previous one. In this case, the student leaves because he has too many mundane things to accomplish and therefore hasn't the time to work on psychological and spiritual obstacles. The difference is that the student doesn't leave for another teaching, but instead asks for a leave of absence with the intention that at some time in the future he will return. Even though the intention is there at the start, after a while the chances of the student returning become slimmer and slimmer.

In only a handful of instances does the student return and then pick up the path and continue forward. Such a student has a strong will and determination to follow through once the mundane things have been resolved. In the cases in which this has happened, the student's Higher Self was very developed and gave the student the impetus and longing to return.

Obviously, it is better for the student to stay in the teaching and continue attending classes. He may stay at a standstill because the work isn't being done, but at least the connection is still there with the teacher and the teaching.

13. Giving Your Power Away

This impasse is about owning your power. When a student reaches a certain place on the spiritual path, he must recognize and start to work with his inner power.

This is one of the main challenges any yogi will have to face. In past lives everyone has had a position of authority and everyone has abused the power of that position. Because of the karma that had to be paid off as a result of the abuse, spiritual people may keep away from positions of authority that can in any way cause them to go off again. This problem is so general in spiritual communities that it can be called a spiritual condition.

This is an impasse where many students become stuck indefinitely. To overcome it requires a student to look at past lives, understand the karma, and fearlessly choose to have the authority again with the inner knowledge that he will now know the way to handle it.

There are many leaders who have run nations who work in minor jobs because of the fear of power. There are many incarnations of people who now see themselves as victims and have in past lives been the victimizers. There are many children who have been orphaned because in the past they have killed people and destroyed homes. All of this is karma that is still being paid off.

To overcome this impasse, which is huge, a student needs to accept responsibility for others, not be afraid of leadership, try to take on roles that make him more prominent, and literally say no to the fears that will arise. Power, when directed for the good, is gentle and loving and comes from inner wisdom. Power, when self-serving, is demanding and strong, and comes from the lower nature. The energy is very different.

You should understand how you react to power. If it frightens you or intrigues you, then you need to look at why. Explore all the ways it works on your feelings. Learn ways to begin to slowly utilize its energy to help others. Look at all the things you can do to start to reawaken it and use it correctly. Then this impasse will become a new start on the path to higher achievements.

The use of power is necessary on the higher levels. To reach them you need to let go of the past and believe in your Higher Self to guide you.

14. Losing Oneself in Emotion

With this impasse comes the need to refine emotions. This means reaching a place where you are in control of your emotions. It means never being out of control or, if you are out of control, having the ability to re-center yourself completely.

Obviously, an emotional person can get stuck on this plateau for a time. So let's try to understand exactly what remaining in control of your emotions means. If you go out of control, your energy can harm another person and cause some difficult karma that would stop your advancement. A spiritual student always has more refined energy because the practice of meditation itself refines your subtle body, which enables you to use energy more directly. The higher the initiate's consciousness, the stronger is the energy. If you haven't curtailed emotions, that energy can be abusive. This is why a student who is emotional cannot grow spiritually until he can control all feelings and not give in to the negative ones.

Everyone on the spiritual path feels this particular impasse, and everyone will be tested time and time again to see if he can move forward. I assure you, anyone who is advanced can control emotion, but sometimes even an advanced person will allow emotion to take hold of him.

In some cases, emotion is used as a means to get through to someone who wouldn't listen otherwise. But if this is happening, the person is in control and only uses the emotion for this purpose.

Since emotion is very much a part of the human makeup, it causes difficulty in a lot of relationships. Some relationships are trapped in a pattern of emotional abuse, and the individuals involved have no clear means to break the pattern. To break free is too difficult, yet the only way a person can grow is to be independent and totally free. The kind of freedom I am referring to is not separation, but the freedom that comes from self-control.

If someone deliberately pushes your buttons, it's probably because the person knows you will respond in a certain manner. To end the pattern, you need to stop responding in that same manner, thus breaking the pattern of expectation. For example, someone yells at you and you always yell back and then the next response is even more yelling. If you don't respond by yelling back, then in all likelihood the person who yelled in the first place will become quiet. In some instances, the person is stumped about what to say because he failed to get the expected response. To change a pattern, it only takes one person in the pair to do the opposite of what is expected.

When you have control over your emotions, it makes you feel very secure in any situation. Since you can handle your own feelings, you will not be afraid of anyone else's emotions. Total control of emotion is the goal of every student.

15. Not Wanting More Wisdom

How can a student not want more wisdom? It seems very paradoxical, but there are initiates who come to this plateau and stay there. The main cause of this impasse is the feeling of giving up. The following can cause this feeling:

- Being too involved in mundane things.
- Having circumstances in one's life, such as illness.
- Needing to take a break as described in impasse 12.
- Looking at the teaching and feeling one can't understand any more.
- Seeing the teaching as old knowledge that no longer relates to today's world.
- Wanting to feel secure with the knowledge already gained.
- Seeing the teaching as something already achieved.
- Wanting to wait until older to delve into it more.

When any of the above happens, the student can be at this impasse a long time. It doesn't mean that the student isn't still striving, but it does mean that he is not growing in knowledge.

What is meant by this? Basically, a student can go to class, do his dharma in every way, even work on all the material the teacher gives out, but if his own wish to understand more falters along the way, then he is giving up the desire for wisdom. This lack of interest turns into apathy and causes the student to stand still on the path. Without a doubt, this is a major impasse and needs to be addressed before the apathy becomes ingrained.

First, it is important to recognize that you are in this state; only then can you decide to change it. Simply studying some more can overcome the impasse, as can going to some spiritual meetings in which there is good lively discussion around spiritual matters. Reading another teaching can provoke thought and interest.

There are many ways to move out of this impasse, which seems very easy to do, but in actuality this can be one of the most difficult ones to move through. That is because the feeling is one of not needing more, especially if you have been in a spiritual teaching for a long time. It means you feel you have learned all you want to learn. This type of person can be very knowledgeable, but the knowledge itself can be part of the impasse of not needing to learn more.

Usually a person who is at this place can recognize it and move through it, but there are people who even leave a spiritual teaching they have been in for years simply because of oversaturation. You may say, why not take a leave of absence? Because if a person does this, the person will usually not return. Such a person would feel obliged to stay away and pursue something else; otherwise, he would feel like a failure for having left in the first place.

In general, we are talking about advanced people who have already learned much and simply need some new stimuli to excite them. When you know someone like this, it can be very astonishing to hear that the person has left the teacher and is never heard from again. Even the best souls have to fight to keep active on the path.

If you should find yourself at an impasse, it is important to first recognize that fact, then try to understand what you need to do to move through it. Each impasse has a different set of dynamics that make it a strong or a weak one. Hopefully, you can see the meaning of the impasse and not let it affect your personality for any length of time. If it does, then you may need to seek help from your teacher or another student so as not to remain stuck. Usually, the teacher sees everything the student is going through, but cannot give advice unless the student asks for it. The teacher can only send good thoughts and prayers that the student understands what is needed to move through the impasse and climb upward.

Every student encounters impasses on the path. Just knowing about them can be helpful in identifying some of the feelings, feelings that can make the impasse much larger than it need be. Be vigilant at all times, and then you will recognize each step of the path and where you are standing.

In reviewing the impasses in this chapter, if you find one you are in, ask your Higher Self what are the steps to overcome the impasse and how to best move through it. Each impasse may need a different type of process, so always ask for each step, write it down, and go though the process. Some impasses will take more time than you may imagine and others take less. Never feel you have to move quickly, since working with one impasse often leads you into another one that is hidden beneath it. What's important is moving through the impasse with a better understanding of the blocks that come up for you.

There are no time limits. Some impasses will stay there even as you move forward. They often need to be revisited later on and may become stronger at that time. The main thing to remember is that you can eventually move through any impasse.

Chapter 12

Looking at the End of Life

DEATH IS A STAGE

A spiritual student does not consider death the end of life. In fact, she looks at death as the beginning of a new life, and death and rebirth as one life that will continue for the length of the earth's cycle and then go forward to the next and the next and the next. Life as we see it has no true end, and even the beginning came from a living form. Therefore, in essence there is also no beginning.

You may ask how can this be. Essentially, all life is energy, and since energy cannot be destroyed, there is no end. Energy, once it is formed from its source, goes through change, but even when it appears dormant, it is still alive.

An example of this is the moon. It seems to be a dead body, but in truth, it is full of life forms that are simply at rest. Another example is winter. The plants and trees appear to be dead, but as soon as spring arrives, these life forms enter a new cycle and start to bloom.

Humans are no different. Life is in all things, and even when something appears to be completely dead, it will return in a new form and continue on.

With a new cycle comes a new surge of energy, and since energy is formless and essentially invisible, there is no true understanding of how this energy, which is called life, occurs. Basically, in each cycle there is a resurgence of the old energy that has taken on new properties. These properties can seem to resemble the old but in fact have indeed gone through change, even if the change is minuscule and unfathomable.

For example, the change a tree goes through is a slow growth for some trees and a substantial growth for others. If the tree dies, either by natural law or by a person cutting it down, the elementals in that tree go on to a new tree that is in the seed stage.

In regard to the stages of death and rebirth in humans, the cycle varies according to the evolutionary path of the individual. Obviously, if a person has lived a spiritual life and accrued good karma, that person will be reborn more quickly, as there is less to learn in her sojourn on the subtle plane.

For a soul that has developed negative karma on the physical plane, the sojourn is much longer and can even last up to several hundred years. This soul will spend a long time in Kama Loka and then have to go to areas in the subtle plane to learn more about evolution and the structure of life.

Even with this knowledge, when this soul is reborn, she will still be pulled into negative karma that is the result of previous karma incurred in other lives. This negative karma continues the same pattern. Only when the soul has absorbed the knowledge of karma can she avoid being pulled back into the pattern and choose not to continue on the wheel of suffering.

With each round or cycle of the earth's evolution, the individuality or soul has to change form and develop itself according to the round's intention. If, for example, a particular round is to end with people taking on more ethereal forms, the individuality will be working toward that outcome. If the soul lacks the ability to evolve to that level, it will not continue into the next cycle but, instead, will incarnate into a higher cycle of a lower planet than the one the individuality was evolving on.

This process is still a continuation of life. The soul must still go through the process and learn more in order to achieve the higher levels.

When a person has entered the realm that is often referred to as Devachan, there is a complete shift in consciousness. The soul at that stage has begun the process of what is called separation from the lower principles and movement into the higher ones. This is after the stay in Kama Loka, where the soul already played out all the desires of the lower in order to reach a point where it is willing to no longer be attached to those desires. For higher initiates,

Devachan is a short stage of divine bliss that enraptures the soul and emphasizes the higher desire of longing for God Consciousness.

During this stage, whether the desire is personal or divine, the individual will develop a karmic longing toward fulfilling this need in the next lifetime. Personal desire will coat the soul and pull it in that direction; the desire for God Consciousness will heavily focus the soul toward this goal in the next life. Therefore, it is of prime importance during life to have fulfilled personal desires so as to leave them behind and only concentrate on the spiritual ones, particularly as you grow older. Such an emphasis is of utmost importance for any spiritual person.

The process of dying varies with the individual. If a person is open and happy at death, then the spirit will leave very quickly. If, instead, the person doesn't want to die, the spirit will hold on and take a long time to leave the body, even when the physical body has taken its last breath. The longer the spirit remains, the more difficult it is to pass through the stages quickly and easily.

When confronted with death, a student needs to let go immediately and allow the heart's action to take over. This means when the physical heart goes through the process of stopping, any resistance can prolong this action and make the process more physically painful.

Some of you may wonder why a person would even think about all this when the first stage of death begins. This is understandable, but in reality, even when a person is dying, there is time to process the stages of death and consciously release the spirit, thereby helping it move quickly. For example, if someone is breathing peacefully at one moment and the next has ceased breathing, the death process has really been going on for several minutes before the last breath, and the individual, even if she seems to be sleeping, is actually conscious of what is happening. That is, if someone is sleeping during this process, the person will have a dream in which she is conscious of dying.

Accepting this process is the best possible way of going. If you struggle to remain in the body, this stage of dying will take longer and the resisting can cause not only pain but also some distortions in the process.

The question remains, is there a way to know what you will do when you begin the process of dying? This is a very concrete question. An advanced initiate could, at the end, suddenly try to hold on because of some unfinished business, and someone who seems to want to stay can go quickly and easily when the time comes. The only way you can help determine how you will respond is to begin the process of letting go of those things that cannot be fulfilled in your lifetime when you are young. When you hang on to unfinished tasks, the spirit does not want to leave.

Let's take time now to analyze what might cause you to not want to leave.

1. First and foremost are the loss of loved ones and the fear of never seeing them again. Even an advanced student can have attachments to others that hold her back, particularly if there was no time to say goodbye.

2. During the process of dying, there can be a moment of remembering something that is unfinished, and the need to complete it pulls the soul back.

3. Sometimes the person feels a renewal of energy and believes that she really isn't dying and can stay in the physical world. This is a false belief that can be so strong the person will momentarily regain consciousness.

4. At the end of the process, there is a time when the soul is caught in a vacuum and feels loss. It is important at that time to stay in the process and have no fear. Fear can cause a person to stay in the vacuum much longer than necessary.

5. Another factor is the sadness of those who are with the person. If loved ones are by the person's side when the death process is taking place and they are crying and emitting sadness, this can cause the soul to want to stay and not leave them. Unfortunately, this is usually the case. Believe it or not, when someone dies in their sleep, alone in the room, dying is much easier. It is up to loved

ones to hold back their grief when they are with someone during the dying process.

6. Lastly, a reason a soul may try to remain is the need to
hold on to material things. Even at death, objects such
as money, art, clothes, etcetera, can make a person want
to remain. Such attachments leave a strong impression
that is carried into the next life.

In the dying process, people, in general, are attached to things
and to others. Thus no matter how young or how old you are, it is
very important to begin the process of letting go in advance. Let's
look at some of attachments and analyze how letting go is possible.

First, get a sense of going through this process right now.

Exercise One:
In meditation, ask your Higher Self to help you imagine that you are
dying. You do not have to experience the stages; rather, just feel the
emotions. During this process, ask yourself:

1. *Is there anyone in my life that I cannot leave?*
2. *Is there anything in the way of tasks that need to be done*
   that would cause me to feel sadness if they are not fin-
   ished?
3. *Are there any material objects that I feel so attached to*
   that I would have difficulty leaving them behind?

Write down your answers, and then ask your Higher Self for a
process that would help you psychologically to let these things go.

Letting go psychologically does not mean you should end relationships and give objects away when you realize you are attached to
them. Psychological letting go is not about living without things
and loved ones; it is about having everything you want with nonattachment. The hardest thing is letting go of loved ones.

Know that it's not about leaving them, but rather, loving them
in a more disidentified manner. Doing so will give you the ability
to love more deeply and not to be attached to the needs involved in
your love pattern.

If you are young, it will generally be most difficult for you to let go of the work area of your life. Since your life is ahead of you, many of the desires you are holding on to relate to the vocation you are either in or are working toward. Again, it is not about letting go of the need to fulfill your vocation, but simply of seeing the vocation in a disidentifed manner and realizing that if you don't fulfill it now, you will come back another time and complete the work you have started.

The same holds true of the yogi's need to grow spiritually and have higher initiations. If you have a great longing for such achievement, this longing too will hold you back, even though it is a lofty desire. The desire for God Consciousness is not part of this attachment, which refers solely to the need to stay alive to grow spiritually by achieving more initiations. The unfinished tasks are the initiations.

LOOKING AT ALL THE STAGES OF LIFE

There is the process of dying, and then there is the actual end of life. Naturally, you are going to question how you can know when your life is going to end. So instead of actually knowing the date of your physical death, whether you are twenty-five or seventy-five, imagine you are now at the end of your life.

In the West, the subject of death is almost always avoided and not talked about unless someone is in the process of dying. In the East, death is very much a part of the spiritual process and looked upon as a continuation of life itself. When someone feels that death is only another stage in life within the totality of lives we encounter on the journey, then death is never important and is looked at in a more realistic manner.

Therefore, if for example you are an aspiring twenty-five-year-old yogi in the East, you see life as continuous and death as being simply one of life's stages. You recognize that death is important only for someone who does not understand this stage of life and fails to view it as one of the goals of spiritual growth. With this view, if the twenty-five-year-old were to suddenly die, she would do so with full acceptance, realizing only that the stage came earlier than expected. There would be no regrets or feelings of incompleteness.

Exercise Two:

1. *Close your eyes and see the stages in your life. Write them down. After you have written them down, review them again. Have you covered every stage? Have you covered things that have to happen in a future stage, that are part of your dharma and need to be accomplished? For example, you are now fifty years old, studying for an advanced degree, which you know you need to do in order to complete a certain work. You would include the future date of when that degree will be attained. Each stage should cover approximately five to ten years.*

     Next, take each stage on your list and write a paragraph about it. What were the essential things that either happened in that stage or you feel should happen in a future stage?

     Lastly, sit with your Higher Self and check each stage, asking the Higher Self whether there is anything you have forgotten or anything that is missing.

2. *When you have completed all of the above, take some time to connect with your inner spirit. Do this for at least a day, through meditation, walking in nature, feeling energy, and immersing yourself in beauty of some kind.*

3. *Once you have taken this time with your inner spirit, look over the stages you wrote about earlier and notice if there is anything within them that you experienced when doing this last exercise. For example, if you experienced beauty, is beauty of any kind included in any of your stages? What about your experiences in nature? If you experienced love and oneness at all, are these present in any of your stages?*

Many times when people design their life's work and strategize the steps, they leave out their need to experience beauty and to relate to others. Normally, their plans are just action plans, but as this particular exercise is your whole dharma plan, you need to include the desire for spiritual growth and for beauty, among other qualities inspired by the Higher Self. Add these to your stages in a general way. For example, "When I go for my degree during this stage, I need to be certain I meditate, I walk, I read light reading, I go out with a loved one," and so on.

Exercise Three:
1. *Take time now to add important aspects of your spiritual striving into your stages in a general way.*
2. *Then, when you end with the stage of death, place that where you feel intuitively it should be and write about your feelings about death. For example, are you afraid to die? Do you avoid looking at dying? How does death relate to your life at this time?*
3. *Finally, check the whole exercise with your Higher Self, asking the following questions:*
   - *Are these stages as accurate as possible at this time?*
   - *Can I see them as stepping-stones on my evolutionary path?*
   - *Have I included the spiritual steps within these stages in an accurate manner?*
   - *Are the future stages as full as possible?*
   - *When I think of the future stages, am I positive?*
   - *Do I have any blocks to doing the future stages? If the answer is yes, ask what those blocks are and ask for processes to overcome them.*

With each answer or process, take time to really feel whether it is accurate or whether your lower desires replaced the Higher Self in any way. If you feel the latter could be true, then ask again at another time; and remember to always shine light on the Higher Self to be certain it hasn't changed in response to any question related to desire.

Now that you have completed the outline of your stages, realize that they are temporary, and, as you grow spiritually, they can change. Life can always change. Be open to the changes as part of your karma as well as part of the karma of those around you, your culture, and your life on earth. Change is part of dharma and is part of everyone's life. It sometimes can cause strange turns on the path.

For example, a stage you need to be in may change completely because of those around you and the conditions in your society. A stage can also take longer to accomplish than the time you allotted. Obviously, if you have some perfectionism within your psychological conditioning, you will want those stages to be completed more quickly. Others may allot too much time to the stages and so need to adjust them accordingly.

When you look at the stage of death, do so with discrimination and conscious acceptance. Can you see it as simply a stage, or is there a finality that keeps creeping in? Can you give this stage just a minimum of attention?

Exercise Four:
To help in the process of seeing death as a stage, try now to go beyond it, starting with the stage after death:

1. *What desires do you have now that you think will be played out in Kama Loka? Can these desires be released during any of the stages preceding death so they need not prolong your stay in Kama Loka?*

2. *What are the other stages that precede rebirth? Usually, you go through a learning process. What do you think your soul needs to learn at that stage? Again, in reflecting on this, do you think some of that learning can be accomplished in any of the stages preceding death?*

3. *Next, consider the stage of rebirth. Write about the kind of family you would like to be born into. What kind of genes will help you the most in your next life? What kind of vocation do you think you will be doing?*

4. *Check your responses to the above questions with your Higher Self. Naturally, much desire can enter in here,*

> *although often the desire will pull you in a karmic direc-*
> *tion to where you need to be.*
>
> 5. *Finally, ask your Higher Self: "Is there anything in my*
> *future life that I haven't included here that you know*
> *about?" For example, you might ask specifically, "Will*
> *I be in a spiritual teaching in my next life?" and if the*
> *answer is yes, ask, "Is that part of my evolutionary plan?"*

Sometimes a spiritual person needs to take a break and live a more ordinary life, or there may be a mission that will keep someone from a spiritual teaching in a particular life. Be open to hearing about what your next life may entail.

Now you are seeing the stages in a more complete manner, and when you see them this way, the death stage is just a small one within the frame of continuity. Life is always a continuity that, like the sea, fluctuates in its ebb and flow. Sometimes it's important to live a short life and be nourished on the subtle plane more quickly, and other times a longer life is required. Seeing life in this manner releases the fears around dying and enables you to see that the end of life, which people call death, is not death at all but rather a continuation of the process of evolutionary growth.

Help yourself go through these stages, and never feel they are static. Every year, look at your list of the stages, and make any needed changes in the future ones. See yourself as energy in motion, containing action and rest. You need both for nourishment. Look at your expectations with eyes of discrimination. Do you really have to accomplish everything in this life, or should some things be carried into the future life? Achieving spiritual growth is of primary importance. Have you put this into your stages? It comes down to two main questions you need to ask yourself:

Do I expect too much?
Do I expect too little?

Your responses will tell you what you need to adjust in relation to your future stages. Make those adjustments with the help of your Higher Self. Realize you can grow spiritually by seeing that life is a continuation and that the continuation is governed by your aspirations and karma.

When you have finished the exercises in this chapter, take some time to relax. Really see life as a joyful process, not one of constant work, but one of joyful renewal. This way, if your stage of death happens sooner than expected, you will leave with the expectation of returning to the process of evolving on your personal journey. Death is only a much-desired rest and helps the soul renew itself.

In conclusion, these exercises help you start to look at life in a more disidentified manner. In so doing, you will take that understanding forward to your next life and it will help you to become more detached from the karma you need to experience. This ability to disidentify is the best tool of all to carry with you, as it opens the way to develop spiritually more quickly and attract the kind of karma that will give you the support needed to fulfill your dharma.

Chapter 13

When You Are Feeling the Sadness of Life

Life, for everyone, has a way of causing emotions that vary from extreme happiness to extreme unhappiness or sadness. The latter is very much a part of the spiritual process and is often the stage where spiritual people become stuck.

Let's explore the ways that a student can suddenly find himself in this stage. For example, you may be walking the path correctly, finding time for meditation and spiritual work, and following your dharma as closely as possible. Suddenly, something unexpected happens, either psychologically or physically, that throws you off the path and locks you in its grip. It can take place with your family or close friends or in your work environment or even with your spiritual family. In any case, it will always be a difficult challenge, even a major obstacle, causing you to lose momentum on your journey.

Here is an extreme example of such a challenge.

Isabella was an aspiring student who was doing very well, and, at the time this event occurred, she was approaching her second initiation with a spiritual teacher. Her story is a strange one.

She had three children and a husband she was very close to. They had been married twenty-six years, and there was still a deep love between them from having been together in many lives and having developed some very good karma together. The negative karma in the family had to do with one of the children, whose name was Jonathan. He was seventeen at the time and was planning to finish high school and become a full time employee in his father's hardware store. Jonathan was a good worker, but not very intellectual. He had to forgo college because of poor grades.

Jonathan was the oldest child, with a sister, Amy, fifteen, and a brother, Erik, eleven. His siblings were both very bright. Amy, an A student, was already planning to become a lawyer.

Both Isabella and her husband, José, had always treated the children fairly, trying never to show favoritism of any kind. Though their intentions were clearly good, they had a very strong love for their daughter, mostly because she had been their child in a previous life and also their mother in a more recent life. In both lives, the relationships were the result of positive karma.

Their youngest son, Eric, who also had good karma with them, had a difficult personality. As a result, he required more of their attention. Obviously, Jonathan got the least attention, and over the years he spent more and more time away from home, with friends. All of this seemed fine until a certain evening in late spring.

Isabella was home alone. José had taken the two younger children to a movie, and Jonathan was out with his friends. Isabella was meditating, when suddenly her teacher appeared to her in an inner vision and told her to leave the house immediately. The warning was so strong that she jumped up and ran out, grabbing the keys to her car. Only when she was several blocks away did she stop near another house to catch her breath and ask, in meditation, what was happening. The answer she received was so shocking she didn't believe it. She grabbed her cell phone and telephoned her teacher, who confirmed the message, which was, "Your son is going to try to kill you. Call the police now."

She did, and waited in the car until the police came. A shot was fired when they opened the door to the house. When she tried to get into the house, the police held her back, called for help and surrounded the place. In the end, they found Jonathan upstairs in a corner of her room. He had shot himself when the police arrived. His last words when he saw his mother were, "I wanted you dead! I hate you, I hate you!"

Nothing had happened to lead her to suspect that Jonathan was so full of hate that he would go to this extreme. Nothing, except she knew about a past life with him, in which she killed him in a duel he had initiated because of a love triangle. She later found out that the woman they both loved was José. When he was younger, Jonathan always acted jealous when his parents were affectionate with each other. Isabella assumed he was jealous of his father's attention toward her and never realized it was the opposite;he was jealous of her attention toward his father.

Obviously, Isabella's life changed dramatically. She blamed herself for all that had happened. As a yogi, knowing their karma, she should have doubled her attention and love toward him. Instead, she had distanced herself from him, with the excuse of having younger children who needed her more. She was overwhelmed with sadness, and it took her several years to work her way out of the guilt and become a practicing yogi again.

Sorrow of any kind will halt the progress of a yogi. Sorrow can lock a person in its grip; to overcome its power takes love and patience. When a student is full of sorrow, it can turn into self-pity, a condition impenetrable by the Masters as well as by others.

Self-pity belongs to the lower nature and keeps a student from progressing into the realm of understanding. To feel self-pity is to give up all hope of striving toward Joy. It is necessary to do something very drastic in order to emerge from it. Self-pity will always be a realm with no exits. It limits any possibility of letting in a fraction of light. Self-pity is a place where the lower nature can enter, but the teacher cannot.

Exercise One:
The following exercise will help you determine if there is any area at all in your life that evokes self-pity.

   1. *Reflect on your current life. List the things that make you feel sad or upset. Include in your list everyday events and relationship issues. For example, you have to walk upstairs with your groceries because the store no longer delivers, or your best friend has moved away.*

   When you have completed the list, take each item and ask yourself: "Do I feel any self-pity around this item?" Also, try to look at your deeper feelings to determine what they are: Ask, "Do I at any time feel sorry for myself?" Make notes next to each item as you proceed through your list.

Finally, check your findings with your Higher Self. Then, also ask your Higher Self, "Do I at any time feel self-pity?" If the answer is yes, ask your Higher Self to help you be more aware when you are feeling this condition.

2. *Now reflect on your life so far. Have there been periods in your life when you felt self-pity? Have there been blocks of time when you were depressed and down on yourself? Try to understand how your body and mind were affected in those periods.*

   Then, with each item, create a reverse scenario. Ask yourself: "What would have happened if I hadn't felt self-pity? What could I have accomplished instead?" Make notes.

3. *Next, consider the impact that any periods of self-pity or depression had on others. Were you in a family at the time? Or did you have a circle of friends? Whatever your situation at the time, try to remember how others close to you felt and also, reflect on whether your feelings in any way affected them.*

Remember, feelings of sadness are very strong and can cause similar feelings to arise in others, especially in someone very close to you. Married couples can float in and out of depression and sadness and keep affecting each other and their children as well.

4. *Lastly, let yourself remember whether you have ever been with anyone who was depressed and full of self-pity or sadness. How did that person affect you? What did you do as a consequence? Make notes about this.*

Now that you have looked at the impact of sadness on yourself and others, let's start to understand how to change the feelings before they become too deeply embedded in the personality. Without a doubt, a depressed person will eventually change his personality and become more and more withdrawn, even becoming intro-verted when he had previously been more extroverted. Such a person will cause negative vibrations to surround him and others who come into that atmosphere.

These vibrations also pollute the environment of every place the person enters. If, for example, you sit next to someone with such negative vibrations at a concert or movie, you can sense the vibra-tions, causing a disturbance that detracts from the performance. Since you may not be able to change your seat, it is important to recognize what is happening and call on the elementals and devas to surround the person with harmony and to replace the vibrations with positive ones. This is one way to deal with such disturbances. There are other ways, including the following:

1. If someone who needs help overcoming depression comes to see you, try to see the person outside, in a neu-tral place. If that is not possible, place a bell around the person by asking permission of his Higher Self to do so. If you get a "no," then ask the person's Higher Self to help contain the energies within the individual. In the meantime, place a bell around yourself and ask your own Higher Self to keep any negative vibrations from penetrating your aura.

2. You are at a party and meet someone who is project-ing negative energy. Instead of leaving or removing yourself from the person, try to encourage him to get into a better place. Talk about beauty and all the things that pertain to it. Tell jokes that make people laugh and break the negative atmosphere.

3. If you are with someone who starts complaining, change the subject and don't listen to him.

4. Without a doubt, watch your own thoughts and state-ments. Are they possibly on the verge of being negative? Are you sad or upset about something? If you feel this way, make a point of not expressing your negative feel-ings if you are with someone.

5. When you begin to feel sad, try meditating and giving

your negative feelings to your teacher or Master. Ask that they be removed, and then try to do something uplifting.

6. In general, become more aware of your inner feelings, and when you know that certain subjects can trigger them, avoid those subjects.

If you are feeling sad over the loss of someone you were very close to, it's best not to repress the feelings, and, when you are alone, let yourself cry and release them. Genuine grief needs to be expressed, and it is often helpful to do so with another person who feels the same way. If someone has died, try to express the loss right away. Grieving for a long time not only keeps you in a place of sadness, but also can pull the departed spirit back and keep it from moving on. The spirit then feels regret about leaving and will try to stay close by. This is often how ghosts come into being.

If you are naturally a sad person who sees all things from a "glass-half-empty" place, then you need to begin to change your personality. A yogi must always be positive. A yogi who is negative can affect many people, not just one or two. Such negativity can cause karma, and this type of karma can continue to affect others. Let's look at an example.

Tom was a very industrious man. He worked hard all day and played hard at night. Everything was fine in his life until his wife died and he simply fell apart. His wife had been his constant companion for thirty-five years, and they had followed a set routine that was an intrinsic part of their lives. Not only did Tom lose his closest friend, but also his whole world had turned around. No longer were there clean linens on his bed. His house was dirty and fell in disrepair. His nightlife also fell apart. Going out with friends just depressed him, especially when they asked how he was doing. He began avoiding everyone and stayed at home watching TV in the evenings.

Tom was still able to go to work every day. He worked as an accountant and loved his job, but he no longer had anyone to talk to about his clients and the finances of the wealthy that had often provided lots of laughs for him and his wife.

They both had been in a spiritual practice, but he stopped going to meetings and even stopped meditating, as, again, it was something they did together.

Finally, after several months, a good friend dropped in and talked to him. He told Tom the following story.

"When I was a child, my mother died. I was only five years old. No one talked to me about it, as they thought I wouldn't understand, so I walked around with my grief for almost a year, sometimes crying privately when no one could see me. I was just starting school. The teacher thought I was retarded because I would just sit and stare into space, living in a make-believe world with my dead mother.

"One day, I was playing in my yard by myself, and a neighbor, an elderly man, called to me. I think Daniel was his name. He invited me into his house for cookies and milk, then sat down next to me, and asked how I felt about the loss of my mother. Can you imagine, that was the first time anyone asked me that question? I cried and cried, and he held me and let me cry. It was such a relief to let out all the tears I had repressed. I spent a lot of time visiting Daniel after that, time spent talking about my mother and telling him all the things I could remember about her. In a few months I was back to normal again, and I surprised my teacher by becoming her best student.

"I'm telling you this story because I've seen you doing the same thing. I'm going to stay here with you every day until you've cried away your loss and can come back to your friends."

Tom followed his friend's advice and spent a month or two grieving. Then, with the help of others, he arranged to sell his house and buy a smaller place that didn't hold all his memories. He redecorated the house, learned to cook, and hired a house cleaner. Within two years, he was dating and having a wonderful time.

Meditation was also back in his life, and, instead of always thinking about his dead wife, he concentrated on the beauty of the subtle worlds and felt how happy she must be there.

Loss and sadness around old memories keep one trapped in the past. Letting go of the sadness is also letting go of the past, allowing a person to continue in the present and future. It's important to have memories of someone you have lost, but each day is built on new memories with new people and new places. When you realize there is no loss, because life is a continuation, then you can go to the next stage, as mentioned in the last chapter. In the past, you had someone in your life that you loved. In the future, that person will return to you in another life, so, in actuality, there is no loss but a continuation. Of course, if you lose someone with whom you had difficult karma, it is important to let go of the person completely, so as to not attract that individual back to you.

Sadness can change into action. If you are sad that your child was rejected from a sports team because he wasn't good enough, you can take action by helping him train to become a better athlete. Of course, you must be sure the child really wants that.

If you can take action of any kind, then you are transforming sadness into another kind of energy. Tom, in the example above, was able to change his energy by taking positive action and buying a new house that had none of the old memories and associations.

Even if a person can't move, taking the action of removing the spouse's possessions and changing the house decorations can be something that not only occupies the mind, but also helps the person feel that a new stage of life is beginning.

If you are sad because you didn't receive a promotion or you lost your job, taking the action of finding a better job will change those feelings very quickly. Also, self-pity can always be dissolved through bringing beauty into your life.

There is little time for self-pity or sadness when a person has a family to care for and continues in that effort.

Generally, there should be no looking back with regret at what might have been. Doing so will only deepen the sorrow and promote feelings of guilt. In the story about Isabella and her son Jonathon, who tried to kill her, she kept looking back at what she should have done for him, and, as a result, it took her longer to return to her life.

One last exercise may help prepare you for sorrow if it comes into your life.

Exercise Two:
Ask the Higher Self: If a deep sadness happens to me in the future, what is the best way for me to a), handle it, and b), overcome it and take the right action to continue my journey?

In essence, sadness is very much a part of the human condition connected to the grieving process. But in reality, a yogi needs only a short time to be sad because the knowledge of the higher worlds makes it apparent that most of humankind evolves and, in that process, there will be times of sadness and times of joy. Letting go of sadness within the framework of the whole evolutionary period makes it easier for the yogi to let go more quickly.

Even when the sadness touches those around you, it is important to not get caught up in others' feelings. If a loved one holds on to sadness, try to help him, but also try not to hold on to your sadness in sympathy. It's right to feel, but wrong to make the feeling the dominant part of your life.

Look to the future as a haven from sorrow. The future is free and full of opportunity. If your sorrow is over a material loss of some kind, see the future as a place to regain what you have lost. If the sorrow is around a lost loved one, see the future as the place to meet others who will be as important in your life. If the sorrow is concerning your physical condition, see the future as a way to focus on more important things in your life. Always see the future full of promise and full of opportunity to grow spiritually. In so doing, you let go of the past, retain the knowledge gained from it, and move through the difficulties and sadness that had encompassed it. The past is past and cannot be changed, and the present holds the key to the future, which is full of possibilities.

Never forgot who you are on the path. You are more than your feelings. You are more than the material world. You are more than your personality. Remember that your spirit is also part of the whole. Believe in the Higher Self and it will lead you onward through the difficult passages in life, onward toward the heights.

Chapter 14

Holding the Wisdom

To hold wisdom requires the special condition that you learn and retain the learning, not just in your mind, but also where it can be accessed easily. This capability comes into being when a yogi has attained a certain number of initiations and her Chalice is open to attainment. The condition depends not only upon initiation, but also on the ability of the student to be disciplined and centered in the "I" that connects to the Higher Self.

To explain this process more simply, if you can open your heart and mind during the learning process, the information is stored in the Chalice. If you can then maintain the heart and mind in a state of repose, you can access the information at any time. Some people have this ability naturally; others need to work at it.

The heart and mind do not have to be fully opened. Obviously, if they were fully opened, you would be a high initiate, and such a person always has access to higher wisdom. Instead, this refers to a student who, in the process of striving, opens the centers occasionally. If you can strive toward wisdom, you will be more open to receiving it when it comes.

This is not about learning in the normal sense of the word; it is about esoteric learning that comes from centuries of experience, centuries devoted to the inner knowledge of the adepts. Such learning includes, for example, knowledge about nature and how to work with the nature kingdoms, or knowledge about the true meaning of dharma and how dharma affects the evolution of the individual, or knowledge about the planet and how it has evolved. Even knowledge about the meaning of energy is very much a part of esoteric studies.

Holding the wisdom means more than remembering what you

have learned. It means taking the knowledge and applying it to your everyday life.

If, for example, you are aware of the existence of the nature kingdoms, then it is important to communicate with those kingdoms on a daily basis. This application of knowledge and learning from those kingdoms impresses the information in the Chalice. For another example, if you have studied cosmology, to hold the wisdom is about beginning to understand the realms of the macrocosm and the microcosm and comprehending the relationships. In other words, it's not just book knowledge; inner knowledge is far more complex.

Holding the wisdom is about being subjected to all the energies that surround you. It means dealing with negative forces that want to destroy the knowledge gained so they can keep the planet from evolving. It means holding knowledge that could disappear as soon as you receive it. It means believing that knowledge about the higher worlds is obtainable and that you deserve to have it. It means many things that are foreign to you at this time.

Exercise One:
Write a list of all the areas in the teaching that you have already learned about. Then prioritize the list so that the most important is Number One. Now, taking that item, ask yourself the following questions:
1. *What makes this the most important area for me?*
2. *How did I hold on to this knowledge?*
3. *Is there more that I have forgotten?*
4. *How can I reclaim what I have forgotten?*
5. *When I am reading or experiencing this knowledge, how has it helped me to grow spiritually?*
6. *In the future, how can I retain more of this knowledge when I receive it?*
7. *Looking at the storehouse of knowledge, has this item helped me retain more about the other areas on my list?*

Usually, you will make your top priority something that relates to all the other areas on your list, and it's important to clarify how it relates. If you had a yes answer for number 7, take a minute to think about how that item has affected the others, or how it has worked hand-in-hand with either one or several items.

Storing knowledge is a difficult thing for a yogi to do. There is always a great deal of abstract or intellectual reading. People who are more right-brained never do well with storing knowledge. If the knowledge is visual, they do better, whereas left-brained people have good storage capabilities but little ability to use the imagination, which is a help in understanding the abstract aspects of the teaching better.

Forgetting what has been given or has been read and digested causes a large store of accumulations to lie dormant. This in itself is not wrong, but it would be better to use the knowledge, thus keeping it more in the consciousness. Therefore it is best to work with another student or in a group, because hearing the words and discussing the different perspectives keeps the knowledge fresh in the memory. Holding classes is built upon this premise, as is using exercises that help students delve into areas of the subconscious.

Stored knowledge keeps the student alert to many possibilities. For example, if you have read a lot of material on the care of plants and applied this knowledge to the plants in your home, your plants have surely thrived. But if instead you have read a lot on the care of plants and have forgotten what you have read, the plants then would be subject to the same treatment as if you never read the material at all. In most cases, you may have applied some of the methods to care for your plants and likely remembered only a few of the things you read. Yet just doing that much makes a difference in how the plants grow. So, in essence, some of the knowledge remains.

The same is true when you study any occult teaching. A few things that excite you or even affect your growth will be recalled. The rest will drop away.

In looking at your list in the above exercise, do you sense a general understanding of each area? Does each feel familiar enough for you to talk about it? If the answer is no, then either you overestimated your learning or you are not retaining the knowledge you should be retaining.

Let's look at what can cause this lack of retaining knowledge. There are a variety of reasons. For example, if you are always preoccupied with other things, your ability to retain is at a minimum. Also, feeling too tired when you are studying can cause the knowledge to go right into storage with little retention. Memory loss due to illness or age can also cause material to be stored without retention. There are also people who seem to be burdened with weak memories; usually, these types have so many thoughts in their minds when they study that all can be lost. Chaotic thinking is a primary reason for losing any material you want to remember.

How does inability to retain knowledge affect the student? Naturally, if you spend a lot of time studying this teaching or other teachings and you fail to remember what you study, it almost seems a waste of time. Yet, that's not true, because your subtle body is also learning, and in the subtle body you have full retention of the information. When you begin to operate with the higher energies, much of this knowledge is there to assist you. However, the more you can retain the material consciously, the easier you will find it to operate in the subtle body when you are more advanced on the path. This is why it is important to study all the esoteric material that is available. Higher Self Yoga is based on Agni Yoga and Theosophy. Both are very important studies to be absorbed, and highly recommended.

Holding wisdom changes your consciousness. There is no turning back and discarding wisdom, because it is an energy that affects every aspect of your spiritual growth.

For example, you have read the first chapter in this book, about sound. When you are in a situation where there is discord, such as an argument, you may or may not remember what to do to protect yourself. Yet instinctively, you will respond to the discord, and in most cases your instincts will follow the knowledge you have retained from that chapter. If you consciously remember the chapter, you will try to recall what to do, and if you can't remember, you will probably look at the chapter again when the argument is over and thus retain more. If you simply remember the main phrase that runs through this book, which is to link with your Higher Self or link with your heart, just doing this will effect a change in the discordant situation.

This kind of memory is more feeling oriented than mentally oriented. A right-brained person will be more apt to remember the chapter because it is experiential, whereas a left-brained person will remember it in terms of the information given out. In both cases, whoever reads that chapter has changed.

When you sit in a class and listen to the teacher talk, you will always retain some portion of what is being said, and this portion can help you remember other related materials. When you are reading material that is intellectual and factual, you probably are going to forget much of what you have read unless the material really interests you and holds your full attention. Even then, there will be certain people who lack retention.

The following exercise can help you assess your retention.

Exercise Two:
1. *When you read a novel, can you remember any details about it a month later?*
2. *When you study a subject that interests you, can you recall the main things you read a month later?*
3. *When you study, do you always prepare by making certain you have no distractions?*
4. *When you talk about something you read a while ago, can you remember the gist of the material?*

If you have a no answer to any of the above, then you probably have poor retention. Yet sometimes a person with generally poor retention can have total memory about a specific book because it is so well written. Keep any such book you have as a good baseline. If you can remember details from good writing, then you can also learn to remember details from more academic writing.

After the above exercise, the probability is that you need to prepare to change some habits that may stand in the way of your retention. Let's look at what some of these habits can entail.

Being preoccupied with other tasks you want to do.

1. Having to study when you would rather go out with friends.
2. In school, lacking study habits and not doing well on exams.
3. Wanting to study but feeling you don't have a good enough mind.
4. Feeling too tired all the time.
5. Having noisy neighbors and not having the time to go elsewhere to a quiet place.
6. Having family around you that needs constant attention.
7. Seeing the material as interesting but preferring to read something else that is more fun.
8. In general, feeling duty-bound to study because your teacher has told you to, but lacking enthusiasm.
9. Feeling it a duty to read material that you find too difficult.

These are some of the excuses that can become habits that keep you from studying esoteric material.

Exercise Three:

Take time to reflect on each of the above statements, and make notes for yourself on any one that relates to you. If there are other circumstances that interfere, make a note of those as well.

Next, take your notes and, with each item, ask the Higher Self the following questions:

1. *When I act out this habit, is there anything that precedes it and lays the groundwork for failure?*
2. *When I am feeling the draw of this habit, what do I need to do to change the feeling?*
3. *Do I have any core beliefs that are underlying this habit?*
4. *Can I replace this habit with a new one that is positive?*
5. *Is there any childhood conditioning involved in this habit?*

6. *In looking at the habit, does anything come to mind that is new to my understanding?*
7. *With each habit, is there a pattern connected to it?*

Generally, everyone will fall into one of these habits on occasion. But it is important to see whether this habit has become standard behavior, which is much harder to change.

An excellent exercise to do now is to choose a book that you find difficult or just one that needs more of your concentration and try to read it. Some people have simply never learned good study habits.

The following are suggestions that always help a student study. If you don't know these techniques, they should certainly help you.

1. Prepare the place you will use to read and study. It should be comfortable, in a quiet place in the house. It should be a space that is yours alone, never used by others. It must be located where there is beauty, such as paintings or a view of outdoor beauty or the beauty of fresh flowers. Take time to notice the beauty and breathe it in.

2. Always do a short meditation before studying. In the meditation, dedicate your work to a spiritual Master or Lord Jesus or Buddha, and ask the Higher Self to be with you and help you to understand the material and remember it.

3. As you read, if there is something you want to remember, highlight it and read it out loud. Seeing words and reading them aloud at the same time always helps you remember the content.

4. After you have finished the required reading, go back and reread the highlighted places and again speak the words out loud. If you want, type or write out the highlighted sections so you can keep referring to them later.

5. Before beginning a new section, reread your previous highlights or the typed or written notes you made. Then begin the process again with the new material.

6. If you have a friend who is studying the same material,

meet and quiz each other and, in general, talk about what interested you in the reading.

7. When you have finished your studies, reward yourself with a fun activity. This is very important for balance.

8. The next time you study, try to look forward to it. Make it an interesting experience by viewing the material as meaningful, stimulating and exciting.

When you study or prepare for an exam, a lecture, or any presentation, it is important to link with your Higher Self and your teacher, if you have one. Inwardly give them your fear and any feelings of insecurity.

Be aware also that you are an instrument for the teaching and can be overshadowed when you are speaking about it. If, for example, a friend asks you what you are studying, immediately link with your teacher and ask to be overshadowed when talking about it, or link with your Higher Self if you do not have a teacher. When you do so, the words you speak will be mirroring what your friend needs to know at that time. If you find it difficult to speak about the teaching, take that as a sign that your friend is only curious and not really interested, in which case the best thing to do is to make a simple statement and change the subject.

Many people will be interested in the Higher Self, as it has been a popular subject in the past few years. When you talk about it, try to explain the teaching in an uncomplicated manner. Again, linking with the other person's Higher Self helps you know how much information to give out. The Higher Self understands if the person is ready to hear such esoteric knowledge as the concept of the Abode of Enlightened Beings, or Shambhala. Reincarnation is also something that many people are beginning to believe in. Therefore, a good way to understand if the person is ready to hear more is to ask if she believes in reincarnation. If the answer is a definite no, then don't pursue the subject. However, if there is even a maybe in the response, you can speak more about it.

Use your discrimination at all times. For the most part, do not recommend this book to others if you feel they aren't ready for the knowledge. An aspect of holding the wisdom is protecting it, so that others will not in any way slander or malign it.

The idea of holding the wisdom can be literal and symbolic.

In a literal way, it is most important not to spread information coming from the Masters to those who would not believe in it or accept it. Such information will only be misinterpreted and held in contempt. This will not hurt the wisdom, as that is always pure, but it will create negative karma for those who treat the knowledge negatively. In order to protect such people, be careful about how you disseminate the knowledge. If you lack discrimination, it is better to keep quiet, or ask someone who's knowledgeable and knows the person in question whether it is appropriate for you to talk to him or her about the teaching. It is natural to want to share with friends and family, so be most careful with them.

Holding the wisdom in a symbolic way is a much deeper concept. Let's look at what is meant by the teaching being symbolic. A symbol represents energy, and the energy has many levels. The obvious level is the first one, but under this are many other levels that aren't very apparent to most people.

For example, let's take the symbol of a flag. A flag represents its country. Because it moves in the wind, it also represents the element of wind, which in itself has many meanings. When the wind is part of the flag, the flag takes on the deeper meaning of giving life and, therefore, represents the living essence of the country. Consequently, the flag is considered sacred. This is why, in most countries, it is against the law to burn the flag. Then, the flag is also part of the military defense of a country. Marching with the flag presents a consensual image that the whole country is behind a military action. The flag represents all the citizens of a country, all the work and labor performed within the country, and, when it flies in front of an embassy, even around the planet. These are just a few of the meanings of a flag.

The concept of holding the wisdom requires a deeper understanding that is mostly hidden. For example, not divulging the teaching without due consideration but holding it sacred, means keeping the symbol of wisdom hidden from most people in order to protect it.

Let's examine what it means to hold the wisdom as a symbol. What might the symbol be? It could be a red flame. It could be the three magenta spheres in a circle, the symbol of the Roerich Pact that is also the symbol of Shambhala. It could be a blue six-pointed star that is the symbol of the Abode of Enlightened Beings. It could even be a red rose or a golden chalice. Choose any of these to visualize, as they represent the Highest. Make certain your color is pure and brilliant, with no gray or black in it. It is important that you hold it symbolically and, in so doing, the essence of its meaning will become more alive to you personally.

For example, if you are talking with someone about the teaching and you start the conversation by picturing your symbol in your mind or heart, this action makes you totally alert in regard to protecting the teaching. Doing this becomes automatic, and you are then more aware of everything you say.

Placing the symbol in your heart when you meditate will help you to understand it better. Try this now.

Exercise Four:
1. *Take the symbol you have chosen and draw it in color. Now stare at it for a few minutes, then close your eyes and place the symbol in your heart. As you do so, tell yourself that this symbol represents to you the Source where wisdom is contained.*
2. *Ask to feel the energy of the symbol.*
3. *Ask to know more about the symbol you chose.*
4. *Ask to understand more about its wisdom.*
5. *Then ask to be given some thought or feeling from the Source of wisdom. This can come in as a personal message or something on a larger scale.*
6. *Finally, take the above answers and check them all with your Higher Self, which is the conduit to the Source.*

Do this exercise sometimes when you meditate and, of course, write down what you have been given and always check the information with your Higher Self. You want to be certain you are connecting to higher wisdom and not to your desire body.

The key to higher knowledge lies within your Higher Self. Connecting with your Higher Self will help you expand your scope of learning and also help you discover hidden resources within yourself. You have had lives of being a scholar, and even if you are not one in this life, the potential is there to be reawakened. Many a student who had little schooling became an astute scholar of the ancient wisdom.

All wisdom comes from the Highest and is part of the evolution of the planet. You are part of that evolution and in the future will have more and more access to this higher wisdom. When you have been given brief moments of connection with it, hold such experiences as sacred and special. Keep them contained within you and hold the wisdom as your heritage.

Chapter 15

Obstacles That Impede Spiritual Growth

Sometimes on the path there are obstacles that keep a student from moving forward. These obstacles are always part of the karma the student needs to face, and most often they come from childhood conditioning and therefore have a psychological basis.. Encountering an obstacle can bring a student to a standstill for a long time. It can even take the student off the path. Such an obstacle, naturally, would be very significant.

Although you have already looked at obstacles that can impede your progress, such as those having to do with emotions in Chapter 8, the types of obstacles looked at in this chapter are the most serious. The main obstacles are:

1. Wanting to grow faster spiritually when you are not ready.
2. Having too many desires connected to the mundane world.
3. Having too many desires connected to love relationships.
4. Wanting prestige and recognition from other students.
5. Needing the Masters to acknowledge your achievements.
6. Looking at the goal as too difficult to achieve in this lifetime.

These obstacles differ from the impasses talked about in Chapter 11. An impasse can stop you momentarily but an obstacle to spiritual growth can stop you permanently. Even though some seem the same, obstacles have much stronger energy. They can be completely hidden and not appear until later on one's path, and because of this can be much more difficult for the disciple to face.

1. Wanting to grow faster spiritually when you are not ready.

Let's look at the first obstacle. Here is an example from long ago.

Andre was a very accomplished man. He had achieved recognition in his field of education. He was a professor at a leading university and was writing a book on the impact of education in a particular third-world society. He had spent several years in that country and had established some very progressive schools, providing him with a fine reputation in his field.

At the time, he was around forty-five years of age and had been studying metaphysics on his own for several years. He was what is called a destined disciple, and he and his teacher both had instant recognition of his having been her disciple in several previous lives.

Having a very good mind, Andre approached the teaching with enthusiasm and the desire to learn everything he could. Within a year he had made discipleship and was on the way to developing a broad base of knowledge. Nothing stood in his way, or at least that is what he believed.

Andre studied, meditated, and followed every advice his teacher gave him. He was the model student. After two years he started questioning when he would be given his next initiation. His teacher explained that when he was ready he would be told. Nothing happened for another year, and he kept asking.

His teacher realized that Andre had many unresolved issues concerning relationships and that he needed to focus on resolving these issues. He started therapy but thought he was smarter than the therapist and dropped therapy without mentioning it to his teacher. His attitude began to be less enthusiastic and less attentive. When questioned him on this, he said he was tired of waiting for the next initiation, and he had begun doubting the teaching and everything connected to it.

When his teacher explained how he was at a serious impasse and needed to realize that he could not progress until he resolved some of his psychological problems, he told her he didn't believe in therapy and had dropped it. She explained that the psychological problems would intensify with future initiations, and that the reason he wasn't progressing spiritually was due to his inability to deal with these issues.

Unfortunately, Andre couldn't accept that this was the case. He felt that all he needed to do was continue his studies of the teaching and his meditative practice.

He went into such strong denial that he broke from the teaching and when last heard of was seeking another Eastern teaching that he hoped would accept his abilities and not question his psychological blocks.

This is an example of someone whose ego needs were stronger than his ability to see his innermost problems. Many students believe they can repress their psychological issues and not have to deal with the outside world when they enter a spiritual path.

In the past this was true. A student could live in a monastery and grow spiritually to a certain level. But in today's world, this is no longer the case. To achieve the higher initiations, a student needs to be in the world and be tempted by all that the mundane offers. If Andre had really probed into some of his background, he would have uncovered the unresolved needs that would truly hold him back spiritually.

No student can move forward without uncovering the psychological blocks. Andre felt he didn't need to do this, but if he finds a true teaching on his quest he will again be faced with these unresolved problems.

When a student wants more than he is ready to handle, he generally needs to spend a day meditating and, in the meditation, ask to see the progress he is making.

Exercise One:

Link with your Higher Self and ask:

1. *Am I progressing on the path in the correct manner and time frame?*
   - *If the answer is yes, ask: As I am working toward my goal, have I jumped any steps that need to be taken? If yes, what are they?*
   - *If the answer is no, ask: What is the right progress and time frame I need to follow?*

   2. Do I have an over inflated opinion of my spiritual abili-
      ties?

   3. Do I have an under inflated opinion of my spiritual abili-
      ties?

Sometimes a student should be moving more quickly but gets stuck somewhere and needs to go through the obstacle and move onward.

2. Having too many desires connected to the mundane world.

The second obstacle relates to desires connected to the mundane world. In most cases students should move faster on the path, but get caught up in mundane or worldly problems. Achieving success in the world can become an obstacle if desire for this becomes stronger than the desire for God Consciousness. It can take a person away from a teaching, particularly if the desire body produces needs such as wanting a lot of money and worldly recognition. Once this happens, a student will put the teaching on a back burner and even forget to meditate. Keeping up with things in the world becomes a priority. Others who are not spiritual may also influence such a student so that he loses belief in the teaching.

When a student achieves worldly success, the ego self can become inflated and cloud the Higher Self. To refocus on the highest becomes more and more difficult, as, naturally, the Higher Self cannot operate when the ego is inflated.

Sometimes a student will fall into this ego trap even when he doesn't receive great worldly success. Even a little success can cause the student to become egocentric.

There is nothing wrong in achieving worldly success of any kind. The test comes when desire for such success becomes more important than the spiritual goal. Many yogis have been successful in the world and still maintained their spiritual life. Striving for success is fine as long as it benefits others. When it benefits only you, be careful to live your highest values so as not to lose sight of what is most important. When you are working successfully in the world, it is important to keep the following values highlighted.

Exercise Two:
Ask yourself the questions:
  1. *Do I live my life according to the teaching?*
  2. *Do I remember to approach my work and friends by always connecting with my Higher Self?*
  3. *If I have a problem, do I always ask for guidance and help from my teacher or Master?*
  4. *Do I question any work that I take on in terms of it being ethically sound?*
  5. *Do I approach my work relationships with honesty and integrity?*
  6. *If I am in a position of authority, am I always conscious of how I deal with others?*
  7. *Do I always feel egoless when others praise me?*

If you receive a no on any of the above questions, ask your Higher Self how to begin to change this, realizing the necessity to always be vigilant around these questions. Many students lose sight of the spiritual goal when worldly matters distract them.

It is important to be aware of how negative forces will try to pull you into your lower nature by inflating your ego when you achieve any kind of success. The challenge is to always remain vigilant and to realize that your success makes you an example of the teaching and a target for the dark ones who want to keep that example from being a positive one.

In addition, there is always a strong pull from the outside world to disturb anyone who is spiritual and successful. This pull comes from the collective masses who operate through the need to vicariously experience the success. Public success is the most difficult to handle, as the energies around it can really invade a person's aura. It is important to remember to protect yourself if for some reason you are in the notice of the public.

Another obstacle emanating from the mundane world is the need for personal gain, whether this be material or mental gain. It is fine to make good money for the work you do. It becomes a fine line when the need for money compromises your values. Am

I doing this work because I really want to, or am I doing it for the money I will receive? This is a question to always ask yourself.

Often a person thinks he is pursuing the right vocation when, in actuality, the material rewards that vocation offers are the prime focus. If a vocation doesn't offer material rewards it may be bypassed and literally discarded even though it really is the correct vocation for the person. To fulfill his dharma, a person must be totally aware of what the correct vocation should be; otherwise the life is not fulfilled and he will have to return at another time to accomplish the work destined for this lifetime. Again, the Higher Self knows the best work for the person to pursue, but often the desire body will cloud that knowledge.

If you know your right work, how can you continue to grow spiritually without having your vocation take precedence over your spiritual practice? This is always a major challenge for every yogi who operates in the world. In this teaching it is necessary to be in the world, and as a result the struggle is usually more difficult.

3. Having too many desires connected to love relationships.
The third area to look at is the area of personal relationships, including romantic ones. The latter are always a deterrent in a spiritual teaching unless, of course, the loved one is also in a spiritual teaching. That is ideal, but it doesn't happen often, mainly because the law of karma creates attractions that are based not on spiritual backgrounds but rather on emotional pulls.

Obviously, having a love relationship with someone who is not spiritual will make it difficult for you to carry on your normal spiritual practice. Often there is resentment from the loved one around time spent with the teaching and the teacher. Unfortunately, this can pull a student away, or, even if the student remains faithful, there can be a loss resulting from the constant pull of the loved one to spend more time together rather than to pursue the spiritual practice. It is therefore very important for a yogi to choose a partner who is at least sympathetic to the teaching and the teacher.

Check to see if there are any blocks inherent in a new relationship that can impede your spiritual growth, and if this is the case, it may be wise to end the relationship before you become more involved.

Naturally, if your tendency is to not be as fully committed to your spiritual work, then you will be pulled away more easily. The situation will be a test of your devotion and commitment. Sometimes a situation arises on a spiritual path to help the person determine whether the teaching is the right choice at the time. If the student decides that it's not, then he will leave in pursuit of the romance, becoming involved in karma, and will not have the opportunity to return at a later time.

When relationships are more important than the spiritual path, you can be certain you are not ready to continue working toward your spiritual goal. This doesn't mean you have to forgo relationships. It simply means that your priority should be more focused on the spiritual rather than the personal.

Many spiritual people are in relationships and still continue on the path. In fact, relationships help the yogi to see in more detail the psychological patterns that need to change and help the student to open the heart when the relationship is a truly loving one.

Sometimes relationships become very negative, and then it is of the utmost importance that the yogi finds a way to end the relationship without accumulating negative karma. It is difficult to change negative karma because it needs to be played out. Some of it can be changed with positive thoughts and actions, but that has to be done with great care. When a yogi has a karmic relationship, it is very important to determine what the karma is. Otherwise there is no freedom of choice.

A good example is a couple that has been married in several lifetimes. This couple's karma is both negative and positive, but slightly more negative. At a certain stage in their relationship they begin to quarrel and fight, causing more negative karma and tilting the balance they came in with even more. If instead they were positive with each other, they could have a good marriage and build positive karma to equal or even exceed the negative.

With relationships in general, it is wise to be careful at the first encounter to determine whether the karma has been positive or negative. At this early point it is much easier not to continue in the relationship if you know the karma is more negative than positive.

Exercise Three:

Looking at the relationships in your life, ask yourself the following questions:

1. *Do I have a relationship that is pulling me away from the teaching?*
   - *If the answer is yes, ask if it is a karmic relationship that needs to be resolved.*
   - *Also if this answer is yes, ask your Higher Self how you can resolve the relationship without making more karma.*
2. *Looking at some of the other relationships in your life, are you aware of the karma involved?*
3. *Is there a relationship that is helpful to you on the spiritual path?*
4. *Are you looking for someone who can be helpful to you on the spiritual path?*
5. *Do you want to be with someone who is also spiritual?*
6. *Can you accept being with someone who is not spiritual?*
7. *Comparing your romantic life to that of others not in the teaching, do you in any way feel deprived?*
8. *Does the romantic or sexual mean more to you than the spiritual in a relationship?*
9. *When you are in a relationship, can you honestly assess whether it is a good one or not?*
10. *When you aren't in a relationship, can you honestly see what you need to search for in a relationship that will make you happy?*
11. *In general, on a scale of 1 to 10, how important is it to you to be in a relationship?*
12. *In general, on a scale of 1 to 10, how important is it to you that anyone you are in relationship with is spiritual?*

If you see relationships as separate from the teaching, then you are not seeing them correctly. Anyone in a relationship needs to have support for every part of his or her life. If you are with someone who doesn't support your spiritual practice, then you will always have negative vibrations pulling you away from the path. Naturally, this makes it more difficult to continue.

Sometimes a student comes into a teaching with a partner who isn't sympathetic. This often causes problems and needs very careful handling. When this is the case, it is best to never talk about the teaching or try to persuade your partner to join, as doing so would be against the partner's will and affect his seed of the spirit, which may not be ready. Women have more of a tendency to go along with their partners if the partner enters a spiritual practice. This can be correct or not. In every case, it is best not to try to use your inner power to convince your partner to follow your spiritual direction. It's always best to remain silent and conduct your practice in the least obvious manner.

Exercise Four:
If you are in a relationship in which your partner is not sympathetic to the teaching, ask yourself the following questions.
  1. *Am I affected by my partner's lack of interest in the teaching?*
     • *If the answer is yes, ask your Higher Self to give you a way to change your attitude.*
  2. *Do I always want my partner to be sympathetic?*
     • *If the answer is yes, ask the Higher Self, how do I let go of this wish?*
  3. *When I am alone with my partner, can I accept him fully, or do I always feel something is missing?*
  4. *Have I thought of leaving my partner because he isn't in the teaching?*
  5. *Can I love my partner unconditionally?*

These are some of the questions you need to ask yourself. Generally, if you are with someone who is not sympathetic toward the teaching, you need to be honest with the person and express how much the teaching means to you. It is important to let the partner know that it isn't necessary for him to believe in it, but that it is necessary for the partner to honor your desire to pursue the path without interference of any kind. Make this a definite agreement that your partner will accept, and if the partner continues to say no, that he will not accept your spiritual practice, then you have to decide the right course of action.

Perhaps going to a couples therapist will be helpful for your partner to hear your innermost needs. This is especially true if the partner will not in any way accept your spiritual desires. Naturally if you come into the teaching and aren't in a binding relationship, it is easier. You will then need to question anyone new coming into your life about whether he will accept your spiritual commitment, no matter what his own beliefs are.

4. Wanting prestige and recognition from other students.

The fourth obstacle has to do with wanting other students, your brothers and sisters, to recognize your accomplishments. This obstacle is very subtle and can be very tricky. Most spiritual people say they are not competitive, but, in actuality, competition is one of the last characteristics to go. Many a high initiate has fallen because of this.

Most people who are striving spiritually compare themselves to others, and often when they do this they perceive others as being not as spiritually advanced or psychologically astute as they are. If, for example, a yogi is aware that another student has more initiations and that student, in the eyes of the yogi, has faults, then the comparison takes place, either consciously or unconsciously.

Many times a student will be chosen for a particular mission because of past accumulations and not necessarily because of who the student is in the present life. Carrying out the mission can often bring out the positive abilities of that student and in the process help the student to grow spiritually.

If, however, another student is envious of the mission and wants it for himself, that negative energy can impede the student who is fulfilling the mission and awakening the positive accomplishments of his past. This is why most missions are given to students secretly, and they are asked not to reveal the mission to anyone else unless it is important to do so.

It is wonderful to have a group of students who can handle competition by looking at it honestly and letting it go. Since everyone on a spiritual path has many obstacles to pass through, it is important that students honor each other's journey and be there to give a helping hand if need be.

Some students can handle recognition without feeling superior in any way; others still need the recognition that hadn't been given to them in childhood. Generally the latter situation comes from having parents who could not recognize the qualities and skills of a child. The need for this recognition carries into adulthood and often becomes focused in a spiritual teaching. It is important to understand the source and then work with those needs in therapy, and not bring them with you on the path.

Exercise Five:
Ask yourself the following questions:
1. *Do I need recognition for my spiritual accomplishments?*
2. *Do I think about myself as being superior to my spiritual brothers and sisters?*
3. *Have I had higher initiations in the past that make me feel I know more than others?*
4. *When I am with my teacher, do I compare myself to him or her?*
5. *Do I feel any competition for the attention of my teacher?*
6. *Do I feel any competition around my spiritual brothers and sisters?*
7. *If I hear of someone's initiation, do I feel in any way jealous?*
8. *Do I compare myself to anyone in my spiritual family and think of myself as being more spiritual?*
9. *When I am in a group of people who are not pursuing a spiritual practice, do I in any way look down on them?*
10. *If I am with people in another teaching, do I think of my teaching as being better?*

In general, a feeling of spiritual superiority comes from wanting to be special, and this need can interfere with a student's progress in any teaching. It comes from an inferiority complex and makes the student vulnerable to attack.

No one likes this kind of person and, unfortunately, such behavior reflects negatively on the teaching the student is studying. If a teacher sees that a student is acting this way, the teacher may even ask the student to leave.

5. Needing the Masters to acknowledge your achievements.
The fifth obstacle, wanting Hierarchy's recognition, is very similar to the last obstacle. The same type of person will also have this obstacle. The student may feel superior to others and also have a strong need to be recognized as special. This kind of student will naturally believe certain things should be given to him.

For instance, a student feels chosen and special, and expects to be given some recognition from the Master, either a sign of some kind, a gift, or even for the Master to appear. When this doesn't happen, the student feels neglected and can even become resentful, especially if another student is given a special gift.

There once was a student who was working very closely with his Master on the subtle plane. This student became so obsessive with wanting his Master's attention that the Master withdrew from him, only to have him then start demanding to see his Master every time he meditated. He became very jealous of another student the Master was also working with, to the point that he began to make sarcastic remarks to others about this student. When this happened, his Master sent him a warning, but even the direct warning didn't make a difference. He was so certain that the Master would never leave him that he suffered deeply when the Master did leave. Later, he realized how obsessed he had become, and saw what an obstacle that had been. The Master could then resume working with him.

The state of feeling superior reflects in every aspect of your life. There is an air of acting more knowledgeable that can even impress other students. Some of the more advanced disciples can have this obstacle.

Other students look up to an advanced disciple. This can cause the disciple to feel even more superior, especially if others come to him for advice. It can become very tricky, especially if the disciple is facing his lower nature and is being influenced by it.

No matter how advanced a student is, there should never be any attitude of either knowing more or being special. Naturally an advanced disciple is given more attention from the teacher and Master, as more help is needed at the advanced stages. But even when this happens, the student should always see others as being co-workers, having the same seed of the spirit within that he has. The path is a long path, and many a person who seems more advanced can get stuck and others who follow can pass him. Remember this.

Exercise Six:
Ask yourself the following questions:
1. *Do I in any way feel I have special attention from my Master?*
2. *Have I in any way compared myself to other students in terms of closeness to my Master?*
3. *When I meditate, do I always expect my Master to be there?*
4. *Do I expect special privileges from Hierarchy that are not given to others?*
5. *When I am not with my teacher, do I forget about him and place my attention on my Master?*
6. *When I meditate, do I always keep my teacher foremost in my mind and heart?*
7. *When I meditate, am I grateful for the help that has been given to me or do I simply expect the help to come?*

6. Looking at the goal as too difficult to achieve in this lifetime.
The last obstacle that can really cause you to leave the path is the feeling that the goal is too difficult to achieve. Along with this feeling is the attitude of procrastinating, giving up and thinking that

making this journey can wait until your next lifetime.

This kind of attitude comes, of course, from the influence of negative forces that know that causing you to stop does not just affect this lifetime but will also karmically cause you difficulties in your next life.

Look at it this way. If you were meant to become a teacher in this lifetime and you gave up striving on the path, then you have affected all the people who were meant to be your students. You would then come back and have a more difficult time and maybe not even become a teacher at all, leaving any destined students in a future life to follow someone else. This not only affects them, it also affects your karma. Each time you refuse to follow your destiny it affects your karma.

In looking at this obstacle, you need to understand that any resistance that comes up usually comes from your lower nature and is attached to deep-rooted psychological feelings. Some of those feelings you will need to look at as you begin to walk the path; others will come into being along the way, having been opened so that you can come to a better understanding of who you are. Right now, you can simply look at the feelings as resistance and not allow your ego self to be influenced by them. Ask your Higher Self to guide you through this obstacle, and realize that it can be an ongoing one throughout the journey.

Exercise Seven:
Ask yourself the following questions:
  1. *Am I ready to move forward toward the goal?*
  2. *When I think of my goal, does it seem obtainable?*
  3. *When I am meditating, do I strive toward more knowledge and understanding?*
  4. *Do I always see myself as being able to achieve the higher initiations?*
  5. *When I think of my teacher, do I believe I can also do his or her work?*
  6. *When I think about this, do I understand what the work consists of?*

7. *Can I honestly relate to doing my teacher's work?*
8. *When I am connected to my Higher Self, can I experience the reality of what it would be like to always be connected?*
9. *Generally, is the teaching the focus of my life?*
10. *Do I feel that walking the path means reaching the goal?*

If you answer "no" to any of the above, it is important to understand why. If you answer "yes" to all of the above, make certain you aren't affected by the previous two obstacles and feeling superior. Also, realize that every question can have a "no" answer, which is based on where you are now, so when you answer these questions, imagine you are more advanced and can understand the depth of their meaning.

When you finish this exercise, look back at all six obstacles and ask yourself if you feel in any way less committed to following the path toward your goal. Some of these obstacles may not be there for you at this time. Keep the list and be aware of when they can appear.

In conclusion these obstacles may seem to be not as important as your deeply psychological ones. Be careful not to discount them, because they are strongly attached to your unconscious and, at a future time, can show up in full force when you least expect. This is why they are more serious. Your teacher can help you see them, but it's best for you to always be disidentified enough to notice these obstacles when they appear.

Chapter 16

Facing Truth

Facing truth means facing all levels of truth.

First, let's look at the meaning of truth. For most people, truth refers to those items that fall into the category of scientific or factual knowledge. For example, it is true that the earth is round. Yet in the Middle Ages it was considered true that the earth was flat. Therefore, when it comes to scientific investigation, truth is relative to what is known at a certain time in history, and that knowledge can change as scientific investigation becomes more refined and better informed. Therefore, since what is known about science is open to change, scientific knowledge cannot be classified as truth.

When we speak about truth in terms of factual matters, again it depends on who is viewing the facts. For example, it is true that in the War Between the States, the Northern states won the war. This is factual truth, yet if you speak to a Southern person who knows the history that goes back before the war, that person may say, "Yes, the North won an unjust war, but we have maintained our heritage and are, in fact, still in charge of the South. Therefore, in reality, the North never won, as we will never be Northerners." Now, this may seem a bit far-fetched, but to some Southerners, it would represent the truth.

You can say, "Well, personally, I can tell you many truths," but while something may be true through your own eyes, through the eyes of someone else the truth may be different. For example, you can express what you believe are facts about yourself and your family. You were born on a certain date and your parents were born on a certain date. Yes, to you that is true, but if you told that to someone who was living under a different calendar, your birthday may be something very different. In fact, in some cultures, the day of physical birth isn't as important as the day of conception, and the birthday referred to is the conception day.

While there are certain facts that are considered true and are recorded that way in history books, in reality, truth is subjective, based on the viewer and the culture.

If you look at everything as not true in reality and hold that truth is open to change, then this presents a certain type of dilemma. It means that all is not truth, but is, instead, a constant flow of objects or facts that can change at any given moment and take on new forms.

All of this can be disconcerting for a person who must be grounded in what they consider reality. If reality itself is in constant change, how can anyone view it as a certainty?

Anything set in time is open to change and interpretation. Some historian can write about a historical figure as being a certain way and sound as if that knowledge is based on truth, whereas at another time another historian can refute those "facts" and write about the historical figure as being completely different. Such "truth" is based on interpretation and evaluation.

When a student asks for the truth, it is difficult to reveal what that is. Even occult law and set principles are only given as truth to certain people at certain times and are given out differently, at other times, to other people. When a truth is given out, by the time it is ready to be revealed it has gone through numerous changes, and many of what are called the hidden truths are set in motion. The so-called truth, then, is only a portion of truth. If the hidden truths were then revealed, they would change what is known and make that no longer true.

Without a doubt, nothing that is in motion can be true at all times, but only for a given period of time. Of this, you may be certain. That is why there is the need to always be open to change. Change is the underlying force of evolution, and therefore cannot be set into a framework or time period. What is true for you at this time may completely change ten years from now. It is the same in terms of looking at the past. What you believed to be true ten years ago would have changed in the course of evolution into new meanings. Even if your belief systems are very set, you will be forced to see new truths as things in the world evolve and change.

To be able to face truth can deeply affect your life. For instance, if it is true that you are alive at this time, is it true that tomorrow or the next day you will be alive? You may say yes, and that is probably right, but there is always the possibility that you may have an accident or a heart attack and die tomorrow. Or, you may find out tomorrow that you have a life-threatening disease and will die within a few months. All of this is part of facing the truth of life. Naturally, as you grow older the possibility of dying seems truer. If you are eighty years old, you may be more comfortable with the idea that time is relative and that you may suddenly die tomorrow or the next day. This would make you more conscious of the need to have your life in order so that when you do die, everything is taken care of. A forty-year-old will not be prepared to die, but, in actuality, the truth is anything can happen.

If you face the truth that your physical body will die one day, you look at life through that lens, and you may conduct your life differently. It's like the story of the hare and the tortoise. If, based on the truth that the hare could run faster, you took bets before the race that the hare would win, it would be a big surprise to find out, in the reality of the story, that the tortoise won the race. The way you perceive death presents a similar case. If you see death as a possibility that is always there no matter how old you are, then you would look at your life differently and perhaps even change much of the manner in which you live.

People who have gone through near-death experiences find that their perspective on life has changed. Even if they are completely well again, the way they see life is very different from those who have not gone through that near-death experience. Life takes on new meaning for them, and generally they also experience change differently. Things that were most important to them previously no longer hold the same significance, and they are generally more able to cope with any obstacles that come their way.

When there is a major shift from the "known" to the "unknown," people tend to become very frightened. This is because the "known" holds a person in a place of security. When truth no longer exists as a set reality and all that once seemed secure is shaken, insecurity prevails. Truth becomes clouded with the fear of the unknown, but only in the unknown can a person begin to look at everything with eyes of awareness. Such awareness then helps a person face truth.

The following questions sound very abstract, but they will help you discover any set beliefs about what is true or untrue. Take some time now to reflect on them and answer them as best you can.

Exercise One:
1. *How do you perceive truth? In your view, how do others perceive truth? What changes truth for you? What causes others to see truth differently from you? How are you able to perceive truth as truth?*
   - *You may find as you answer these questions that more questions arise. If so, write these down and answer them also.*
2. *Next, take a moment and look at your life. What do you consider true in your life? List these things, and then take each one and ask your Higher Self, "Is this true? Or is this open to change?"*
   - *Then for each item, ask yourself, "If this changes, will that in any way change what I consider to be true?" You may be surprised at some of the answers you receive.*
   - *Take the answers even further: "If this is truth, can it change? How can it change?" And so on.*

What you should discover is that everything you value as being true in your life now may not necessarily be true in the future. Most of you will find this very unsettling. Naturally, you want those things that you feel secure about to be stable, yet nothing is stable.

Some of the most interesting stories are about people who find themselves in situations that they never imagined. These stories usually end up revealing that truth is relative to the moment, and when you read them, you discover creativity exists in the unexpected and excitement in the unknown. This type of story, called an adventure or mystery story, is very popular because the reader cannot imagine what will happen next. Yet, if the same reader found herself actually a living part of the story, enormous fear would arise around what might happen next.

How strange it is that reality that is dull and full of familiar things always feels more secure and preferable to the unknown. Most people will choose such a reality over any possibility of facing life from a different viewpoint, that of looking at life as a vast adventure, full of exciting changes and emotional extremes. The majority would choose a life set in routine and full of known resources that make them feel comfortable.

Exercise Two:

Take a typical day in your life in which you get up, go to work, perform your job, come home, and continue on into the evening. Live through this day in your imagination.

Now redo the day. Change everything in it. For example, imagine you go to work at a different job, doing something related but not the same work. If there is something you have always wanted to do, see yourself doing that. Then, when you imagine going home, try to create scenarios that are very different from your usual ones. For instance, see yourself with other people. See yourself with children if you don't have children, or see yourself without children if you have children. Try on another partner, not necessarily anyone you know, just an unknown person who is very different from the one you are with. If you don't have a partner, imagine you have one. If you have a permanent partner, see yourself without one, living alone. Put on as many different hats as possible.

Throughout the different scenarios, notice how you feel. Is it scary doing or having something new? Is it exciting? What are the differences between the new and your regular routine? Do you like your normal routine better? Or is the opposite better? Experience all your feelings about what it would be like to make big changes in your life.

After you have done the above, look at both scenes. Is there something in the new scene that you really want to have? Or is there something in the old scene that feels much better, but needs to be made more exciting?

In doing this exercise, sometimes you will see how just a little change in routine can make your life more interesting. If everything new feels better for you, you really need to look at your life differently. Even if it means doing something new, try to make your life more alive. Maybe the truth doesn't lie in either scene but in a combination of both. For instance, if you have a partner you are comfortable with, maybe it's not about finding a new partner but more about looking at what needs to change in the relationship to bring more adventure into it.

If you don't have a partner, and it may be difficult to find one, just developing new friendships or changing your evening routine can be beneficial. The reason why people travel is to bring adventure and excitement into a dull life, but you can bring the same into your daily routine.

Look at things differently. Take the time to stop and examine a flower or to look at a sunset. See nature in every form as being beautiful. Take the time to listen to music you like, and simply enjoy the feeling of being one with it.

Approach your life as if every day is a new day, full of promise that can help you feel the benefit of being alive.

At some point, take the time to look at all the things you have accumulated. Sit down with old books or old files and picture albums. Discard those things that are no longer benefiting you. Help yourself find new things that will bring beauty into your life, be that a new plant or a new picture for your wall. Most people never change their homes but like the familiarity of being in the same setting every day.

Exercise Two:
Walk around your home and see everything in detail. Look at the walls, the floors, the lighting, and the furniture, and really notice

the things that make you feel most comfortable.

Next, see your home in your mind's eye, and remove all the things you can live without. Redecorate your rooms using the same furniture. Take notes.

Now imagine redoing the scene, this time redecorating your house with new furniture. Even repaint the interior and try different colors; create different lighting and floors if you like. Imagine living in this completely new place. How does it feel? What's good about it, what's not so good? Let your imagination really enjoy everything new.

Finally, compare all three visions. Was there something in the last two scenes that you really would like to do? If it is something completely new and you can't afford to do it at this time, see it as a possibility in the future. This is something you can plan for. Even if you can't do something completely new, perhaps there is something in the second scene that you can do now, by rearranging furniture and perhaps also ridding yourself of things that are no longer necessary.

If you don't like anything in your visions, try going to a library and looking at some decorating books. See some homes that appeal to you, and imagine taking some of the ideas and applying them to your house or apartment.

If you have a partner or family, ask them to do the same exercise. Compare everyone's ideas and agree on a few, or even complete changes. Often, just changing the color on the walls makes a huge difference. If you have old furniture, you may want to invest in something new.

Look for sales and auctions. Sometimes a new table or a new lamp can bring a sense of change. What's important is not to conform to sameness year after year. This brings a dull feeling to the home and keeps your energies forming into the same patterns. Just rearranging furniture changes the energy, and this type of change can eliminate the monotony of conformity.

Some people are the opposite extreme; for example, constantly changing furniture around and never able to leave it in the same place for more than a couple of months. In such a case, the person's life needs changing, and by changing the furniture, the person feels better. But what really needs to happen is that such a person needs to make changes in those areas of life she is afraid to look at.

Exercise Three:
If you feel constricted in doing the above exercises, then consult your Higher Self:
- *First, ask your Higher Self: Is there something blocking me from making changes in my lifestyle?*
- *Then ask: Does my lifestyle make me comfortable?*
- *If it does, then ask: Is this comfort based on a false reality?*

The above exercises should have helped you determine what you would like to change in your lifestyle. Once that is clear to you, ask for verification from your Higher Self. Primarily, inquire whether the change is indeed good, or whether you are doing it just to make a change.

When you are ready, continue with this next exercise.

Exercise Four:
Ask your Higher Self the following questions:
1. *When I look at what is real and true to me, am I seeing it correctly?*
2. *When I look at my life, do I see it as fulfilling? If the answer is no, ask, what is there that doesn't fulfill me?*
3. *When I look at the people in my life, do I see them in a realistic manner?*
4. *When I look at my family, do I see it in a realistic manner?*
5. *Can I accept those around me, or do I want them to change?*
6. *Can I feel what it would be like to make major changes in my life?*
7. *Can I accept that life is constantly moving and changing and this is good?*
8. *Can I accept that in ten years I will be very different?*

9. *Can I imagine what I will be like in ten years?*
   - *If the answer is yes, write down the description, then put it in your heart and ask, is this true?*
   - *If the answer is no, ask your Higher Self to show you one changed aspect of yourself.*
10. *Am I able to accept the instability of what I think is true?*
11. *Am I able to accept that truth never conforms to set patterns?*
12. *Am I able to accept that truth always changes according to individuality?*
13. *Am I able to accept that truth is part of the patterns of time and space?*
14. *Am I able to accept that truth is relative to all things?*
15. *Am I able to accept that truth, as we know it, is not truth?*

When you have answered these questions, take time to feel what it is like to be insecure. Is insecurity really a bad thing, or does it have some good qualities? Take time to feel the good qualities, and describe them. Then, ask yourself how these qualities can benefit you at this time.

When you are finished, spend a day or two just adjusting to the feeling of what it would be like to never be secure again. Work with your Higher Self on how to overcome feelings of fear, and work with the process given to you by doing a nightly review.

Much of the fear is based on the unknown, so allow yourself to accept that instead of the unknown being a realm full of uncertainty, the unknown can be full of creative possibilities.

In facing truth, the ultimate reality is that truth, as you know it will always vary within the framework of what is happening at a given time. What is truth even within the world framework can change rapidly, and we have seen this in the last century with the rise of new technologies that have changed old, established scientific viewpoints. In the new century ahead, there will be just as rapid a change in technology, so that what you know now as being established will disappear and be replaced by new forms difficult to imagine.

When you face truth in your life, it is important to remember that what you see as truth is coming from your viewpoint, and that another person would see the truth very differently. This is why it is so important to ask for advice and seek help in situations that feel closed, with no hope for change. Usually a person is so caught up in such situations that it's not possible to resolve anything.

Exercise Five:
Take a situation in your life that looks as if it is completely blocked and ask the Higher Self the following questions:
1. *Can I get through this block?*
2. *Is there something I don't see that is making me stuck?*
3. *When I look at this problem, can I feel hope that it will be resolved?*
4. *How do I let go of any feelings of hopelessness around this problem?*
5. *When I see this problem, can I look at it from every viewpoint, including the viewpoint of the person I consulted?*
6. *When I am in this situation, what is the best way for me to disidentify from it?*
7. *Most of all, can I let myself be free of the feelings around this situation, so that I can see it more clearly?*
   - *If the answer is yes, ask how to do this.*
   - *If the answer is no, ask what is keeping you from doing this, and also what steps to take in order to free yourself.*

Usually, a person can't let go of the feelings because the feelings are what create the block in the first place. Try to follow the Higher Self's advice, because only when the feelings are dissolved can you clearly discern the best way to handle the situation.

In conclusion, it is important to be flexible at all times and, in that state, to realize how liberating it can be. Holding on to old truths can make your life full of set patterns, patterns that keep you bound to the mundane realities. Instead, liberation gives you the feeling that life is full of possibilities and joyful experiences.

Even difficult blocks don't seem so difficult when you see them this way. In the words of a very spiritual yogi, "There are many realms that lie dormant to the eyes of humanity, realms that would give life and hope and joy to those that enter them. Make your eyes open to the beauty of the unseen worlds and, in that opening, realize your true Self."

Chapter 17

When Life Is Lacking in Love

The main wish for most of humanity is the desire to love and be loved. This need comes from the Higher Self and relates to opening the person's heart chakra. Even though love can be difficult for many people, it still holds the key to developing that center, and in so doing it opens the person to all avenues of spiritual growth.

Why is personal love so important, even to a spiritual person? A student may feel it is part of the mundane pull that keeps him from developing spiritually. Even when it is explained that personal love relates to the heart chakra, the student may believe that personal love isn't the love that is needed, but rather, that opening the heart can be done through meditation practices or through impersonal love not identified with a specific person.

Such discipline is carefully thought out by many spiritual practitioners and is part of the old traditions that believe and teach celibacy as necessary on the path to God. But, in reality, personal love can be essential for spiritual growth. Buddhists will claim that Buddha found enlightenment another way, but Buddha had lived many lives of personal love, and even in his youth he had that experience. His heart was fully opened when he saw the suffering of others, but had he not already opened his heart, he would not have felt their suffering and would have simply returned to his palace to live the life his family had envisioned for him.

Buddha came into that lifetime having achieved many previous lifetimes of higher initiations. He had already opened his heart and was spiritually awaiting his next step in enlightenment. His was a mission to help others understand the law of karma and how the mundane can trap a person from fulfilling his or her dharma. Buddha's enlightenment had already happened in previous lives, and his mission was to share this with others.

Most people on the path to enlightenment need to experience all the aspects of being human, and through that experience learn to understand their true nature. Love is a major part of this path, and personal love has to be part of it also in order to open the heart enough to begin to transcend the personal and experience unconditional love. If you have not experienced personal love, you cannot experience the latter.

Let's look at what is meant by personal love. When you have this, you feel emotions, emotions that can be ones of love or even emotions that can be full of hate. Why is this? How can one side of love that is full of joy be also the opposite? Personal love expresses fully what it is–that is, personal. If you love someone passionately, caringly, lovingly, then you have a full emotional involvement. But if your love is unrequited, it can turn negative and make you very angry at being rejected. Even if the person loves you but does something you find hurtful, your response is full of emotion that can also be hurtful to the loved one. The old saying, "We always hurt the one we love" is very apt.

Karmic relationships are pulled by love and hate, hate and love, causing people to be attracted to each other lifetime after lifetime. When I say that personal love is necessary to open the heart chakra, I am not referring to relationships based on these strong karmic ties, but rather to relationships that are about the simpler acts of loving.

There may be karma involved, but the karma is mainly positive, and also there is a strong bond of friendship that makes the relationship very worthwhile and helpful. This, of course, is the ideal relationship, one of sound companionship and good feelings.

You may ask, how does one find such a relationship? Generally a relationship is full of emotions and feelings of attachment, whereas the relationship I am talking about is based on mutual respect and love that is open and unfettered by personal needs.

This is still a personal relationship, but it differs in that the emotional needs are not prominent; instead, the feelings of love are based on genuine caring. With this type of relationship, each person can grow spiritually without feeling bound by the other. This, of course, is ideal and rare to find.

Most people have to go through many relationships before they discover the meaning of a genuine uncompromising one.

If you are in a karmic relationship, it is important to establish strong boundaries that keep you from causing the karma to erupt. I am talking about the kind of karma that pulls you into repeating old patterns and deepening attachments. These attachments can be very strong, especially if the karma is at all negative. Even if the karma is positive, that too can cause a strong pull and keep a person from maintaining his or her individuality. In both cases, clear boundaries have to be established and kept at all times.

If you are in such a relationship, talk to your partner about this, as it is important that both people be involved in setting up the boundaries and keeping them.

Exercise One:
Ask yourself the following questions about the relationship:
1. *Is this relationship basically positive karma?*
2. *Is this relationship basically negative karma?*
3. *Am I able to set up boundaries with my partner?*
   - *If the answer is yes, what should they be, on your part?*
   - *If the answer is no, what needs to happen for you to be able to do this?*
4. *Can I keep the boundaries, or will I have problems keeping them?*
5. *What needs to happen for us both to maintain the boundaries?*
6. *If my partner goes over the boundaries, how do I best handle it?*
7. *If I see myself going over the boundaries, how do I change this?*
8. *Do I have any other attachments to this person of which I am not aware?*
9. *Can I know a little bit about our past lives together?*
10. *How can I be more disidentified in this relationship?*

Try to keep a good review of how you are doing with these boundaries. Also, make certain you keep your end of the agreement, and if you are not doing this, look more deeply into why.

Finally, try to be lighthearted and bring this lightness into the relationship to make it more fun and loving, especially if you are aware of negative karma that holds you and your partner together.

Exercise Two:
If you are in a relationship that is more ideal, to keep the relationship growing ask yourself the following questions:
1. *How can I continue to work positively in this relationship?*
2. *Is there something I'm not aware of that could come up as a problem?*
   - *If the answer is yes, ask what it is and how to change it.*
3. *When I am with this person, do I acknowledge my love for him or her?*
4. *Can I do anything else to improve what we have together?*
5. *Are the boundaries clearly defined?*
6. *If the answer is no, ask if they need to be.*
7. *When I am with this person, can I always be in my heart?*
8. *If the answer is no, ask why not, and then, how to be in the heart.*
9. *In holding this person in my heart, can I feel more love and inner peace?*

What happens when you find yourself in a life without a loved one? You may have lost a loved one, or you simply may never have found one. How do you handle this in terms of opening the heart through personal love?

What happens when there is a lack of love in a student's life? How can the heart chakra be developed, and is it possible to grow spiritually without these types of relationships?

This problem is very personal and, indeed, difficult for many students. Some have gone through personal love and have rejected permanent relationships. These students may or may not be at a place where personal love is no longer necessary. A student sometimes needs personal love, and if this doesn't happen, the student may feel bitter and unfulfilled as a person.

Unfortunately, this lack can cause the student to have difficulties later on the path, difficulties around relationships in general and specifically around relationships with higher teachers. A lack of personal love can cause negative emotions, and unless these emotions are understood and released, they can come up at any point on the path.

Some initiates deny themselves love in order not to be distracted on the path. But experiencing the distraction of love can be helpful in understanding yourself, and if a student hasn't experienced this, it may be more difficult to come to that deeper self-understanding.

When a student has chosen to avoid personal love, some consequences can arise that need to be looked at. These consequences fall into three general areas: denying the karmic implications of relationships, not dealing with or adequately understanding sexual energy, and not recognizing the limitations of asceticism.

1. Denying the Karmic Implications of Relationships

There is the possibility of denying an inner need that plays itself out in other ways in the student's life. For example, some students will not have a permanent relationship with another person but instead will have many relationships. Doing so can lead them to make negative karma, especially if the other people expect the relationship to be more permanent. In some cases, a student will live with someone for years yet not get emotionally involved. This is fine for the student, but if the partner becomes emotionally involved and develops more needs, the student may withdraw or leave, which would make negative karma even if the relationship were clearly defined at the beginning.

All relationships cause karma, whether it is good or negative karma. Most students who are in denial about basic needs around relationship or about the emotional impact of relationships will cause karma, whether they want to or not.

Even in the first instance, where the student has many relationships, the need to fulfill desires can bring him more and more
into the desire body and keep him from developing spiritually.
When such a block happens, the student sometimes does not see
how it relates to karmic consequences, and indeed believes there
will not be any karma, especially if there has been a verbal agreement defining the relationship. However, in actuality the student's
actions themselves will nullify this belief.

For instance, a student having an affair believes he is free of
karma because at the beginning he told the lover that the affair
would only be a casual one. But the student, in the act itself, is
passionately involved and clearly gives that message to the lover
who, in turn, begins to believe that the initial words are no longer
in effect. Karmic ramifications ensue if the student is intensely
involved with someone and then leaves.

However, if he is completely disidentified from the lover and
always keeps the affair casual, then he will not have any karma
when he leaves. The intent has not changed, but the actions are
ones of disidentification, enjoying the sex, but not acting over-
whelmingly with love and passion.

This is a fine line for a student, and one that usually is crossed
no matter what the initial intentions. It is better to choose someone
as a lover you know you have no karma with so you can handle
the attraction without deeper involvement. Most partners of students easily fall in love with them, mainly because the students
have qualities of the heart and spirit that cause love to blossom
and develop. To turn these qualities off is very difficult. Therefore,
it really is important to make certain that strong boundaries are
established from the beginning and to break off the relationship
right away if the lover starts crossing those boundaries.

Obviously, having an affair with another student is the best
combination because both parties have an understanding of
karma and can be more careful to keep the affair lighthearted. In
some cases, the students find real love and decide to marry and
continue on the path together, working spiritually. This, of course,
is very good because they can help each other and learn from any

difficulties that arise in their relationship. In this case, the students are not denying themselves love, but they are learning more about their inner selves from personal love.

2. Not Dealing with or Adequately Understanding Sexual Energy

When a student chooses the spiritual path over personal love and truly keeps to this path without adequately dealing with feelings and needs around personal love, then he will be faced with some inner blocks to overcome. These blocks relate to various needs that have not been fulfilled. One need, of course, is the sexual desire, which in many ways can become stronger in a spiritual person. The reason for this is that the body's functions are heightened through meditation, and usually the sexual drive can become stronger as a result. Most students experience this and deal with it in different ways.

When students have strong unfulfilled desires, they can suppress them and become fanatical in their beliefs. They think they can use sexual energy to intensify their striving, but, in actuality, the intensification goes more into the realm of religious fervor. These students need to be more in touch with their sexual need and either fulfill this need with a partner or through other means. Sublimating the sexual energy is a difficult route, but some students can do this by using the energy creatively. Any of the creative arts, such as painting or writing, provide excellent outlets, or any practices that relate to nature, such as gardening or landscaping.

Sexual energy can also be dissipated through certain meditation practices. These practices are more related to Kundalini Yoga and are definite ways to use the sexual energy to work on the various chakras. Since using Kundalini is a different practice from Higher Self Yoga, it is not recommended, mainly because it forces the energy up the middle spinal channel. Done incorrectly, such practices can cause the energies to go to the other spinal channels and become unbalanced. This can bring about physical harm. Using the energy creatively is a better route to go.

A lot of sexual energy is necessary for developing the use of the will. The will is a strong source of energy, and if someone has a weak will, then the sexual drive is also very weak. The relation-ship between the two is difficult to describe. An athlete is a good example. An athlete is using energy all the time to move the body functions. Prana is flowing throughout as the athlete exercises and can even continue when he is resting. A great deal of energy is needed, and usually the athlete, when tired, will not have enough energy to have sex. In general, this is so unless the athlete has an enormous amount of natural prana, in which case the sexual desire may be heightened.

The same is true with the use of the will. If a person has a strong will and uses it throughout the day, at night he will feel very tired, with little sexual desire. If, instead, he has a strong will and also a great deal of prana, he can have stronger sexual desires. It all depends on the amount of natural prana a person has and is using at a given time.

Exercise Three:
To determine your level of prana, ask yourself the following ques-tions:

1. *When you mentally work hard all day, do you usually come home and relax, or do you still have enough energy to go out, exercise, or do other things?*

2. *On weekends, do you feel you deserve to just relax with a good book or TV, and don't want to do any work around the house? Or, do you want to be more active?*

3. *When you are involved in a creative project, can you con-tinue this kind of work for hours at a time and not feel tired?*

4. *When you are engaged in a sexual relationship, do you want to have sex more than twice a week?*

5. *Do you generally have a reputation as someone who is full of energy and can go, go, go?*

6. *When you meditate, do you feel energy throughout your body?*

7. *At the end of the day, do you feel tired, or could you stay up all night if you set your mind to doing any given task?*

If you can say yes to any of the above, you have good prana and have the ability to direct it to your will and thus develop a strong will. The will is very much the driving force to help you accomplish anything in life, and that includes striving spiritually. Without a strong Will, a student is apathetic and can become mired in the feelings of being too tired to do any of the work.

Naturally, even a person with a strong will can become depressed and enervated. This happens even to the most striving yogi when he encounters some difficult blocks to overcome. The use of the will to work through these kinds of blocks is very important.

In addition, there is the need to have a good supply of personal prana. In order to develop a full storehouse, it is important to eat proper food, not indulge in alcohol or drugs, and, in general, exercise and maintain a healthy routine that takes care of the body. It is also very necessary to meditate and restore your energy this way.

The following exercise will also help you to restore your energy when you feel at all tired.

Exercise Four:

Imagine yourself flying through the sky, and you are doing this by using your personal prana. You can direct your flight because your energy is strong and has the power to make dives and help you fly upward to higher places. As you fly, try to feel the prana in your body and feel how it is working. When you experience this, see a beach you can land on. Then ask the prana to stay in your body, to flow through all your organs and through your bloodstream, vitalizing you and making you feel strong.

3. Not Recognizing the Limitations of Asceticism

The need to become an ascetic grows in an initiate as he moves upward on the path. It is a need that is coming from past lives in which he believed that, in order to progress on the spiritual path, he needed to give up any of the desires coming from the desire body. These desires cover a range of things: sex, rich food, alcohol, wealth of any kind, close relationships, and any material possessions, no matter what they are.

The ascetic goal is to let go of any bodily needs and just live as simple a life as possible. Students on this path do their work with as little interaction with people as possible and make no friendships. The only thing that remains is the teaching itself and the student's connection to the teacher and Hierarchy.

Such a student is regressing into the old traditions that no longer are valid in today's world. This kind of student is better suited to live in an ashram in which these kinds of practices are enforced. But if the student is planning to live in the world and to do so in an ascetic manner, then he will find himself in constant conflict.

"To be in the world and not of it" is an old spiritual saying that means just that. It means to have all the things the world has to offer: a good job, a relationship, money to live on, and material things. All these are all right and even necessary. What is important is not to be in any way attached to those things. The ascetic does not share this view, and the ascetic way of life is a much easier way to live as a student.

To have nonattachment to your surroundings is the goal of a high initiate, but to be in the world is also necessary in order to live out karma and accumulate good acts, which also help you on the path. An ascetic, sitting in an ashram or at home, will not have the ability to move mountains. To move mountains means to do the impossible, and do it with great courage, heart, energy, and love for others. Asceticism is not part of the path of Higher Self Yoga.

Exercise Five:
To determine how much you are an ascetic, ask yourself the following questions:
   1. *Do I prefer staying at home reading a book rather than going out with friends?*
   2. *Do I reach out to others and develop new friendships?*
   3. *Am I content to just meditate, study, and work?*
   4. *Do I think parties and outside gatherings is a waste of my time?*

5. Do I join community groups and participate in community events?

6. When I am alone, am I completely happy and do I know that I prefer to always be alone?

7. Some days, would I prefer not to go out of my house even if I have to?

8. At work, do I keep to myself and avoid talking to others unless it is part of work?

9. When I think about the teaching, do I wish I could be in the higher realms and never come back?

10. Did I initially think that a spiritual teaching would make me feel happy because I would have an excuse to not participate in outside activities?

11. When I have to see my family, do I try to stay as short a time as necessary?

Answering these questions should give you an idea of whether or not you have any of the ascetic within you. The asceticism may not be as prevalent as shown here, but take the time to look at your life and see if some of the qualities mentioned exist in your behavior.

Lack of personal love in your life can cause you to become lonely, sad, and even full of self-pity. A yogi who experiences this can often use the teaching as a substitute for having no love relationships.

When I speak of love, I do not simply mean sexual relationships. I am referring to all close friendships. You can let go of the sexual, but you cannot give up the need for love. As long as a person is in a human body, the need for personal love is very strong and does not leave a person until he achieves the higher initiations. This is because at first the lower chakras contain more energy and the higher chakras have not been fully opened. When those chakras are fully open, the need for personal love and sex diminishes, but this does not happen until you become a high adept. Therefore, if a yogi is substituting the teaching for these needs, they become internalized and projected onto the teacher and the brothers and sisters. In other words, a student who desires personal love will be very demanding of the spiritual family to fulfill those needs.

When you look at your life, try to determine if there is a lack-of-love feeling within you that has not been fulfilled. If this is the case, it is important to bring out the feeling and see it more clearly.

Exercise Six:
Ask yourself the following questions:
1. *When I look at my life, can I honestly say I have experienced personal love fully?*
2. *When I see others in relationships, do I ever feel envious?*
3. *Do I accept the people with whom I feel I have a love relationship, or do I desire more?*
4. *If I am not in a relationship, do I have a strong desire to have one?*
5. *When I am alone, do I feel comfortable, or do I have a strong need to be with someone?*
6. *If my life is full of activities, do I still feel there is something missing in terms of a relationship?*
7. *As a yogi, do I expect my spiritual family to give me personal love?*
   • *If the answer is yes, ask: Am I disappointed if my spiritual family does not give me the love I need?*
8. *When I am with others, do I need to feel that they love me?*

The desire for personal love can come from unfulfilled needs of the inner child, but even if this is true, there is still a genuine need for love that is part of the human condition.

Humankind is different from the animal kingdom, not just because the brain is more fully developed, but also because the need for love goes beyond the sexual desire to procreate. It involves the higher, more spiritual need to have love and to give love. This relates to the seed of the spirit and to the Higher Self. Naturally, the ultimate goal is to go beyond personal love and be able to love in a more compassionate and disidentified manner, but to achieve this it is first necessary to experience personal love. Such love is an energy that runs through a whole scale of feelings, from the most passionate to the most refined. Love opens the doors that lead to the path of enlightenment, and, certainly, the state of enlightenment is love in its purest form.

When love is lacking in your life, it is necessary to change that condition. If you are alone and have no one, reach out to the world and volunteer in children's hospitals or recreation centers. Loving children can be a first step in opening the heart. Even having a pet that you genuinely love will help you in opening the heart. Make your life loving, and in so doing you will have love everywhere around you. The heart energy is the highest energy for a student, but it needs to be used and developed in daily life.

Chapter 18

When You Think You Are Doing Well

When you think you are doing well in a spiritual teaching, you need to stop and look at where that thought came from. Usually, the lower nature will try to make you feel this way, and in so doing it will keep you from striving more. Even if you have achieved higher initiations, it is necessary to always be striving and never feel you have achieved enough. No matter where you are on the path, there is more to walk toward. Even the Masters have their own path, and They never stop moving forward to higher goals.

Satisfaction in your spiritual work can be a deception coming from negative forces. Naturally, these forces will look at every student. They focus the spotlight especially on the student who starts achieving the higher initiations, trying to stop her by sending egoistic thoughts or negative feelings to keep her from striving.

The following is an example of a very high initiate who not only stopped striving but also eventually left the path entirely.

This student, whom we will call Jim, was working toward a higher initiation. Everything was moving correctly. He was focused on his striving, he had full devotion for his teacher, and there seemed to be very little preventing him from achieving the initiation.

One day he met an old friend he hadn't seen for many years. They had been in college together and somehow had lost touch, but through the Internet they had reconnected. When they met, they shared all the things they had been doing.

Jim's friend, Adam, had been in Jim's classes and had continued on to higher degrees, earning a PhD in anthropology at Harvard, where he was became a professor. He had written a textbook that was being used in most of the major colleges. In other words,

Adam had done very well and, in addition, was happily married, had two children, and was financially secure, having invested well in the stock market. Everything about Adam exuded success, and his personality was happy, well-rounded, very intellectual, and full of optimism.

Jim, in turn, had a difficult time talking about his life. Professionally he had a master's degree in social work and was working at an agency for very little money. He liked his job, but it was no longer stimulating and had none of the glamour he was hearing about from his friend. He also had written a book, but was never able to get it published, and self-publishing was too expensive. He married when he was young. The marriage was one of negative karma, and had ended before Jim came into his spiritual teaching. There were no children. Since then, Jim had little desire for marriage even though he did date and have affairs on a regular basis.

Both Jim and Adam were forty-three years old, but the contrast in their stories was very obvious. Jim did mention that he was in a spiritual practice that he found very rewarding, but since Adam didn't ask him any questions about it, Jim never offered more. They spoke mainly about school and other people. Adam had kept track of others, which Jim had not, and it seemed that most of their old friends had achieved successful careers and were well established.

Jim started feeling more and more inadequate, and by the time the dinner was over, he was really seeing his life through Adam's eyes. It was clear that he and Adam had very little in common, and when they parted neither one made any overtures to meet again.

For the next few days Jim was in a very depressed place. Why did Adam have all the luck, why was he so successful in his career when Jim had worked just as hard and had never really felt happy in his profession? Jim chose social work because he had wanted to help others. But, he thought, look at Adam. He also helped others as a teacher and received recognition for his work, something that never happened to him. Jim kept thinking about his life. His main focus had always been his spiritual practice, and in that he had grown considerably, achieving the respect of others in the same group. But now that didn't seem to be enough.

Jim felt that if he asked his teacher for help, the teacher would tell him that he was being challenged with mundane nonsense, that he needed to let go of his competitive feelings, everything was karma, and worldly success had little value in the eyes of the Masters. His teacher would say Jim needed to be happy for his beautiful heart qualities and he needed to see how material things had distracted his friend. This is what Jim felt his teacher would say, and he knew it was true. All that Adam had was connected to worldly success. Jim's path was more difficult, but it would give him the greatest joy.

When Jim connected with his Higher Self, he felt content, but day after day negative thoughts invaded his mind. What if he had chosen a non-service career? He had wanted to be a lawyer, but spiritually he felt that wouldn't fulfill him. Yet, neither did his work. If he had become a lawyer, he would not have met his wife, would not have ended up in a disastrous marriage, and would be making good wages instead of always scrounging to save money. He felt that he could not even date successful women because they would not be interested in him. Many made double his salary, and women on his level were mainly losers like him.

On and on he kept listening to negative thoughts until he finally thought, "If I had never come into this teaching, I would have a better life."

In the meantime, Jim's teacher tried to talk with him on the subtle plane. His teacher knew that negative forces were invading Jim, but even on the subtle plane Jim wouldn't listen to his teacher.

Shortly thereafter, Jim left the teaching and his teacher. He told his teacher that he loved him very much and loved the teaching, but he needed more. He broke his discipleship.

He never came back, nor did he find himself. He went back to school and became a lawyer; he made lots of money and even married again. Only when he was fully in that world did he realize that he had lost his real purpose. He also knew it was too late to go back; he had made his karma and had lost his journey to God.

This is a sad story but one that happens very frequently on the spiritual path. You may ask why did this have to happen. Couldn't

Jim have become the lawyer and still be in the teaching? Why did he have to leave?

The answer is that, yes, Jim could have done any professional work he desired. But, like many New Agers, he felt that the spiritual thing to do was to be in a specific service-type job, not realizing that it is just as important to have spiritual lawyers.

If Jim had talked to his teacher about his feelings, his teacher would have suggested that he go back to school and follow his dream; however, his teacher would have questioned whether this need was coming from a genuine feeling or simply from feelings of competition with his friend. Jim had never expressed a dislike for his job before, and since he felt that money issues were not relevant to the spiritual path, he never complained about not having sufficient funds in order to live.

Jim presumed that his teacher wouldn't understand his feelings, and this was his basic mistake. His teacher knew that Jim was being psychically attacked and could have shown him how to combat the negative influences. Also, his teacher could have helped Jim look more closely at his dissatisfaction with life.

Often, even advanced students will not turn to their teacher for help at a critical time in their development. If they don't do this, the teacher cannot offer advice. It is always up to the student to strive toward the teacher. This is an occult law. The teacher can try to help a student on the subtle plane, but, usually, as in Jim's case, the student won't even talk to the teacher there. Then there is nothing else the teacher can do except send love and pray that the student will listen to her Higher Self instead of the lower nature.

At a certain stage on the path, students question why they are on it. With some, it is a fleeting thought when an obstacle is very difficult to go through. With others, it can be a long period of questioning, and in their case the questioning can end up in their leaving the teaching. In general, these kinds of thoughts come from the lower nature and are influenced by negative forces.

Sometimes the questioning comes from having had a past life in which the student was severely scarred by a religious order. These memories can arise, and if they are not dealt with can cause the student to worry that the teacher or teaching will be destructive. To overcome these feelings, it is necessary to identify where they are coming from. If it is from a past life, it is important to see the past life and understand how it is influencing the present life.

It is best to always talk to the teacher if these feelings are coming up. Since it is part of a natural process, never feel ashamed or embarrassed talking about them to your teacher. She can help you understand where they come from and even help you examine them in more detail.

For example, you may feel that the teaching will keep you from having personal love in your life. This feeling can come from many lives of living in monasteries, or it can come from inner fears that a teaching of any kind will prevent you from having a normal life. All of these fears are false, and come from hidden beliefs. Karma plays a very large role in personal lives, and often it dictates relationships and success on a worldly level.

Many factors come into play when a person enters a spiritual path. Destiny is one of these factors, and karma is a major one, and also the mission a student has been asked to fulfill in this life. It is important to know this; otherwise, a student may want to do something else and never see the true dharma that has been agreed upon before birth.

Doing well relates to knowing one's dharma and, in knowing that, following a plan to fulfill it. Sometimes it isn't possible to know one's dharma because karmic circumstances stand in the way and need to be taken care of.

For example, a student's dharma may be to become a spiritual teacher, but it would be wrong to tell the person this before she is ready to know it. If the student's karma pulls her into a relationship that involves having children, then the student needs to fulfill this karma and will only be ready to work toward the goal of being a teacher when the children are raised and no longer bound to the parents. If the student knows about being a teacher ahead of time, then she may choose not to have a family in order to achieve that goal earlier. This choice would be wrong, as the student needs to complete the karma in order to be free to pursue the goal. Everything is according to destiny.

Another example is a student getting married to someone who is not part of the student's destiny. By using free will, the student may then head off the path in another direction. In this case, it will take longer for the student to get back to the path and continue working toward the goal of being a teacher. The destiny is there, but the free will can change it. If this student knew about becoming a teacher, this information could keep her on the path and help in the decision about marriage. In this example, it is good for the student to know about becoming a teacher and about the importance of using discrimination when it comes to free will.

When students get diverted from their destiny, this causes many new energies to form and take shape. These energies then will try to redirect the students back onto the right path and help them regain the destiny that was discarded.

For example, Julie was meant to marry a very nice man when she was in her early thirties. Instead, she married someone at the age of twenty-five and had two children. This marriage was not part of her destiny, and it wasn't even a karmic relationship. It was simply the pressure of her family and friends that made her choose to marry, even though she was not very attracted to the man. After several years of marriage, Julie decided to divorce her husband. There was nothing in the marriage that excited her, and she wanted out. At the time, she was in her mid-thirties, and it took several years to resettle herself with her children and make a new life.

In the meantime, the man she was actually destined to marry hadn't met anyone he wanted to settle down with. He liked the freedom of being single and considered himself a confirmed bachelor. When he and Julie finally met, he was in his early forties and she was thirty-eight. It was instant love, and even though they had lost the time frame of their destiny, they did marry and begin a new life together.

This ending happened to be a good one, but there have been many more endings in which the chance was lost entirely and both people went off the path of their destiny. When this happens, the energies are readjusted, and hopefully the other destined events will still take place. If, for example, Julie and her destined man couldn't meet because she was still married or he had chosen another woman, then at least she could still follow the path of her vocation and follow that destiny.

How do you know whether you are following your destiny or have instead taken a sidetrack? Let's do the following exercise to check.

Exercise One:
Ask your Higher Self the following questions:
1. *Looking at where I am now spiritually, am I at the proper place where I should be according to my destiny?*
2. *Looking at where I am now, am I in the destined place where I should be in my work?*
3. *Looking at where I am now in terms of my relationships, am I with people I am destined to be with?*
4. *Looking at where I am now, can I understand where I am meant to be in the future if I follow my destiny?*
   - *If you receive a no answer to any of the above questions, ask the Higher Self to show you, or tell you, what is missing, and whether it is still possible to resume the destined path.*
   - *If it is too late to return to the destined path, ask the Higher Self if there is anything you can do to compensate for the loss.*

Most people's destinies are changed because of free will. If the planned destiny is not fulfilled, then the person will have to return in another life and try again. When I say planned destiny, I mean just that. Before a person is born the destined path is laid out and shown to the person according to her karma.

Negative karma on the destined path can be changed through the positive use of free will. For instance, understanding that a relationship is mainly negative and refusing to become involved requires a strong will to say no to the vibrations of the karmic pull.

It is always possible for you to change your course of destiny if that destiny takes you into some dark and negative terrain. It is better to begin a new path that will build good karma and make your destiny one that is positive.

You may say, "But how is this possible? How is it possible to change karma, especially negative karma?" The answer is that it is always possible to change negative karma, especially if the karma is in a relationship that can cause more negative karma to occur. Obviously, if it is time for you to pay back karma, you still need to pay it back, but you can do so in a different way than being with someone who will harm or abuse you. Your karma can be paid off by good acts that lessen the karma. Then, maybe you would not be in a terrible relationship, because you would not be with the original person who would have hurt you more deeply.

Everyone is open to change, and this can even cause karma to change. Difficult karma has to be paid off, but it can be done more gently than originally destined.

When a yogi is faced with difficult karma, it is important to understand the karma and never be drawn into its depth without understanding its source. By understanding the karma, you will eliminate any suffering that goes with it, and it can then be paid off more quickly.

For example, illness is always caused by karma. If you should come down with a disease that makes you handicapped in any way, it is important to accept having the disease by acknowledging that it is karma being paid off. Then, learn how to work positively with energy, directing it to the illness and adjusting your life to the handicap without complaint. In so doing, you will attract positive energy that will help you in the healing process. If the illness is a permanent one, it is best to work with energy to help the illness stay in regression.

With each step on the path of destiny one is faced with decisions that involve the use of free will. Always take the time to determine if the decision you are making comes from your destiny or from your free will.

Ask the Higher Self to help you in doing this, just to check your decisions.

Exercise Two:

Try looking back five years at some of the important decisions you have made. Write them down.

Then, taking one at a time, ask your Higher Self the following questions.

1. *Was this decision coming from my destiny or from my free will?*
2. *If the answer is that the decision came from your free will, ask: Was it the right decision?*
3. *Also ask if this decision in any way affects your future destiny.*
4. *If the answer is yes, ask how, and also ask how to change this so the future can be the destined future.*

Part of knowing your destiny is to understand that a destiny can change and still be your destiny. This happens when your destiny is involved with another person. For example, your destiny might be to do some special work with another person, but the other person goes off in another direction and therefore will never work with you. The work may actually have been based on the two of you doing it together. Your destiny would change because of this, and the work you were meant to do will also change.

The next stage would be for you to do some other work that may or may not be similar to the original plan, and to do this work either alone or with someone else. This type of backup often takes place. As a result, you are still fulfilling your destiny even though the other person dropped the ball.

Much of a person's destiny relates to karma, and within that framework there are other ways of fulfilling the karma and also fulfilling one's destiny. In some ways the process resembles a ball game. You are the pitcher, and you work with the catcher to strike out a player. If your catcher isn't playing that day, you have to work with a substitute who may not fully understand the signals you used with the regular catcher. Then, the person at bat can also change the game. If this person is a new player and a good hitter, then even your position as pitcher can change if the person can always hit your pitch. Life is like the game. Anyone on the team can change the outcome, and you are just a player. If you take on the job as pitcher and do your best, then you are fulfilling your destiny even if you get kicked off the team later. See yourself as always open to change, and your destiny plays a big part in change. If you aren't open to change, you can lose your destiny.

When I talk about doing well, I am referring to following one's destiny, understanding one's karma, and, most of all, being open to new possibilities. Doing well can be one thing for one student and another thing for another student. Do not compare yourself to anyone else, as each person's path is very different.

Let's try an experiment.

Exercise Three:
1. *Take a good look at all the things you are doing in your life. Write down the things that you regard as positive actions, and then write down all the things you think are negative actions.*
2. *Compare the two lists. Do you have more good actions than negative ones?*
3. *Next, take the list of positive actions, look at each item, and think about whether it is your destiny or free will that is doing the action.*
4. *Then, take the list of negative actions, and do the same. Ask yourself: Is this destined, or is it free will? Generally, you will find that the negative actions are under the category of free will.*
5. *Finally, look at both lists and ask your Higher Self the following questions:*
   - *1. Does my positive list feel correct to you?*
   - *2. Does my negative list feel correct to you?*
6. *When you receive a no, ask your Higher Self to either remove or add to the relevant list.*

Without a doubt, the negative will be the most difficult to change. This means changing all the actions even when they are destined.

Destined negative actions can be changed. They generally are due to karma, and, referring back to what was said earlier in this chapter, they can be changed.

Now, when you look at the positive list, realize that even that list can change. If it isn't your destiny to do a certain positive act, then you need to stop doing it. Your time needs to be spent doing your destined positive actions and not to be sidetracked.

In looking at who you are in terms of doing well on the spiritual path, think about yourself in terms of someone else. Take the best example of an initiate person you can identify with. This should be someone you know, a spiritual brother or sister, but not your teacher.

Exercise Four:
Look at the person, and ask yourself the following questions:
  1. *How does my striving compare to this person's?*
  2. *How does my devotion compare to this person's devotion?*
  3. *Is this person more focused than I am?*
  4. *Is this person more centered than I am?*
  5. *Is this person more often in the Higher Self than I am?*
  6. *Do I think this person is following her dharma?*
  7. *When I look at this person, do I feel respect and admiration?*
  8. *As I grow spiritually, do I think this person will always be at a higher level and an example for me to follow?*

In conclusion, this comparison should not in any way be competitive. You are mainly following the example of someone you admire as a yogi. The teacher should obviously be someone you esteem, but sometimes it is easier to observe a fellow student who is sincerely striving and proceeding successfully on the path. Ask her about her personal practice. Get to know the person better and talk about the blocks and the joys of the teaching. Learn from the person, and it will help you to do better. Remember, there are always those who precede you; learn from them, and you too will ascend the ladder and grow spiritually.

Chapter 19

The Importance of Boundaries

The world you live in is divided into many planes, and within those planes there are boundaries, be they between nations or continents or even cities and towns. This is your physical world, a world so physical there have to be boundaries in order to live. There are these obvious physical boundaries and also human-made personal boundaries that people put in place so they can have lives that are not flooded with other people's needs and emotions. All of these boundaries constitute the world as you know it.

A student has additional kinds of boundaries. His boundaries need to extend to other realms and planes of existence that are not physical, but exist in the subtle worlds. In those worlds there are boundaries that exist only upon entering each level, boundaries are very few in number and exist only as differentiations rather than being definite and conforming.

When you enter those worlds or planes, you feel freed from all constraints, and you are able to travel in any direction and encounter no or little opposition.

Even if this feeling is generally correct, there is a limitation. The vastness of space itself makes a person feel boundless, yet as you pass to higher levels there are definite distinctions and requirements of your subtle body. If those requirements are lacking, then psychically you will be stopped and will have to turn back. So, the freedom that is part of your expectation of the subtle world does not fully exist.

If you direct yourself toward a particular place, for example flying to another country, you might suddenly feel some constriction, particularly if you are not meant to go there. That constriction could stop you from going, and if you force yourself to go anyway, then you could encounter some difficulties you hadn't anticipated. How could this happen if there are no set boundaries?

Try to envision boundaries on the subtle plane in a different way. Let's look at them through the eyes of Hierarchy first, and then you may realize that these boundaries are not only different in kind, but also different for each individual, similar to the personal boundaries I mentioned earlier.

When you look at boundaries through the eyes of Hierarchy, you see a combination of things. There is a boundary that involves proper discrimination and also a boundary that relates to how the heart energy is being used. For example, if there are strong personal desires are present they can overtake the heart. An example would be a student asking the teacher if he could come and stay for a week and study privately with him. If the teacher lives in an ashram where there are other students, then this request is fine. But if the teacher lives alone, to ask to be alone with him for such a length of time would not be appropriate, since the teacher has many students and does a lot of personal work with them on the subtle plane.

In an ashram, the teacher's sole mission is to teach, and to teach all the students. Even in that setting the teacher has very little interaction with a student, and when that happens it is only for a half hour or so.

If the teacher who lives alone allows students to come for periods of alone time with him, then, naturally, all the students will want such time, which would leave little time for the teacher to do his personal dharma.

Usually, a teacher who lives alone has a separate mission besides being a teacher, and therefore he needs personal time. Otherwise, he would have an ashram-type setting and devote his full time to teaching.

Let's take time now to understand the student's needs and how boundaries are important for that student with the teacher.

Exercise One:
If you have a spiritual teacher, ask yourself the following questions:

1. *Do I have a personal need to always be in the presence of my teacher?*
2. *When I am not with my teacher, can I still feel his presence?*
3. *How often do I ask my teacher questions in meditation?*
   - *If I do this, do I receive answers I can accept?*
4. *When I am with my teacher and other students, do I crave more attention?*
5. *If I need time with my teacher, do I use that time by asking him spiritual questions, or do I ask questions that will help me progress in my personal development?*

Take these answers and check them with your Higher Self to see if you have evaluated yourself accurately. If you do not have a teacher at this time, think about how you would like to relate to a teacher if you should meet one, and answer the questions accordingly. For example, for the first question, ask: If I should meet my teacher, would I have a personal need to always be with him?

Boundaries of the heart can relate spiritually to the use of energy on the subtle planes. For example, if you are traveling in the subtle world and see someone in need, again you need to use discrimination along with your heart energy to know if it is all right for you to help the person or if the situation calls for another approach. For instance, there are ghosts on the Lower Astral Planes who will not move on and will always be demanding help. There are all kinds of pretenders on those planes, so it is important to always guard the heart energy and not use it unless your guide and Higher Self say it is all right.

Heart energy is a very strong energy, and any spirit on the subtle plane will respond to it, so it is important to protect that energy and not use it unless you know it is all right to do so.

You open the heart and use its energy when you encounter your teacher, your Master, or any other High Being you recognize as being real and not an illusion or a pretender. To check what is real or not real, always ask the being to show you light, and if he cannot do this, then question if he is a pretender.

When you start to use heart energy in your personal relationships, it is very important to always use it with discrimination, even with the people you love the most and with whom you have the closest relationships. Overpowering a person with love can be very controlling, so when you use the heart, never force love to a person but simply ask the Higher Self to direct the love according to what a person needs at a given time. Use love in a disidentified manner and it will always be right and never forcing. How does one use love in this manner?

Exercise Two:
Ask your Higher Self:
1. *When I am with someone I love, how can I send him love in a disidentified manner?*
   - *Then ask: What happens if my love is not disidentified?*
2. *Next, try visualizing a scene with someone you care about and send the person love with the identified, personal approach. Experience how that feels.*
   - *Then, redo the scene by sending love in a disidentified manner, and experience how that feels.*

The difference should be very apparent. In the disidentified manner you can feel genuine love with no personal needs attached. In the identified, personal manner, love is always given with a need for something in return.

Placing boundaries on your love or the way you love may sound strange for a student. You are taught to always open the heart with love to all people, but that kind of love is always a disidentified love that has no attachments. To achieve this type of love, it is important to learn to deal with the heart energies in a discriminating manner. Too often love is sent or given with personal needs so hidden that the student is convinced the love sent is pure. To really be clear on this issue, you need to examine what love means to you and reach a stronger understanding of your personal needs. Do the following exercise with this is mind.

Exercise Three:
Ask your Higher Self to answer these questions:

1. *Do I consciously have a good understanding of what real love is?*
2. *When I am with someone I love, can I really love the person without any expectation of having any personal needs fulfilled?*
3. *Am I aware of what all my personal needs are when I love someone?*
4. *In the beginning of a relationship, do I have personal needs about how the relationship needs to be formed in terms of love?*
5. *When I have been in a relationship with someone for a long time, do I ever review the relationship in terms of love?*
6. *Is love always apparent to me?*
7. *When I need love, can I easily ask for it?*
8. *When I am in a relationship that is a friendship, can I unconditionally love my friend?*
9. *Can I love someone without any fears arising within me?*
10. *In any relationship, can I love someone unconditionally?*
11. *If you receive a no answer from your Higher Self to any of the above questions, then ask the Higher Self why, and also ask for a process to change your response and a first step to help you do this.*

It is very difficult for most people, even longtime initiates, not to have conditions around loving. The open heart usually can only be achieved by a high adept, so do not be discouraged if you receive a no answer many times to the above questions.

Exercise Four:

Look at your no responses and prioritize them according to what you would most like to achieve. Then, take the top one and just work with that aspect of love. Give it your attention on a daily basis, and even do a nightly review to determine how you are doing with it. Remember to ask the Higher Self to give you a first step, and when you have completed that step satisfactorily, ask for a second step.

Just realizing and working on one aspect on your list will open many of the others for scrutiny.

Without a doubt, using the heart on a daily basis is a goal for all students, but it is vital that using the heart be accompanied by discrimination and disidentification. Without these, you cannot have the strong boundaries that also are very important to keep when you are striving upward.

When there are no boundaries, the student doesn't know how to use the energies of the heart. Boundaries are necessary for becoming aware of outmoded ways of thinking. In a changing world and a changing universe, there will always be new ways to look at things and new forms to encounter. This is also true for spiritual people. Ancient information may or may not be correct in the present world. Truth is relative, and only when a student can remain open can he understand this.

If a teaching says a given thing in one century, that same information may change in the following century. Information available to only a few in the past will be given to many in the following century. This is certainly true of any teaching. For example, in the nineteenth century the term Shambhala was known only by high initiates and spoken about among a few with great discrimination. The home of the Masters was sacred and, of course, it still is sacred, but now the masses hear the name all the time. It is written about in books and spoken about on television and radio. Even the Dalai Lama has talked about Shambhala and the Masters in public lectures.

This information is only widespread at this time because it is meant to be. If it were not supposed to be known, it would not be known. This example illustrates the boundaries of information coming from higher sources. When information is meant to be disseminated, that will happen, and not before.

Information has energy and provokes energy, and since energies govern the evolution of the planet, it is necessary for Hierarchy to carefully control what is given out. Humankind can only handle certain information at any given time. The masses are moving in an evolutionary pattern that is tightly controlled.

That is why truth is relative. Truth relates to what you can absorb at a given time.

In general, it is important to reflect on new information given to you that relates to spiritual matters. Put the information in your heart and ask your Higher Self whether it is true just for this time or is part of the cosmic laws. If it is part of the cosmic laws, it will be one hundred percent accurate and will never change. An example of a cosmic law is the law of opposites, or balancing the Masculine and Feminine Principles. Another example is the law of karma.

When you receive new information, make certain the source is a sound one. Some of the people doing channeling are not being given correct information. It might seem correct but is off in a small degree, and that degree will distort truth. People who are channeling cannot be given truth unless they are initiates with a direct link to the Masters. Thus, when you hear or read something that seems to be new information, always put it in your heart and ask whether it is true for this time. If the answer is no, then question where the information came from. Be certain to always add "for this time" because, as stated before, truth is relative to the evolutionary period.

Boundaries are very apparent to the Masters. They live by them not only in their private domain but also in the work they do with the nature spirits. It is most important to maintain good boundaries with any of the spirits in the subtle world as well.

First, concerning the nature spirits, if you are able to connect to a nature spirit, whether it is in a plant or a tree, or is simply a spirit in charge of a certain portion of land, then it is important to approach and maintain that relationship in a designated manner. If you feel the vibration of the spirit, always ask it to let you experience its energy for a definite period of time, for example, a minute. Never make the time indefinite, as that is not in keeping with the very defined structure of nature spirits. If you hear a spirit, ask very politely if you can talk with it and, again, give a time frame, or ask it how much time it can give you that day. Follow the spirit's guidelines always, and be certain to first ask if it is okay to communicate with it. At the end, be certain to thank the spirit and ask to hear or feel it again at a later time. The same holds true if you see a nature spirit; then, you can communicate through hearing or feeling it.

When a nature spirit contacts you, the rules change. Sometimes, if you are very friendly with a certain spirit, it can come through to you and give you a special message. Never set boundaries on this type of communication, as it is being freely given. After the message has been given, you can communicate with the spirit and ask questions. Do not do this for long, as that is taking advantage of their rules in being open to you. They cannot end the conversation or communion, so it is up to you to thank the spirit and say goodbye. This type of conversation should not be longer than ten minutes, so keep that time frame as a good rule of thumb. Remember, nature spirits have work to do and little time just to chitchat. After the time is up, you can ask it whether it is possible to continue for a few more minutes or whether you can set up another meeting to continue the conversation.

If you have difficulty connecting to nature spirits when previously there was no difficulty, then maybe you are not following their rules of etiquette. Try to reconnect and apologize about not understanding the boundaries of their world.

Second, communication on the subtle planes is far more difficult to understand or to explain. Let's look at this with a different model in mind. If, for example, you are taking a trip to another country, you fly from one location to another, arriving on time, and then you take a car, bus, or train from the airport unless a service or friend picks you up. This procedure is normal when taking a journey anywhere in the physical world. Your destination comes after a certain amount of time spent traveling.

When you start a journey on the subtle plane, you will be doing the same but in a much shorter amount of time. Your subtle body will fly through the lower levels and arrive at a higher level where you can experience a plane higher than the ones you traveled through. This journey is directed either by your own spirit consciousness or by your guide or teacher. When you arrive at the higher plane, you can access the information you want or discover something new that is exciting for you to take back.

Now, in the physical-world journey you will encounter people on your flight, and when you land someone may be helpful and give you the assistance you might need. The same is true on the subtle plane. The difference is that there help is automatically given to you without your asking for it, whereas in the physical world there will be times when you may need to ask for help. The subtle world is full of beings who are most helpful and will always be there to assist anyone striving toward the higher realms. These beings are the subtle-world helpers who are mostly invisible, so that you are not even aware of their assistance. This is the reason a person can never get lost in the subtle world, because these spirits will guide anyone who is going in a wrong direction. Never try to talk to them. When your journey is finished, the subtle world guide will leave you, as you will be safe there. Always thank the guide for its help. Returning to your body is a direct route, and sometimes you will be assisted again, but usually your own guide will take you there.

Lastly, you need to have boundaries with the Masters. Some students have direct communication with a Master whereas others do not and instead will link their heart to Hierarchy and to the Masters. The following are the boundaries that are part of both ways of connecting.

- Always think about the Master with respect, devotion, and gratitude.
- Never refer to a Master by His full name unless you are meditating or need help.
- When a message is sent to you from your Master, be certain to write it down and try to follow it if it is guidance of some kind.
- Be aware of your actions and thoughts any time you think about Hierarchy.
- Always be careful to maintain a clean living environment if

you want the Master to visit you.

- When you meditate, feel the vibration of the connection to your Master.

Boundaries on all levels are very important in helping you to see yourself better. When you are aware of other people's boundaries, you have a better idea about the boundaries you need to make to help you on the spiritual path. Students need to set up strong boundaries in order to be more focused in their work and personal relationships. Things cannot go wrong if proper boundaries are made and followed.

Exercise Five:

Make a list of those areas in your life where you need to set up boundaries. Then write down the boundaries you need to create in order for that area to function fully.

If, for example, you are in a relationship that is very demanding of your time, it is important to set up boundaries so that this does not continue. The same is true about your work. If you are in a job with people who are dysfunctional, then it is important to set up boundaries to help you be successful in the work.

Take time in doing this exercise, and when you are finished make certain you discuss the boundaries with the people who will be affected by them. Maybe a boundary you are setting up will offend someone. It is important to know this and discuss it thoroughly. Maybe your boundary is too stringent and needs to be less strict, or maybe the person needs to set up some boundaries with you. It is good to have agreement; otherwise there can be resentment. Certainly, if you are living with someone, it is important for all concerned to have boundaries that are maintained.

When you have boundaries that are easy to follow, you are at a good place that enables you to have a full life and maintain your spiritual practice. If boundaries of any kind cause you or others to suffer, then something is wrong with those boundaries and they need to be adjusted. People who are fanatical have a tendency to develop fanatical boundaries, and they use them for control rather than to make life easier. Be careful not to do this. Boundaries should make life easier, and they can make relationships better because then there is nothing hidden in the relationship. Boundaries make for full awareness, and that always results in a more focused and happier life.

Chapter 20

Seeing the God Within

This chapter refers to the Divine as "God" in keeping with Western tradition, but the way that term is used relates solely to the divine spirit, or Source, not an amorphous being.

A student knows that the seed of the spirit comes from the Source, or God. This seed is part of the divine principle, and it is within all people no matter how long they have been human. But what is this seed, this divinity within, and how can you even relate to the fact that God is within you?

Many initiates who know this fact do not think about it, or even try to relate to it as being Divine.

A disciple told this story:

"When I was a child, I remember asking my mother to tell me about God. Like most Christians, she referred to God as our Father who takes care of us throughout eternity.

" 'But, how does God take care of us?' I asked. She replied that living in a beautiful country, having food and clothing and all the pleasures of life, is how He takes care of us. She also told me that He inspires us to do good acts of kindness.

"All of these things made no sense to me. Then I asked, 'But what about others who have none of the things I have, and what about the children who are starving to death—why isn't God taking care of them?'

"She couldn't answer this question, and I continued to ask, "If God is up in heaven, how can He know what I need?"

" 'Oh, he just does,' she replied.

"My typical religious upbringing never answered any of my questions, and only when I read about reincarnation, and even started having memories of past lives, could I begin my relationship with God.

"When I first realized that God was pure energy that was within all my friends and within me, I saw the world through different eyes. I had this realization when I was eight years old. By then I had met a wise woman who could answer all my questions, even the same ones I had asked my mother, and this wise woman was the one who told me that I had God within me. That probably was the deepest religious moment in my life. It filled me with a moment of divine grace, as I felt God's energy in my heart."

The disciple who told this story continued her quest to find God and is now a teacher. Her revelation at a very young age indicates that she came in with this knowledge and it was waiting to be opened.

In the past it was very important to relate to God as being outside of one's self. Heaven and hell were places where the spirit went. If you were in heaven, you would meet God, or if the opposite, then you would meet Satan. This belief system made people morally aware of good and evil. A believer did good deeds in order to go to heaven, and this was making society a better place. This moral control was in keeping with the restrictions of the church. It made people completely dependent on the church fathers. As a result, there was little regard for a person's spiritual journey unless it was in keeping with the church doctrines. Anyone with different views was considered a sinner and was damned

Christ talked about the God within, but many believed that as a reality this only related to Him, because He was Divine.

There have been major shifts in consciousness as we enter this coming age. People can now accept that to look for God outside oneself does not necessarily help to find Him. Having Him within adds another dimension that changes a person's consciousness. If, instead of the church, you were responsible for your personal moral codes and sanctions, then the whole spiritual process would no longer be only about outward behavior but would now also be about the inner process of connecting to the Source. This process is very personal and relates to a person's evolution. It contains all possibilities and has within it true knowledge and the potential for finding true wisdom. For if God is within, then wisdom is also within.

Let's now start a process that will help you to understand what it means to have God within. As a statement and even as an experience, the phrase "God within" connects to a person's inner beliefs about God. To examine these concepts, you need to examine your conditioning and even some of the past life beliefs you have carried with you. If, for example, you have had many lives in a Western religious order, you would still think of God as a white-haired man; instead, if you have had lives in the Eastern religions, you would think of God as energy. Some lives are stronger than others and play a greater role in how you feel and think about God. Let's look at these personal beliefs.

Exercise One:
Reflect on the following statements and ask yourself if there is any part of you that believes them.

1. *God is always a personal God whom I see as a heavenly being.*
2. *When I think about God, I think of it being a man.*
3. *When I relate to God, I pray to someone outside of myself.*
4. *When I try to connect to God, I do so from a religious point of view.*
5. *I believe that God hears me when I pray.*
6. *Sometimes I think of God as being too far away for me to connect with Him.*
7. *When I think of achieving God Consciousness, I think of becoming one with a Being.*
8. *God Consciousness seems too far away for me to even think about.*
9. *I see God Consciousness as belonging only to very high initiates.*
10. *If you tell me that God is within, I can believe it only in the abstract.*
11. *Believing in God has never been important for me.*

12. *I want to believe in a Divine Being, not in divine energy.*
13. *Sometimes the whole concept of having God within is overwhelming to me.*
14. *Some day I hope to understand more about God, but now it is impossible.*

The above statements may not be complete for you, so try to write your own analysis of how you believe in God and what you believe in terms of having God within. You may be surprised that even as a yogi you hold some beliefs of a personal God.

When someone thinks about the Divine, usually the person thinks about something in the abstract. Since God is a mystery, it is natural to think about it in this abstract way. Instead, let's look at the Divine as unmanifested energy, which is beyond anyone's understanding. Even the word "energy" in this concept is beyond understanding. Unmanifested energy in some religions is called Chaos, or Parabrahman, Brahman, Jehovah, or God as we are using it.

Take for a moment the concept of energy, as you know it. One aspect is that energy is always in motion, is always changing, and has no form, yet we talk about the seed of the spirit being a seed. If unmanifested energy is within and is in the shape of a seed, how is this possible? So again, our minds look at all things as having to have a base in physical reality in order to understand them. Instead, let us think of the seed not literally as a seed but as a divine spark.

Some students believe that the seed of the spirit comes not from God but, instead, from a Higher Being, such as a Kumara. Such a belief is partially true. The seed of the spirit comes from the chalice of this Higher Being, which contains the spirit of God. Therefore, the immediate source is from the Higher Being, but the seed itself is still from God.

Now that you are totally confused and are looking at God in a different manner, let's try to put God into yet different terms. If you see God as spirit, then to hold the concept of worshipping spirit is not valid. If spirit has no form, how can you worship it? You can only worship a concept, or a Being, but not a changing form.

Since humankind has always needed a Higher Being to worship, this need has clouded the true realization of what constitutes God. Instead, if you worship a lesser God who has form, then it is much more comprehensible, and you have a personal relationship with someone and not just with an elusive energy. This is why religions have made an amorphous God into a Being, who has form and is divine and all knowing. It is easier to relate to the Masters, or to Jesus, Buddha, or even to the Lord Maitreya, who is the highest Being that can be visualized.

This is fine to do, and it is also good to realize that these Higher Beings are the closest reality to God that a person can relate to. Yet, in doing this, remember that the seed of the spirit is from the Source, and this divine Source is part of these Higher Beings and is also in you.

Sometimes people have difficulty in believing that God is within. You may say, for example, "If I truly believe God is within, then why can I not access God on a regular basis? If I truly feel God is in everyone, why can I not feel God in those people when I am with them?"

All of these thoughts make the knowledge of God being within unacceptable when someone is faced with the reality of being one with the Divine. Because of this, the statement of God being within, even when it is believed, becomes, "I know God is in me, but it is beyond my reach. I have to be a Master to even feel it. Therefore, it is best not to think about God being within."

Take a moment to see if this statement resides within you. If it does not, I ask you: "Can you really think of becoming one with God on a regular basis? Can you really believe you have the ability to make that happen? And most of all, can you consciously feel God's essence within you?"

You may say, "That is impossible, but I can feel my Higher Self and that is equally as important because the Higher Self is part of God."

While it's true that the Higher Self is part of you, God's essence is also part of you, and though it is connected to the Higher Self, it is still separate and can be experienced separately.

Let's look at the God within as a symbol. It can be a dove, a flame, a spiral, or a pyramid. It can be a six-pointed star or a rose, any of the mystical symbols, or it can simply be a brilliant white light. Take a minute now to choose a symbol that you want to represent the essence of God within. Make the symbol strong, a symbol you can readily see, not just energy or anything in motion. Check with your Higher Self, and ask if this would be a good symbol for you to use to represent God within. If the Higher Self says no, then ask it what would be a better symbol for you to use.

When you have your symbol, draw it in color. After you have drawn it, put it in front of you and just look at it for as long as you can without any thoughts coming in. As soon as a thought comes in, throw it out and refocus on the symbol. Try doing this for at least five minutes, then place the image into your heart and say the following words:

May my heart connect to the God within and let me experience its essence.

Keep working with this every day if you can. It may take time, and if you experience any fear coming up, just visualize the fear as a black ball and hand it to your Higher Self.

The experience is very different for each person and relates to your spiritual development. Naturally, a higher initiate will experience it more easily than a novice, but eventually everyone can experience God's essence within.

The importance of doing this cannot be emphasized enough. To know that you have God within in an abstract way is very different from experiencing it. This experience makes you more responsible in the quest of becoming one with the God within. It also gives a moment of joy and the wisdom of what God Consciousness really means.

Once you have experienced this, it is impossible to think of the God within in an abstract manner. The goal of achieving God Consciousness becomes more defined, and, therefore, it gives you the impetus to strive forward on the path. Without this experience, the goal seems unreachable, especially when you are experiencing feelings from the lower nature. With this experience, it is easier to see the goal through the obstacles and know that someday you will achieve it.

When the goal is achieved, it is possible to review all the twists and turns of the journey. Then you can see the complete pattern of your personal evolution. You will have full knowledge of how you have grown, and in that knowledge comes an understanding of the importance of acknowledging at all times that each and every one is part of a whole and the whole far exceeds any individual. This constitutes true wisdom. When you have come full circle from the beginning of humankind to the final merging with God, then you will have fulfilled your destiny.

Chapter 21

Dealing with the Outside World

A spiritual student has a mission in the world, especially if he believes in the need to be in the world to serve. But how can a student become immersed in worldly values and worldly causes and still remain spiritual? This has always been a problem for a spiritual person—to be in the world but not of it—especially if his mission requires significant participation in worldly matters.

With the new age comes a need for more and more spiritual people to take roles in politics and industry. To do this type of work is very difficult because of the lack of morals that prevails in these areas. Indeed, it is very difficult to achieve recognition in these fields without major adjustments. How much should a student protest the moral issues, or how much should he give in to the pressures of this type of work? So the big question becomes how to remain spiritual while at the same time aspiring to achieve worldly recognition.

When your mission is politics, the moral issue is especially large. How can you become well known without using political gain to help you up the ladder? There will be situations that present difficult choices, and sometimes spiritual people will not take the risks that would help them achieve their goals.

Working in industry presents similar challenges. Often false claims about products and price maneuvering put a yogi at karmic risk. If you stay in an ashram, then there are no karmic risks, but to achieve the higher initiations one has to be in the world and take these risks.

Let's look at these challenges in the light of karma. For instance, what do you do if you have to support someone politically in order to further your own political career but the person is someone you feel is not good enough for the office? If you support the person, then you can make negative karma for yourself. But if instead you oppose the person, you may make positive karma, but at the same time hinder your dharma and the possibility of moving forward politically. Which is more important? Sometimes a yogi gets stuck trying to understand what is the best choice karmically, and as a consequence does nothing. This is very much like the situation faced by Arjuna in the Bhagavad Gita, who cannot decide which army to fight. In such a case, it is important to weigh the odds and the consequences involved in the decision.

First of all, when a student worries about making karma, he is forgetting that every action has a karmic consequence, and it is important to always look at the outcome in terms of karma. If you have to make difficult decisions that will affect others, then it is best to weigh the effects the decisions will have on all those involved.

For example, you are meant to take a job in a corporation that is very progressive and would give you the opportunity to do some highly creative work. But in the job interview you realize the person you would be working with is very difficult and could make trouble for you. Would you still take the job, or would you refuse it?

To arrive at the correct decision, it is important to know what your relationship with that person has been in the past. If the two of you have incurred negative karma from a past life, you would be wise to refuse the job and to try to find something else. If, instead, you have no karma with the person, but he has a difficult personality, then you would take the job and deal with him as issues arose, doing your best not to incur any new karma along the way.

The same is true in similar situations where you have to be involved with difficult people. If you are a student and must take a particular course with a difficult teacher, you should go through the course doing your best while trying not to feel any anger or resentment toward the teacher. The main thing is to have your goal in mind.

Life itself will have many challenges, and the main ones will be around ethics: what to do when confronted with moral decisions. Sometimes a student will have to accept some negative karma in order to follow his dharma, knowing that the negative karma will be offset by positive karma when the goal is reached. It means carefully walking a fine line.

Obviously, you do not want to hurt or abuse anyone along the way, but inevitably someone will be negatively affected if you are striving for a leadership role of any kind. That person may be a rival, or simply someone you will overlook in the process. You can't arrive at the top without making enemies, whether or not you have done anything wrong. The challenge is to always do your best with discrimination, knowing you are bound to meet some old karma along the way, some of which will be negative.

When you see yourself working toward your dharma and you know it will bring you to the attention of others, how do you handle this? Are you aware of how powerful your effect on others can be if you are an initiate? Such energy affects others whether or not you realize it. You may have a simple job, one that isn't in the public eye, yet you may still make a significant impression on your fellow workers. An initiate has vibrations that penetrate the atmosphere and will draw out either the best or the worst in others. Remember, you can change situations just by using your heart. Do you do this? Or, do you simply consider your work life separate from your spiritual life and fail to realize how one overlaps the other?

The exercise below will help you understand this issue better.

Exercise One:
Ask yourself the following questions:
1. *When I am doing my job, do I in any way affect the people I work with?*
2. *When I am at work, am I always careful to try to be positive and to send that energy out into the room?*

If you supervise others, ask:
3. *When I am supervising someone, am I careful to link with my Higher Self and the other person's Higher Self in order to help that person in the task ahead?*

4. *Am I conscious of others' vibrations and how they affect me?*

5. *When I speak to my boss or supervisor, am I careful about the manner in which I say something?*

6. *Do I always link with the Higher Self during the day in order to make the best decisions?*

7. *Do I have a good understanding of the karma between those I work with and myself?*

8. *When I look at my actions while I am working, am I aware that they are in sync with others?*

In regard to your relationships with friends and family, are you aware that as a student your vibrations are different? These vibrations will definitely affect others. Therefore, you need to be careful that they are directed only in a positive way. If you should get angry, your anger will be much more powerful than the average person's anger. The same is true if you are loving. That loving vibration will make others feel very happy.

So often students look at life as a glass half empty rather than half full. This attitude can cause others to view you negatively simply because the energy you put out is so much stronger than someone else's. Most students don't realize how powerful they are. This is unfortunate as it can create karma when least expected. If you realized your effect on others, you would be more careful and even make some changes in the manner in which you talk about something. The following exercise is to help you start to see your influence on those around you.

Exercise Two:
Ask yourself the following questions:
1. *When I am in a negative mood, am I careful not to project that onto others?*

2. *If I feel happy about something, am I careful not to overpower others with my feelings?*

3. *Am I conscious of how my words affect others?*

4. *When I am centered, do I focus on sending positive*

> *thoughts to others?*
>
> 5. *If I am working with difficult people, do I send them love?*
> 6. *When I am alone, am I conscious of having positive thoughts about others?*
> 7. *As I grow spiritually, do I always try to be more centered and conserve my energy so as not to overpower others?*
> 8. *When I am working with others, do I try to be receptive and not take charge?*
> 9. *In a work situation, do I always focus on using my energy to enhance the work?*
> 10. *When I am using my will, do I moderate its energy?*

Sometimes a student will think he is talking from the heart when in reality he is talking from the will. The heart and the will have some common features; both are focused and both have strong energy. The heart's energy is always positive when coming from the Higher Self and not from the desire body, and the will is always positive when coming from the Higher Self and not from the need to be dominant. Someone once said, "The difference between being in your heart and being in your will is that the heart requires no acknowledgement, whereas the will needs to be listened to."

The focused will can be creative and determined at the same time. When it is not in a positive place, it loses its creativity. There is a big difference in the time it takes to focus the will or to focus the heart. Focusing the will requires more concentration and takes a few minutes longer. Focusing the heart can be instantaneous.

For most people the latter is more difficult, because they don't even realize they can focus the heart. Focusing the heart is different from connecting to the heart. It requires more concentration, and it even requires using the will to do this. For example, someone close to you asks you to do something you don't want to do, but you agree to do it because of the relationship. If you only focus your will on doing the task, you can complete it but may feel resentful because your ego self felt forced to do something it didn't want to do. If, instead, you undertake the task with a focused heart, you can accomplish the work with joy and without resentment.

How can you focus and use the heart in this capacity throughout the day? It takes time and considerable effort to learn how to do this.

Let's start with a simple exercise.

Exercise Three:
- *Take an object you love, concentrate on this object, and give it all your attention. Then move the concentration to the heart chakra.*
- *When you feel the energy in your heart chakra, then again focus on the object from that place.*

What you should feel is a different kind of energy than you experienced from simply concentrating on the object. The concentration is there, but it is more relaxed, with no strain, yet it still is concentration without other thoughts coming in.

Do this exercise every day, and when you feel you have achieved heart focus, do the following exercise.

Exercise Four:
- *Pick one person you know very well. When you have a conversation with this person, instead of concentrating on the words with your mind, move to the heart and try to concentrate with your heart.*

Remember, this is different than linking with your heart. Instead, it is using the heart as an instrument. Notice if what you are hearing is different from your normal reception. Try this for a period of time, until you feel you have mastered the technique.

Ultimately, you will first link your heart with someone and then use the heart to concentrate on the words of that person. Using both of these faculties gives you the true ability to mirror the person. The concentration and focus help you to listen accurately, and linking literally puts you in touch with the person's Higher Self, giving you more access to the person's inner needs.

After you have mastered the concentration of the heart with

people, then begin to use your heart to focus on work. Use it even when you read, and notice the difference.

If you concentrate with your heart in this manner, it doesn't mean that you are not also using your mind. The energy of concentration comes from the heart, but the reasoning around what you are doing comes from the mind. The difference is that you are less opinionated when you use the heart for concentration, and thus you are centered in and connected to the Higher Self.

The following story relates to heart concentration.

Many centuries ago, in the country now known as Afghanistan, there lived a king in a small kingdom that was very prosperous.

This king had seven children and he loved all of them equally, which made him uncertain about whom he should choose to be his heir. He didn't want to follow the tradition that left the kingdom to the eldest child; he wanted it to go to the one who could best govern it. He was a very good and progressive king for the age in which he lived, and was very much loved by his people.

One day the king was walking in the forest, and a large insect landed on his hand. The insect was almost five inches long and looked like a cross between a butterfly and a fly. It was brilliant blue in color, and its wings had patterns of gold in the middle and were delicate and lovely like a butterfly's, but its body had the coarse shape of a fly.

The king was startled by the insect and tried to shake it off his hand. But the insect clung more tightly to the king's fingers and said, "I think you need to listen to me. Do not try to shake me off your hand."

Amazed, the king replied, "All right, but please sit across from me and not on my hand as you frighten me by doing that." The insect consented. It flew to a rock in front of the king, and began to speak.

"You are a very wonderful king because you have a good heart. Some of your children take after you, and some take after your wife, who does not have the same warmth of the heart. It is important that you leave your kingdom to a child who is more like you. Otherwise, your kingdom will eventually fall into ruin. I am going to give you a test that you will present to all your children. You will explain to them that the one who succeeds will be your heir, while the others will serve him or her."

"Yes, what is the test?"

"You have four sons and three daughters. You are to tell each one, separately, that he or she needs to put on a disguise, leave the kingdom, and find someone who can show him or her how to change a piece of iron into gold."

"But that is impossible! No one can do that! They will all fail!" the king said, frowning at the insect.

"Do I look possible?" The insect spread its beautiful wings. "A butterfly from an ugly fly?"

"Yes, but you are magical," the king protested.

"But what I am talking about is also magical, and you have only one child who has a big enough heart to make magic happen."

"All right, but only my sons should go. My daughters are too frail to wander into city streets."

"Leave that up to them. If any one of your daughters wants to go, tell her she needs to disguise herself as a man and take a strong servant with her."

The king followed the insect's advice and sent his children to do this impossible task, telling them that if they could not find the person within one year they should then return home. Only one of his daughters, Beheshta, wanted to give it a try. The other two preferred to stay at home. One was married, and the other one was very unadventurous.

Naturally, all the children were stumped about what to do. Each one spent some time wandering around asking people if they knew about a man who did magical things.

Aarif, the eldest son, gave up trying after two months. He was tired of living on the land and missed the luxuries to which he was accustomed. He felt that his father was only indulging a foolish whim anyway and that when it came time to choose an heir he would naturally fall back on tradition and make him, as the eldest, king. Aarif believed he could better convince his father by staying at home where he could prove how qualified he was for the job.

The second son, Omed, lasted five months. He too felt tired and irritated with the impossible assignment. It was difficult to wander the streets, going from town to town, only to be looked upon as some kind of nut. He didn't think he was in line to be king anyway, as he was considered not as bright as the others. He was content to take a back seat.

The third son, Edris, gave up after ten months. He believed that everyone else must already have quit because the mission was hopeless. It had to be a stupid mistake. He was in love with one of the maidens who served his mother, and he missed her terribly. If he married her, his father would never make him king anyway, and to lose her was unthinkable. So, he returned home.

This left one son, Nabi, and his sister, Beheshta.

Nabi was determined to succeed. He had a strong will and used it to his advantage by focusing on every possibility. Traveling far and wide, he sought out and questioned every spiritual man he could find, for he discerned that such magic had to come from someone who was spiritual. Nabi had one servant with him, and he'd sent the servant out to ask everyone where spiritual nomads dwelled.

On one occasion he met someone who said that changing iron into gold was possible. This person had heard of a holy man who did it, and he told Nabi where he believed the man lived. When Nabi went to the indicated town and inquired, he found only a couple of people who knew about a holy man who had lived there, but the holy man had moved and they didn't know where he had gone.

One day, Nabi was sitting alone under a tree and a small boy walked by. Nabi called out to him automatically and said, "Do you know any holy men living here?" The boy stopped and said, "Yes, I know of one, but it is very difficult to get to him."

"What do you mean?"

"He lives way up that mountain."

The boy pointed to the top of a steep mountain nearby. "There is a trail over there." Then he pointed to a cluster of trees. "But the trail is very steep and no one even tries to reach him anymore."

"I will try." And Nabi got up and started toward the trail.

The boy was right. The trail became steeper and steeper, and the dirt of the path was dry and full of stones. As his feet touched the stones, they kept rolling down, making the climb very slippery. But Nabi continued, determined to find this holy man.

Nabi was a strong man and fortunately very agile. After three hours of arduous climbing, he arrived on a small plateau where there was a stone cottage. In front of the cottage sat a very old man with his eyes closed, meditating.

Nabi stood looking at the old man, waiting for him to finish. When the old man opened his eyes, he smiled and acknowledged Nabi, even calling him by name. This man was a great holy man and knew much about magic. When Nabi asked him if he knew how to change iron into gold, the holy man said yes, and that he would teach him. For the next month he taught Nabi, who worked hard and learned everything he could. When it came time to do this great feat, he accomplished it without a problem. He thanked the holy man, and said that in return he would give him anything he wanted: A beautiful home, servants, anything.

The holy man just smiled and said, "Don't you see, I could have all of that?" He pointed to the gold they had just made, saying, "It means nothing to me. I prefer the gold being in my heart."

Nabi didn't understand this remark, but it didn't matter to him. He left to return home and win his kingdom.

Meanwhile, Beheshta did not give up trying to find someone to teach her the mystery. She, too, traveled far and wide and finally came to the same mountain her brother had found earlier, and after she had climbed the steep mountain the holy man greeted her by name. He also showed her how to change iron into gold, and as she was getting ready to leave, the holy man made the same remark, "I prefer the gold being in my heart."

Beheshta asked the holy man what he meant by that. He replied, "It is a more difficult process. It means changing your gross energies, similar to iron, into the pure energy of gold, not in the literal sense as you now know, but in the spiritual sense. This is the esoteric meaning of changing iron into gold, and it requires a person to go through a whole transformational process."

This fascinated Beheshta, and she asked, "Can I be taught this great art?"

The holy man replied, "But my child, it will take several months to learn this, and now you have only a short time to return and claim your kingdom."

"What you are saying means more to me than the kingdom. Please teach me."

In the months that followed, Beheshta proved to be a wonderful student. She learned quickly and devoted herself to finding the keys to real wisdom. When she had learned this true alchemy, her teacher told her it was time for her to return home: Her father was worried that something terrible had happened to her, as it had been almost two years since she had left.

Meanwhile, at home, Nabi miraculously turned iron into gold in front of the whole court. But when he tried to do it a second time, he was unable to repeat the feat. Everyone interpreted this to mean that the holy man had not wanted this gift to be used unwisely, and allowed it to be used only one time. The king happily bestowed the title of heir apparent on his worthy son.

Beheshta arrived home late one night and immediately went to see her father. He was delighted that she was well and unharmed. When Beheshta told her father that she had also learned how to turn iron into gold within the year's time, he asked her why she hadn't returned sooner. Beheshta replied that she had stayed on to learn about the purity of energy within the heart and that had meant so much more to her than the gold. And she told her father about the great teacher and what she had been taught.

"But you lost the kingdom; I have made your brother the heir."

"I know," she replied, "but, Father, this knowledge is so much greater than ruling any kingdom."

When Beheshta described the holy man, her father knew he was the same one her brother had seen. The king called his son and asked him what the holy man had told him when he was about to leave. Nabi responded, "Some crazy words about the real gold being within."

"And you didn't want to know that?"

"Why should I? I had done what you asked."

"Yes, you had the will and determination to take an enormous task and achieve it, but if you had listened with your heart, you would have known, like your sister, that the real gold is spiritual, not merely material. The difference between you and Beheshta is that she also had the great will and determination to complete the task, but her heart told her that there was something else that was much more important. She chose to stay and learn the true meaning of changing iron into gold, even though it would lose her the kingdom. She is the true ruler, who will rule not just with her will, but also with her heart."

"But, that is not fair! I did the task asked for in the given amount of time."

"You are right," his father agreed. "If the holy man will agree to work with you, and you are able to succeed in learning true wisdom, I will let you both rule as co-rulers."

So Nabi returned to the mountain, where the holy man agreed to work with him. In that process he changed his determined will to a will flowing from the heart, and he realized that his sister and father were right.

The two ruled peacefully for many years after their father's death, and both tried to pass on to their children the holy man's wisdom. As for the holy man himself, after teaching Nabi, he left his mountain home and traveled on, to continue his teaching elsewhere.

This story illustrates how the strong will can be used in conjunction with the heart and, in so doing, how one can change oneself into a more spiritual being. Obviously, the process takes more than a year, but, depending on what you have accumulated over many lifetimes, it doesn't have to take as long as most people might think. The process is about looking at all those things within the lower nature and transmuting them into the higher nature, using the powerful combination of the will and the heart.

When confronting the mundane world, a student often forgets that he is on a spiritual path and, instead, falls into the routine thinking and behavior of his peers. It is very difficult not to do this, mainly because he has been brought up in a specific society and follows the accepted customs of that society. For example, if you are a woman brought up in a Middle Eastern household, you are expected to marry, have children, take a back seat to your husband, stay at home, and be a good housewife. Even if you are spiritual, you will have to keep that to yourself and not join any groups unless your husband approves. Certainly, an esoteric teaching would be likely to provoke disapproval. This pattern also can be true if you are brought up in a strict Catholic or orthodox Jewish household. Many European cultures also have similar constraints.

On the other hand, if you are brought up in a more liberal household, such as might be found in America, your challenge may be having too many choices and too many things in your life that keep you from moving forward spiritually.

The physical environment also presents obstacles for many students. To live in the country and to enjoy the freshness of the air and the beauty of the surroundings is the ideal setting for a student. If, instead, you must live in a city in order to work, then the challenge of being surrounded by the vibrations of many types of people can sometimes be overwhelming.

You need tranquility in your environment. If this is lacking, it can affect your spiritual practice and interfere with your meditations. Therefore, where you live is very important, and it is especially important that you make it a calm and beautiful place.

Certainly, if you are fortunate enough to live in the countryside, you have a better chance of being surrounded by positive vibrations. If you have to work in a city, it would be best to have a home in the suburbs, where you can have a garden and trees and the natural beauty of nature. But if you really must live in an apartment in a city, then you need to try to keep the vibrations pure.

In addition to burning incense and sage, there are other methods that can change the vibrations, and in some cases these will prove more beneficial. Lavender Aroma Diffuser oil and Euphoric Aroma Diffuser oil are Ayurvedic solutions that are very potent and act as good purifiers. There is also a combination of several herbs: lemon grass, lavender, camphor, and essences of violets and roses. Place equal portions of the herbs and essences with a few drops of camphor in some water, boil them down into a strong solution, and spray it into the air.

The main source of the tranquility a student needs comes from being surrounded by people who have positive vibrations. This is especially true for any student who is married and has children. Living in a calm environment that is without disputes or fights of any kind is extremely important. It is up to the student to contain any feelings that come up in order to keep the atmosphere peaceful. If there is an argument of any kind, the student needs to cleanse the vibrations almost immediately. This is sometimes difficult to do. It is best to be vigilant and not take part in any argument that may arise. If there needs to be a confrontation with a loved one, then plan to go for a walk and sit somewhere in nature surrounded by grass and trees and do the confronting there. The vibrations of nature are so strong that they can absorb human vibrations and keep the atmosphere pure. This way you do not disturb the elementals in your home.

The same is true if you have children you need to reprimand. Take the child out into the yard and try to talk in a calm manner.

Most nature spirits are very kind when it comes to human frailties. They see that we lack understanding of the elementals and that we are not careful in respecting their domain. Unfortunately, this is true. When you argue or become angry in nature, remember to thank the nature spirits for changing the energy back to one of calm. At all times, it is important to give them recognition; they surround everything you do. Thank them for their help in every kind of situation.

This is all very foreign to most people and even foreign to some students. Remembering to say thank you to the nature spirits for cleaning up the atmosphere is most rare, yet the more you do so the more opportunities you will be given to communicate with this kingdom. Your positive vibrations help to enhance their work. They love such vibrations and will make them even stronger. If you meditate in one place on a regular basis, the vibrations will be very strong in that place because of the combination of your vibrations being sent out and the positive elementals enhancing them. When you walk into a room where there are good vibrations, you can sense it immediately. Even someone who isn't a student will comment on how nice it feels in the room.

When you go to your office, you will encounter many different types of vibrations, which may prove more difficult to handle, especially if you work with or near someone who carries strong negative energy. The best thing to do is to imagine a glass bell around your body so that you can see everything that happens but not take in the vibrations. Usually, when you do so it feels as if you are an active participant in all that is taking place, yet, on another level, you are in a distant place. It is important to do this practice in most situations, unless you are in a good and happy atmosphere. Burning sage in your office in the morning can also help, but make certain there is an open window, as others may think you are wearing strange-smelling perfume. If you are the last to leave, do this at night instead so that the sage smell has time to dissipate.

In general, a student needs to be aware at all times of the surrounding vibrations. Too often students are inundated with negative vibrations and don't realize what is happening. The result is an intense feeling of fatigue. If this happens to you a lot, it means you are not protecting yourself. Sometimes even people around you who seem centered and well adjusted can carry some old resentment that comes out once in a while. The person could even be an old friend who has unspoken feelings toward you that have never been resolved. I suggest that you always try to resolve any differences. If you pick up on something that's unclear, simply ask if there is something wrong. Many people are reluctant to express their true feelings.

In general, the vibrations given off by others are the main cause of a student's feelings of unrest, irritation, and helplessness. Be cautious of those people who keep you in a place that feels burdensome. Remember to protect yourself. Do not give up the friendship, unless it is a truly negative one; instead, protect yourself when needed.

The world is full of people who look at life with blinders. Sometimes these people can have a breakthrough and come to a better realization. It is important to have friendships with many people and not just those who are spiritual. Often a person has opened the seed of the spirit but is not activating it in a given lifetime, instead choosing to have a mundane existence without the pull to the spiritual path. Students choose to rest between spiritual lives just to reclaim their humanity, feeling that in so doing they will be more balanced. This is both true and not true. It is better to work and have relationships in the world and still pursue a spiritual path. That is far more difficult to do, but it is the only way a person can achieve adeptship. In comparison, a spiritual practice in a monastery is easy to do.

Therefore, I suggest that you reach out to all kinds of people, have many friends outside the teaching, and develop compassion for all beings. If you just have other yogis for friends, it is more like living in a monastery. No doubt reaching out will challenge you to look at different things than if you surround yourself only with other yogis.

Remember to think about people with an open heart and realize that no one is perfect: no friendship, no love relationship, no child, no parent–none are perfect. Keep standards for yourself so that no one can take advantage of you or abuse you, but also be open to anything happening.

Sometimes life surprises you in the strangest ways. See the surprises as ways to grow and ways to make your life more meaningful. The outside world is your world. Be conscious of all that it contains and enjoy all the advantages it bestows. Both the good and the bad help you on the path toward understanding yourself and others.

Chapter 22

Letting Go of Expectations

When you see beyond expectations, then you can let them go. How is this done? First, let's analyze what expectations mean to you. If you have an expectation, it means that you want something you feel you should receive, and this desire is usually strictly personal. Someone else may believe you shouldn't have what you desire and may even believe that another person should have it instead. So, it is all relative.

For example, Martha wanted her husband to buy her a fur coat. She felt she deserved to have it, because she worked long hours in the home and took care of three young children. Martha told him this, and he refused. This made her very angry, as they were wealthy and money wasn't a problem. Arguments arose and, naturally, the more the matter was disputed the more stubborn her husband became. Some of his anger was caused by the manner in which she asked for the coat. Her attitude that she deserved it came off as a demand rather than a request. If she had simply said that she could use a fur coat because she was cold in the winter, and would it be okay with him if she bought one, her husband would more than likely have agreed to it and not made it into a big thing.

Now, unfortunately this story is true. Martha and her husband ended up in a divorce over the fur coat. Naturally, there were also other tensions, but Martha had many expectations and couldn't understand why that made her husband defensive. This scenario is not just about women; men also have expectations. In fact, this attitude that is prevalent among many people.

Where does such an attitude start in the first place? Obviously, in childhood there are expectations from the child toward the parents. The child expects to be loved, fed, clothed, and taken care of. If the child feels deprived in any way, then that child will grow up with unconscious unfulfilled expectations. If the child felt unloved, then there will be a need to be loved. If the child was never given enough food, then she will have a need for food, and so on. All these needs are projected onto relationships in the guise of expectations. If you feel a true friend should always be there for you, that need could come from feeling that no one was there for you as a child.

Now, the opposite can also hold true. Perhaps you had doting parents who met every one of your needs. This spoiled you into believing that all of life is like that, and when you grew up, you expected all the people close to you to act this way. So the feeling of expectation can come from not having been given enough or from having been given too much.

In general, everyone has expectations of some kind. The media gear much of their advertising toward those needs.

It is important to see how expectations stand in the way of a student. For example, if you have expectations of any kind, you will most certainly project those onto your teacher and Master. If, for instance, you feel you strive and work hard spiritually and do what you think is required of you, then you may have expectations of being given more initiations and having more attention from your teacher. In fact, any expectations of that nature will automatically keep you from progressing on the path. One requirement for the higher initiations is to have no desires or expectations. The only desire to have is the desire for wisdom or God Consciousness. Yet, students are full of unspoken expectations that make for hidden resentments when those desires aren't fulfilled.

Here are some of the expectations that students may have.

1. I should be helped at all times, even when I probably can do it myself.
2. I need you to help me in the mundane things of life.
3. When I am in my Higher Self, I expect to have wonderful visions or be given something special.
4. I think of my teacher as a parent who will take care of all my needs.

5. I think of Hierarchy and my Master as a parent who will take care of all my needs.
6. I know it is impossible to be given certain understanding because I'm not that advanced, but, in actuality, I feel I deserve to be given it anyway.
7. When I am with my teacher, I expect her full attention.
8. I know I am loved, but if this is true, my teacher and Master should tell me this often.
9. When I meditate, I expect to be given some kind of message.
10. If I do all my work for class, then I expect to be acknowledged in some way by some kind of praise.
11. With time, as I become a devoted follower, I expect that others, and especially new people, will look up to me.
12. With time, I will become closer to my teacher. This closeness will make me special and everyone else will then consider me special.
13. When I become a high initiate, I expect my Master not only to guide me but also to take care of all my needs, including financial ones.
14. With each initiation, I expect more to be given to me.
15. When I think about Hierarchy in general, I feel not only protected but also that the protection extends to every part of my life, including protecting me from getting into karmic relationships.

None of these expectations is based on reality and certainly none will be fulfilled. Take this list and ask yourself if any of these statements ring true for you. After you have done so, then check it all with your Higher Self. You may have some hidden expectations you are not aware of.

Let's clarify the help that is given to students. All help that is given is based on the student's striving. If a student is striving, she will be given spiritual and psychological help, mainly on the subtle plane. If a student is not striving, the student will not be given any help. This is also true of the teacher's help. The teacher only helps those who are genuinely striving spiritually and psychologically.

Included in this is help given to those who have special missions to fulfill, missions that will benefit humanity. If a student is working for a corporation or company that is helping humanity, she will be given creative ideas to further that work. A student who is an artist or scientist and is working for the betterment of humanity by bringing in beauty or curing illnesses will be given help and guidance. If a student is in politics and can help bring in laws that are beneficial, then help will be given. If the student is in a profession that will uplift humanity in any manner, then she will be helped in that work. But if the student owns a commercial enterprise or works for a company that makes commercial products or produces other things that are not directly benefiting humanity, then the student will not be helped in that work.

Usually a student chooses work that will benefit humanity, but for some that is not the case. This is important to understand, because some students will expect assistance when they see help is being given to another student, and will feel resentment if they are not also helped.

Students working at a job that benefits humanity will be assisted. But even in these cases, if there is too much expectation from the student, the excessive energy of these expectations prevents the help from happening. This occurs because the energy of expectations comes from the lower nature.

To understand the difference between the energy of expectation as opposed to the energy of cooperation, think of a child who willfully wants candy and cries for it over and over again, in contrast to a child who asks for a piece of candy and, when told that the candy will be given after dinner, accepts this and later is given the candy. One is a strong energy of need coming from the lower nature, and the other is an acceptance and gratitude for what is given.

When the Masters see a student with the neediness of the first example, they cannot help her. But if the student asks for help with an open heart, with gratitude for whatever help is given, and with no expectation, then she most certainly will be helped. The first need comes from the lower nature and the latter from the higher.

Most often help is sent when it is least expected. This is because there are no expectations and the energy can flow unencumbered. This help can even come in the form of material rewards when a student is in real need, but always when it is not asked for but freely given. The Masters are friends, not parents—remember that—and as friends they respond to real needs that, if not fulfilled, would stop a student's spiritual growth. The line is a fine one, so in all cases it is best to expect no help whatsoever, and if it comes, it comes naturally as a gift from a true friend.

The energy of expectation takes on a certain energetic form. It literally has a very murky shape and color, sometimes forming a large ball that moves between the person who expects something and the person to whom the expectations are directed. For instance, if you expect a friend to help you move, then the ball would be a light green-gray, and it would move between you and the friend. This ball of energy can become very large when the expectations are large or very small when they are not as demanding in energy. If you could see these balls, you would see a string of them surrounding most people, varying in size and color. It is fascinating to watch the balls form and dissolve. It is like watching balloons flowing and bursting in air. When the Masters see a lot of these balls around someone, they cannot get through to the person and therefore cannot help even if they want to. It is best for the person to understand the expectations and let them go.

Most students have formed patterns of expectation that revolve around spiritual help. These patterns can cause some major obstacles to form that keep the student from moving forward. If, for instance, you expect to receive higher initiations because you are striving and doing the work, then those expectations can form an obstacle. If you have a need to be taken care of by the Master or the teacher, that also is an obstacle to your growth. When you have any needs based on expectations, those needs impede your ability to move forward. The list earlier in this chapter can help you discover what those needs are. It is very important to work on any needs and change the expectations.

Let's look at why a student has expectations. Starting with a full realm of expectations, a child grows up in a family environment that generally is full of needs, which are sometimes answered and often not answered. If those needs are unanswered, the expectations come to the fore again when the student is an adult and is working spiritually.

An example would be that if you were not nurtured as a child you would look for a nurturing teacher to give you what you never received. In every case, expectations tend to cause undue anticipation, and disappointment when they are not met. If you feel any of these longings, it is important to discover the source and go for help from a therapist, and to not project those needs onto the teacher.

In some cases a student comes from an abusive background. Physical and mental abuse can also cause the student to seek a teacher who is either very strict or the opposite, very lenient. The first type reflects to the student the strict attitude of the parent, and the second reflects the need for a parent to be just the opposite. Anything in between sometimes seems ineffectual and not right. Unfortunately, seeking a teacher who fulfills one's psychological needs is not choosing correctly, and the student can make the wrong choice because of that.

If expectations are part of a student's desire body, how can she correctly change and transmute them rather than simply repress them? First, it is important to identify all the expectations you may have.

To start, ask yourself the following questions.

Exercise One:
When I am with my family, do I have any expectations toward them? If the answer is yes, list them and prioritize them, starting with the strongest one.

1. *When I am with close friends, do I have any expectations? List the friends and work with each one separately, listing the expectations.*
2. *When I am at work, do I have any expectations of my co-workers other than what is work related?*

3. *When I am with others who are more like acquaintances, do I have any expectations?*
4. *When I am with my spiritual family, do I have any expectations?*
5. *When I am with close friends in my spiritual practice, do I have any expectations? Again, make a list and work with each name separately.*
6. *When I am with my spiritual teacher (if you have one), do I have any expectations?*
7. *Do I have any expectations of my Master (if you have one)?*

After you have answered the questions, take some time and look at the lists of expectations. Notice if some of the expectations are the same on the separate lists. Prioritize the expectations. You should end up with a list of expectations, the top being the one that comes up for you the most.

Exercise Two:
Taking the top expectation on your list, ask your Higher Self the following questions:
1. *How long have I had this expectation?*
2. *What is its origin?*
3. *Do I want to let it go?*
   - *If the answer is yes, ask the Higher Self to give you a process and a first step to do this.*
   - *If the answer is no, ask the Higher Self why you need to hold on to it, and then ask for help in order to overcome this.*
4. *When I am feeling this expectation, how can I immediately recognize the feeling?*
5. *When I am feeling this, what is the best way for me to release the feeling?*
6. *In general, if I am meeting someone with whom I have this expectation, how can I best prepare myself before the meeting?*

Work with this first expectation, and when you feel you have transmuted most of it, then move on to the next one on your list. To overcome these takes time, but in so doing you will find that people will respond to you more, because that energy is no longer bouncing back and forth from you. You attract more spontaneity from others, and usually things are given freely because the expectations no longer exist. Obviously, this isn't always true, but just letting the expectations go is very freeing.

If you truly need something done and you directly ask for help with no expectations, you will never be disappointed if the person says no. If that happens, then ask someone else to help you. It is always best to be direct.

Now that you are more aware of your inner needs, let's explore what happens to you when you feel someone else has expectations of you. To begin, take the questions given earlier, and this time reverse the questions.

Exercise Three:
1. *When I am with my family, do they have expectations of me?*
   - *If the answer is yes, ask: What are they? Make a list and prioritize them.*
2. *When I am with close friends, do they have expectations of me? List the friends and, working with each one separately, list the expectations.*
3. *When I am at work, do my co-workers have expectations of me, other than what is work related?*
4. *When I am with others who are more like acquaintances, do I feel they have expectations of me?*
5. *When I am with my spiritual family, do I feel they have expectations of me?*
6. *When I am with close friends in my spiritual practice, do I feel they have expectations of me? Again make a list and work with each name separately.*
7. *When I am with my spiritual teacher (if you have one), do I feel she or he has expectations of me?*

8. *Do I feel my Master (if you have one) has expectations of me?*

After you have answered the questions, take the lists of expectations that others have toward you and prioritize them. Take the top one and answer the following questions.

Exercise Four:
1. *When others have this expectation of me, how do I feel?*
   • *If the feeling is negative, ask the Higher Self how best to handle the situation.*
2. *Have others always expected this of me?*
3. *If this is the case, have I done something to cause it?*
   • *If the answer is yes, ask: What have I done and how do I change this?*
4. *When others have this expectation toward me, is my response different depending on who is expecting it?*
5. *Is there a part of me that likes others to expect this of me?*

Some people want others to have expectations of them because expectations make a person feel important and can inflate the ego self. For example, a person is always chosen to be the leader of a group, or a person is always chosen to take on an important task. These types of expectations can make a yogi feel happy, and this is fine as long as the happiness isn't around being more accomplished than anyone else. Spiritual pride is a real challenge for any student.

When you have your lists of expectations and can see them clearly, both the ones you project and the ones that others project toward you, take both lists and compare them. Do you project expectations onto others that are similar to those projected onto you? If this is the case, then you can really start to understand why you do so. In most cases the expectations will be similar. When you find they are not the same, it may be that they are the opposite because you dislike the expectations projected toward you.

When you have finished your comparisons, take a moment to notice if any of the expectations relate to one person more than others. Obviously, you may have more expectations toward your spouse or a child, or even someone with whom you are a close friend. Take time to determine the main person who falls into this category, and then ask yourself the following questions about that person.

Exercise Five:
1. *Does this person have too many expectations of me, or are they what I would consider normal?*
2. *Does this person accept my expectations, or are there problems around them?*
3. *When I am connecting to this person, do I feel an old karmic pattern coming into play? If so, ask your Higher Self what this pattern is.*
4. *When I am with this person, do I want to play out the expectations fully, or can I accept that it is better not to do this?*
5. *Looking back on the relationship I have with this person, can I honestly say that it has not been built on expectations?*

Sometimes a personal relationship is built on expectations and to let them go can cause a major shift in the relationship itself. Look at your list and determine whether there is anyone with whom such a shift could occur. If there is, then ask yourself the following questions:

Exercise Six:
1. *If I let go of my expectations of this person, and she lets go of expectations of me, would we have a relationship at all?*
2. *If I try to let go of my expectations of this person and try not to follow her expectations of me, can I accept her completely, or would there be difficulty maintaining the relationship?*
3. *Would this person be open to talking about expectations?*

4. *Can I honestly accept this person without any expectations?*

5. *When I am with this person, can I be open and not in any way want more?*

6. *Looking at the history I have with this person, can I honestly feel that our relationship can change when I let go of expectations?*

7. *In general, is this person willing to change?*

All the above can start the process of trying to institute change around expectations.

Next, it is important to determine whether you are willing to let go of expectations or whether it would be too difficult for you to do. Sometimes the intention is good, but the pattern of needing something takes over without you being aware of it. When a person is caught up in the pattern, it is very difficult to stop it, but when it starts, you can interrupt the pattern and keep it from going forward. The easiest way to do this is to create a key that triggers your mind into awareness.

Usually, it is best to take someone you have expectations about and work with that person first.

Exercise Seven:
Ask your Higher Self:
1. *Am I ready to let go of my expectations of this person?*
   • *If the answer is yes, ask for a process that will help you do this.*
   • *If the answer is no, ask why you are not ready.*
2. *Then take that answer and continue asking, going deeper into the cause.*

There may be some hidden agendas preventing you from letting go of inner needs. If this is the case, determine whether those needs are coming from your childhood conditioning, and if they are, then maybe it would be best to get some outside psychological help to process them. If the needs are coming from a past life, then it would be very helpful to see the past life and look at the patterns that are continuing. In any case, it is important to determine the true nature of your expectations and begin the process of letting them go. A student has to be free of all attachments, and expectations are a major block to spiritual growth.

When you work with the expectations of others toward you, change can become more difficult. You can consciously want to change, but you cannot expect others to want this. It is important not to expect others to change if only you make the changes. First and foremost, it would be good to talk to those you feel expect the most from you. Directly ask them what their expectations are of you. Really clarify the expectations and discuss them. If the expectations are what would be called right action, then you can agree on them, but if they are more the demands of the other person, it is important to say no and set some boundaries. Let's look at an example.

John was married to Marilyn. He was an old-fashioned man who expected his wife to do everything, from cleaning the house to cooking all the meals, and, of course, to caring for their eight-year-old child. That was fine in the old days when women did not work and housework was their primary responsibility, but Marilyn had a very difficult job as a corporate lawyer. Not only was her job tiring, but she also had to work long hours.

None of this mattered to John; he still expected her to do the household chores, and he never helped at all. Marilyn became very resentful of this, and arguments and fights became part of their daily routine. John was stubborn in his beliefs. How could he cook? He had never learned to do so; but mainly he felt it wasn't manly to do this. The same was true of taking care of their daughter. What did he know about shopping for her clothes? And only mothers took their children to school. The cleaning problem was solved by hiring a cleaning lady, but nothing else could be resolved. In the end, this couple divorced. Marilyn was already doing all the work, so why bother with John as an additional burden?

This case is extreme, but believe me, there are many men in relationships in which the women do all the work even though they also go to an office and work long hours outside the home.

The opposite can also be also true, but it is usually more in relation to taking charge of the children. The father may work long hours, yet he always has to be the one to take the children to sporting events or Little League in the evenings and on weekends.

When there is an imbalance of any kind in a relationship, whether it be a marriage or even a friendship, then you need to talk directly to the person about changing the pattern. If it is about what is happening in a marriage you may need to go for outside counseling. In a one-sided friendship, it is important to understand whether the friend is in any way taking advantage of you, and then determine how best to handle the situation.

Going back to the John and Marilyn story above, let's look at what happens if they could have avoided being pulled into those dynamics. When Marilyn married John, she was working and had the same long hours. Because they didn't have their daughter at the time, they could go out to eat. They lived in a small apartment rather than a big house, so the upkeep was not very difficult. The problem was that Marilyn, from day one, did all the work, and never looked at it as such a burden. Only later, when they had a child and moved into a big house, did it become a problem. John was used to his routine and wouldn't change it at that point. If at the beginning Marilyn had established boundaries around chores. Had these been set up differently, then the additional work of the house would have been taken care of.

The lesson in this example is to make certain that in a relationship there is some balance, and if there isn't, then it is necessary to determine how best to change any imbalance.

Sometimes you may believe you don't have expectations and you become very surprised when someone does something you disapprove of. That something can develop from a minor detail to a major one. If, for instance, you expect a person to follow through on a task you are responsible for and the person not only doesn't follow through but also feels the task is not necessary, what do you do? Usually, you would quickly try to do the assignment yourself. However, the result could be anger and resentment toward the person you are dealing with. This situation can happen in an office setting or around any project you are working on. In the office setting, it is important to establish what needs to happen, within a framework of written assignments and timelines. That way the person cannot later claim that it wasn't her job. In a personal relationship, if someone is meant to do something and fails, then it's important to tell the person clearly what you want to happen, and if she can't do it, then ask someone who can. Kind people, in general, over-volunteer, and then sometimes they can't follow through. They mean well, but what is important is getting the job done.

Look at your tasks in general and do the following exercise.

Exercise Eight:
1. *Make a list of those things you think are important to follow through on.*
2. *If the list is too long, prioritize it and put some of the tasks in a later time frame.*
3. *If you feel there is someone who should share these tasks, then simply ask the person to help, and go over the list together.*
4. *If the other person agrees to take on part of the list, then both of you can make time lines for your respective tasks.*

It is important to ask the person to help you; do not demand. This is also true if you are living with someone. Suggest that you go over what needs to be done together. Make separate lists and compare them. Perhaps there are tasks the other person feels are important that you don't even recognize as such, and vice versa. If both of you agree the schedule should be flexible, don't assign any task a particular day for it to be done.

For example, if your housemate does the laundry for the week, don't designate that it be on any specific day and then become upset if the laundry isn't done on that day. It is better to say that sometime in that week the laundry will be done. At the end of every week have a meeting to determine if tasks were completed, and if they weren't, find out what the problem was. Try never to get angry with someone who doesn't do something on time. If you do, you are moving into the realm of expectations. Instead, try to understand why this is happening. Perhaps the person really hates that task and is procrastinating. If you can reassign the task, that would be better. If the person still procrastinates about doing the given work, it is possible there is a psychological block, or it can simply be pure laziness. Handling that moves into the psychological realm, and, as in John's case, the problem may be affecting the whole relationship and outside counseling is required.

This process sounds very detailed, and it often makes people feel that sometimes it is better just to do things themselves. This is the pattern of a workaholic who will just do and do and do and, of course, overdo until she gets ill or overstressed. It is, therefore, very important to avoid asking too much of a workaholic, which is difficult to do with someone who has the reputation of getting things done. In general, try to keep all things balanced, unless, of course, there is a problem that needs more help.

Living with a workaholic can seem good, as things are accomplished, but it can also be difficult if the workaholic is a perfectionist and demands that things be done a certain way. A perfectionist is never happy, so even if you agree to work on a task, the perfectionist won't like what you have done and will want more. How does one live with either of these types? Try the following exercise if you have this problem.

Exercise Nine:
Link with your Higher Self and ask:
1. *How can I remain calm and centered when "so and so" wants me to do things a certain way?*
2. *Then ask: When I am calm and centered, what would be the best way to approach "so and so" with my observations of her?*

Generally, workaholic and perfectionist personality types know they have this problem, so when you point it out to them, they can accept it. If they cannot, and it is a live-in relationship, then the next step is an outside counselor. Otherwise, do not get involved in any work program with this type of person, or, if you must, then try to deal with the situation in a peaceful manner.

When someone expects you to do something you feel you should not have to do, it is important to always talk to the person in a calm clear way. Point out the expectations, and, if the person feels she has a right to have them, then try to explain the effects of expectations and, in general, how the energy of expectations surrounding someone makes it difficult to do anything for that person.

Even doing all of the above, you may find yourself in relationships with people who don't understand and still have expectations and demands that are difficult for you to handle. Confronted by this situation and finding that no amount of talking changes it, what do you do? The question becomes how to handle the expectations in a disidentified manner, doing what you can do and not following the demands of the person. If the demands are too strong and too much, it is important to calmly say no and walk away; otherwise you become a victim. This response should happen only when you have tried all the above methods and none of them have worked.

Being disidentifed at all times is a big test. In that calm place you can see what is happening and not be affected by it. Only then can you deal with someone in a clear manner. As soon as you feel you are not centered, it is important to link with the Higher Self and ask it for help in regaining your center. If you become too emotional, you cannot reach the Higher Self, and then it is best to leave the situation until you can recover your composure and again be linked.

Every situation has moments when you can lose calmness. It is a good idea to have a plan to follow in case that happens. Do the following exercise:

Exercise Ten:
Ask the Higher Self:
    1. *When I am with someone who is demanding and I lose*

> *my calm manner, what can I do to regain it?*
> 2. *Also ask: Is there anything I can do to prevent losing my link with You when I know beforehand that I will be with someone who makes me feel emotional?*

Take your answers and experiment with them. Purposely try to see someone who is difficult for you to deal with. The more you practice this in little ways, the better prepared you will be if you find yourself in a situation of extreme circumstances. Be aware that the small things can be just as irritating as the large ones. When you feel irritation, deal with it immediately and do not let it fester in any way.

Now that you have looked at expectations you have toward others and they have toward you, it is important to continue the process, and this time look at the expectations you have for yourself. This area is very large for most yogis, in particular because the spiritual practice is a disciplined practice and there are many rules concerning the discipline. In fulfilling these rules, yogis will place many expectations on themselves. Let's look at some of these areas:

1. Expectation to meditate daily.
2. Expectation to study the teaching.
3. Expectation to go to classes.
4. Expectation to be of service.
5. Expectation to always be respectful toward the teacher.
6. Expectation to give freely of one's time to help others.

These are a few of the spiritual requirements expected of disciplined yogis. They are part of the spiritual practice and certainly should be fulfilled. The expectations come in when the yogi demands of herself that they be done. What is the difference, you may be asking? The difference is the fine line between fulfilling one's dharma in a conscious way and fulfilling one's dharma in a demanding way. Working in a conscious way comes from working with the Higher Self and striving toward oneness with It, and working in a demanding way comes from the spiritual subpersonality that demands that you fulfill these actions in a fanatical manner. The difference is the intensity of the demand. Generally, if a student is identified with a spiritual subpersonality, the demands become overwhelming and the student will stop doing anything at all and go into a state of apathy.

As a rule, expectations of any kind can cause a student to give up, causing someone who has unworthiness issues to feel totally insecure or a student who simply is busy with family or work to feel overly stressed.

Balance is the answer, but how does a person know what balance is? The answer is that balance has no expectations or demands in it. It simply comes from an inner knowing of what needs to happen at any given time. If the spiritual practice is a priority, then someone who is very busy with mundane tasks will have an inner need to at least meditate and maybe do less studying and reading of spiritual material. In so doing, the person will not have any guilt feelings. If the spiritual practice is not a priority, then the person will simply stop most of the practice and follow outside interests and never have a problem with spiritual expectations.

Balance is about keeping the priorities clear and never giving in to outside things that interfere with the priorities. Again, it is not rigid. If you meditate every morning at a certain time but you have a guest in your home and that prevents you from doing this practice, then you work around that by trying to find another opportunity to meditate before the guest awakens, changing the time if need be. A spiritual subpersonality would demand that you meditate at your time even if the guest is up.

Everything is balance. Discipline that is balanced has no demands in it. It just is. The need to accomplish spiritual goals comes from the heart and, therefore, is open to all things, all change, and its focus is always being in the striving heart.

If you have inner urges to accomplish something to the extreme, then question where these are coming from—from the heart, or from the subpersonality? If you want to work on a project that will help you spiritually, do you do the work because it is important to your heart and you love doing it, or do you do it out of a need to please the teacher, thus making undue expectations upon yourself?

Exercise Eleven:

Keeping this in mind, ask yourself the following questions:

1. *Looking at my spiritual practice, do I accomplish it from a sense of spiritual desire coming from my heart, or do I do the work from feelings of demand on myself?*

2. *When I meditate, do I really want to do it because it brings me closer to the higher planes, or do I do it because I feel I have to?*

3. *When I study the teaching, does it make me feel happy, or is it a boring task that I need to do because I think it is expected of me?*

4. *When I go to class, do I do so with feelings of desiring to learn more and to be with my brothers and sisters, or do I go from the feeling that I am expected to go?*

5. *With each day, do I look forward to doing spiritual work that can benefit others, or is this just a duty to be performed?*

6. *When I am with my spiritual brothers and sisters, do I feel happy and at home, or do I see them because I feel I am expected to want to be with them?*

7. *In my daily work, do I think about my teacher with happiness in my heart, or do I think about the teacher because I know I should be doing this?*

8. *With each stage of my personal development, do I question my beliefs and change them if necessary, or do I accept everything "as is," expecting that nothing can change?*

9. *When I relate to others in the teaching, do I have expectations that I should be more like them?*

10. *When I look at my teacher, do I have expectations that I need to be more like her?*

If you find that you have many expectations concerning your spiritual practice, you will probably carry those expectations toward everything you do in life. For example, if you need to have a tight routine that can never falter, you probably will also need to keep to a tight routine in your housework and your social life. Someone who is rigid about life is not open to change, and when something happens that necessitates change, that person will get stuck and not know how to handle it. If you are like this, then you are someone who has strict expectations of yourself, and you may also have a strong spiritual subpersonality.

Naturally, all of us have some expectations about ourselves. The problems come when someone governs their whole lives this way. Such a person will easily fall apart if she cannot live up to the expectations. It is either all or nothing, no balance, no in-between. A person like this generally exhibits some of the following:

1. Has perfectionist characteristics.
2. Has no patience for those who aren't disciplined.
3. Wants recognition from others. (This may be an unconscious desire.)
4. Feels lost when not working.
5. Can be judgmental toward others.
6. Wants to change others.
7. When giving advice, feels annoyed if it is not taken.
8. Has expectations toward everyone, and when disappointed, gives up in a futile manner.
9. Needs others to side with her.
10. Is critical toward herself.

Obviously, such a person is very rigid, but sometimes will not show this trait this to others, and will seem very light-hearted. The rigidity is turned inward. This type of person has problems with authority in general, unless the authority is someone the person accepts completely. Of course, the authority has to be perfect, and when that isn't the case, there is deep dissatisfaction.

In general, having expectations is having a need for perfection in one's life. Since life itself can never be perfect, it is also true that having expectations is not realistic. To expect anything from anyone is not realistic; seeing expectations in that way may help you to let go of expectations in general.

Instead, if you simply hope that someone will follow through on something or you hope that a task will be completed or you hope for help to be offered, the energy is different. Hoping is always better than expecting. If the hopes are not fulfilled, then the disappointment is not the same. However, even hoping can have a fringe of expectation, so it's good to notice if that creeps in. For instance, you may hope that a friend will offer to help you do something, but in reality you expect this because you have done her a service. If the friend doesn't offer, you may become disappointed and even angry. But, instead, if you simply hope, you may be disappointed, and maybe even strongly disappointed, but not angry. The energy is different.

The other possibility is to simply ask for help. The worst that can happen is that the friend will say no. You may be disappointed, but there is no outgoing energy of expectation or even hope. This way you are direct and the answer is direct. Maybe the friend has a good reason for not helping, a reason you may not even know about. In general, it is important to simply ask for what you need or would like. If you are someone who asks out of expectation, that is another story.

For example, a man goes to a department store with a friend. He expects the friend to wait for him while he is trying on some pants. Instead, the friend gets bored and says that he is leaving. The man expected his friend to wait and even help him choose the right pants, so he is disappointed and even angry. If, instead, he asks his friend to help him pick out some pants when they go to the store, the friend can say either yes or no, and then the man has no reason to feel angry or disappointed. It is much more direct to simply ask.

If you choose the route of asking, then do not expect to be told yes every time. Remember also that asking is not demanding, and there is a major difference between asking in a nice manner and demanding something. Often a person doesn't realize that she is demanding and becomes angry when there is a no response, and when she approaches the same person at another time she fails to understand why the person doesn't want to be asked. The consequences of always asking for help and expecting it can cause a rift in friendships. Be aware if you are someone who often asks for help, as people may think you are too demanding. Again, do everything in moderation. Always try to do the task yourself first, unless, of course, it requires others to join in or the task is not yours to do in the first place.

When you come from the place of being centered and in your Higher Self, you will know when to ask and when not to. It is important not to try to do everything yourself, which is the opposite extreme of the person who asks too much.

No man is an island; everyone needs help at times. Be careful to ask the right person to help you, or even mention to a group of people that you need help. That way you are leaving it up to them to offer, and if no one offers, you may have to go elsewhere. Also, do not ask for help when you have the means to have the task done professionally.

People need to examine their behavior when it comes to expectations. The energy is always strong, and often negative, and can make the receiver back away and not follow through. Be careful to always examine your motivations when you ask for something.

Exercise Twelve:
Ask yourself the following questions beforehand:
1. *Do I expect this person to say yes?*
2. *Will I be okay if the person says no?*
3. *Do I expect this person to follow through with my wishes?*
4. *When I ask for something, is my voice nice and nondemanding?*
5. *Can I accept excuses as being genuine?*
6. *Do I feel comfortable asking for help?*
7. *In general, is it easy for me to accept help?*

When a person genuinely needs assistance, the energy is different and you will find that people want to be of assistance. Obviously, an older person needs more help than a younger one. A yogi should always try to help those who need assistance, and a yogi should also be conscious to offer help even when it doesn't seem necessary. It is part of the path of service to help others, but even yogis can become caught up in everyday life and not think about helping someone who needs assistance. It is a good policy to become more conscious of those needs by asking yourself the following questions at the end of the day.

Exercise Thirteen:
1. *At the beginning of the day, did I ask to be of service during the day?*
2. *Was there anyone today who needed help, and I didn't offer it?*
3. *Did I have an opportunity to help someone and fail to do so because of personality differences?*
4. *When I look back on today, did I overlook an opportunity to be of assistance?*

In doing the above exercise, be aware that you are not meant to help everyone who needs help, and also be careful not to offer to help someone out of your pleaser subpersonality. Any offer of help should be a genuine one coming from the heart; otherwise, it is false, and feels false to the person on the receiving end.

On the other hand, if you are constantly the one who is asked, then maybe you are being too generous. This also relates to your physical family. If you are the child from whom the parent always needs help, then it is expected of you because you are the generous one. Next time ask the parent to speak first to a sibling or a friend. There's a fine line between being taken advantage of because you are nice and actually being the only one who can help. Be conscious also of the feeling of being taken advantage of. If you feel this way, then any help you are giving is not from the heart.

When you genuinely want to help a friend or a relative, do so with an open heart and with no expectations of being helped in return. Just the act of helping is a good enough reward karmically. The energy of expectation changes the karma and takes from it the good results. Realize that everything is karma and that every good act produces good karma. If you weigh everything with expectation, then the karmic results will be diminished.

The last basic expectation is the expectation of love. If you love someone, you expect love in return. Unfortunately, this is one of the most difficult expectations to deal with. Loving someone unconditionally is the goal of a yogi, but it doesn't necessarily happen. It is part of the human makeup to expect love in return, and when love is unrequited, there is a major feeling of disappointment and loss. Again, karma plays a major role in this play of expectations.

Attraction is a strong energy, and attraction comes from old karma, which isn't necessarily good karma. Rejection is also very karmic. A person falls in love and pursues the loved one only to be rejected. This causes a lot of heartache and disappointment. The individual usually doesn't understand that the karmic pull is causing this to be played out. Maybe in the past the person did the same to the loved one. Even understanding this doesn't make it less difficult because the expectations are very strong.

How does a yogi accept this type of karma and let go of any expectations? To answer this question, it is necessary to look at the whole picture. Love is energy, and when it is dealt with as pure energy, it has many benefits. When it has attachments and expectations, the energy becomes encased in even stronger energy, and the purity of the love is diminished into need and desire.

If you find you love someone and the person doesn't have the same feelings toward you, it is wise to ask your Higher Self to help you understand the karma, and at the same time give away to your teacher or to your Master any expectations or attachments. Try to simply love the person unconditionally and let go of the person psychically. Realize that it is not meant to be, and it is still okay to simply love the person with no attachments. You will find that, if you release the expectations and attachments, you will not suffer any disappointment or hurt from not having the love returned.

Many people drive a loved one away because their expectations are very high, expectations that are caused by insecurities. Simply expressing love isn't enough for such a person. There is a need for more and more, and that overwhelming need can cause the loved one to leave.

Humankind is very destructive when it comes to love and

expectations. Most karma is a play on this, and the wheel goes round and round.

In conclusion, looking at the expectations you have toward others is very important. Expectations keep you from being dis-identified and instead cause you to get caught in the karmic pull. Walking the path is letting go of attachments, and one of the major ones is expectation. Look at the expectations in your life and let them go. Letting go of them will bring you freedom.

Chapter 23

When You Feel Lost

Every student on the path at some time feels lost and alone. It is part of the journey to encounter such feelings and to try to work through them. The feeling is one of absolute aloneness, that there is no one you can truly connect with. Even if the yogi has a family, a teacher, and many friends, the feeling is the same: you cannot reach anyone and no one can reach you. An example was Jesus crying out on the cross, "Why hast thou forsaken me?"

When a student encounters this feeling, it is very difficult and often becomes a major block that keeps him from continuing. The feeling can be a small nagging one, or it can be the larger feeling of being forsaken. In either case, it is important to understand what is happening and how to overcome this experience and continue to move forward.

Let's examine the feeling itself. When a student is moving forward he will encounter resistance from his lower nature. A major resistance is the fear of being alone, and the negative forces emphasize this by making the student feel more and more isolated, particularly if he succumbs to the negative feelings. It is true that some of these feelings are based on reality. The path does need to be walked alone because each person's process is different. No matter how close you are to others, their experiences will be personal and different from yours.

If you are in a spiritual teaching that has initiations, every initiation is done alone, and the degrees of initiation vary according to the consciousness of the student. Since each initiation takes you to higher levels, be aware that even if each level you attain is parallel with that of a spiritual brother or sister, the obstacles and challenges will be completely different. What one student may find very easy to do, another student will find difficult. As you grow spiritually, your personal challenges will become more refined and more tuned to your consciousness. That is why no two students are alike and why the teacher has to treat each one individually.

The nature of the challenges the student faces as he advances into the higher levels is the experience of personal struggle and the feeling that no one can help or be a guide. Even the teacher seems to take a back seat and watch, and only advises the student once in a while on what is happening. Often a student feels the teacher doesn't understand, which of course is not true, but the struggles the student is going through make him feel this way.

When such feelings occur, it is important for the student to reinforce his energies and confront those feelings and understand their source. Since the path must be taken alone the initial feeling of aloneness is correct, but in actuality there is always guidance and help, even when the student feels it is not forthcoming. The problem comes when the student listens to the lower nature, feels abandoned, and doesn't recognize where the feeling is coming from, thus making the feeling even stronger, until he is in real pain.

In some cases the student may seek outside pleasures for distraction, and some of these pleasures may cause karma and change the outcome for the student. However, if he recognizes the process and accepts the feelings as part of the path, then those feelings will diminish in time and never appear again. In all the other cases, the feeling is partial and, in some way, is preparation for higher initiations.

Often a student has an inner sense of aloneness that stays with him for many years. In those cases, it is important to recognize that the spirit within longs to return to God and in that longing feels separate from others, even close loved ones. It is a natural feeling of the spirit and, therefore, cannot be changed. It is necessary to allow the feeling, with the depth of understanding and realization that the feeling of aloneness isn't necessarily true, except in terms of the spirit. One can experience the connections with others and accept the aloneness as part of the spirit's journey. The difficulty lies in distinguishing what is coming from the spirit and what is coming from the personality and lower nature. The following is a true story that illustrates this.

In the East there lived a man called Pandu. Pandu was very wealthy and big-hearted. Not only did he provide his family with all the necessary luxuries, but he also gave generously to the towns-people and those who worked for him. In every way, he was much loved by all and had many good friends who enjoyed his company.

When Pandu was forty-five years old, he decided to enter a spiritual life. His children were running the business, and his wife was very happy tending to the many grandchildren. He found his spiritual teacher in a monastery near his home and began his stud-ies. In just a short time Pandu had achieved several initiations and was working on the higher ones when suddenly his teacher left the monastery in order to travel and visit other monasteries. This trip was to last five years. Pandu felt at a loss when his teacher left, and even more so after he offered to accompany his teacher and was told no.

The monks in the monastery were a group of ascetics, and because they had lived that life from childhood, they were very unworldly and therefore had little in common with Pandu, who had been a successful businessman and married with a family. The inner group always considered him an outsider. The monks were courteous and kind when the teacher was present, but when the teacher left, they were much more distant. Pandu soon found the atmosphere in the monastery unwelcoming when he came for his daily meditation.

He stopped going to the monastery and, instead, used a small room in his home as his meditation room. This was separate and apart from the family, and he spent many hours a day in the room meditating and studying the books his teacher had given him. Often he would feel his teacher with him, but just as often he did not feel his teacher's presence, and when that happened, Pandu began to feel abandoned. There was no one in his family he could talk with. They considered him odd for pursuing a spiritual prac-tice, and he slowly had less contact with any of them. Even his wife went on long visits to the children's homes, and Pandu found himself more and more isolated and alone.

Since he had been accustomed to a house full of people, their absence became more and more troublesome to him, and he was no longer happy in his meditation practices. Instead, he would wander down to the village and talk to his old friends, drinking with them in the evenings, and even sharing their food. This routine was fine for a while, but more and more he felt separate from them because they lacked spiritual awareness and he couldn't share what was important to him with them. Being in such a crowd made him feel even more alone.

Finally Pandu decided to try the monastery again, this time taking a room there to live full time. He sequestered himself completely, only joining the other monks in meditation and in spiritual practices. Since he was now living in the spiritual community, he was accepted more and he found that there were some monks with whom he could really communicate. Yet, even that didn't seem to help because the monks viewed the teachings differently. His years in the world gave him a broader outlook that was unacceptable to traditional monks. Even though he was now accepted in the community, he felt even more alone and his feelings of being lost were heightened.

Pandu then felt the need to travel as a wandering monk. He decided that maybe he would find solace in new places. He wandered into remote villages and monasteries and was always welcomed, and he even began to teach a little wherever he went. Soon he had followers who became his students, and some accompanied him on his journey. But even with his students, he felt separate and apart. They were novices, and he had grown spiritually to a place where he was dealing with higher energies and subtle beings in the other worlds. Every so often he would see his teacher and even his Master, but he knew he was not at their level, and his longing to be with them only made him feel more alone.

One day, as Pandu sat under a tree eating his food with his students, a small boy nearby saw him, ran to him, threw his arms around his neck, and called him "teacher." The boy told him that he had been seeing him in his dreams for a long time and that he was so happy, as now he had found him. The boy laughed and cried as he told his story, saying how lonely he had been without him. In that moment, Pandu felt all the feelings of being alone leave him, and he realized for the first time that those feelings came from the boy's soul.

When Pandu looked at the students gathered around him and the small boy clinging to him with love, he knew he would never be alone in the world. When he closed his eyes, he saw his teacher smiling at him and his Master was also there, and he knew he would never be alone in the subtle world. The strangest thing of all was his sudden knowledge that it was all right to feel alone at times, that it was a wonderful challenge of the spirit's need to grow, and that it was very much part of his spirit's growing pains.

Pandu became a high lama and eventually established a monastery that always welcomed outsiders and householders who wished to study the teaching. His spirit accomplished its purpose. When he died he joined his teacher and Master on the subtle plane and became part of the ashram of Shambhala.

Pandu went through the turmoil of separating from the mundane world, and only when he felt unconditional love from the young boy did he realize that a person is never alone when there is love. He had experienced the love of companionship and the love of his teacher, but when he was going through the separation process, he lost contact with that feeling, and only the love of a child could force him away from feelings of loss and give him this understanding. The child had been his student many times, and in the reawakened connection came the realization that although a person travels the path alone, it is filled with others from before and after who are there with love, and that in actuality you are never alone.

It is important to understand the concept that, yes, you walk the path alone, but you are always surrounded by love. Pandu achieved this understanding when he was a teacher, but everyone can come to the same understanding when faced with feelings of being lost and alone.

First, let's examine what those feelings are like.

1. You can be surrounded by people, but in your heart you feel apart from them.

2. When you meditate, you long to go into the higher planes and stay there.

3. Some days you want only to meditate and not do anything else.

4. When you are with a loved one, you sometimes see the person as never being able to understand you, and knowing this makes you feel totally separate.

5. When you talk about mundane things with others, the subjects feel unimportant.

6. You find yourself at a loss for words when others ask you about your practice. It feels so private that it is something you cannot share.

7. You look at your spiritual companions and see them as being very different, so different that you have little in common with them.

8. It is important for you to meditate alone and not be with anyone else, even if you are living with others who meditate.

9. When you study the teaching, you feel separate from others, having an inner feeling that no one can really understand the teaching the way you understand it.

10. Sometimes you look around and feel like an alien and not part of the world.

11. When you are with your teacher, you feel the teacher as separate and not part of your world.

12. When you are with your teacher, you long for the teacher to understand you better and sometimes feel he doesn't understand you at all.

13. Looking at your past, you feel you have grown more and more apart from your family and friends.

14. You find you have less and less in common with those with whom you always felt close.

15. At the end of the day when you go to bed, you feel totally alone, even when there is someone in bed with you.

Often the person who is going through this experience feels not only lost but also abandoned by others. In some cases the feeling of abandonment is so strong that he has to reach out in order to feel even a little better.

Sometimes this reaching out can be done in a negative manner. For example, he may phone just anyone who is available and deepen the abandonment issue by choosing someone who doesn't respond well. Another time, he may stop in at someone's house or apartment without calling first, hoping that the person is at home. This, of course, is a real imposition and causes friendships to fall apart. He may also send someone many e-mail messages that make the receiver tired of responding.

If he lives with someone, he may not allow the companion space, but needs to be with the person all the time. This can cause couples to split up, resulting in his feeling even more alone. Loneliness is a difficult condition and certainly one that needs to be looked at with compassion.

If you can relate to any of the above statements, then it is important to analyze whether or not you are becoming lost. To become lost is to feel the emotions and act on those emotions by giving in to them. Since it is part of the spiritual condition to go through some of these feelings, let us look at the best way to handle them when they happen to you.

Initially, recognize the feeling when it happens. You can use the above statements to get in touch with this.

Once you have recognized the feeling, it is important to ask your Higher Self the following questions.

Exercise One:
   1. *Why am I feeling this way? Is this feeling coming from a hidden source? If so, what is the source?*
   2. *Is this a feeling I have experienced before? If so, when?*
   3. *Is this a feeling I have experienced in past lives? If so, when?*
   4. *How can I begin to overcome this feeling? What is a first step?*

In general, just recognizing the source of the feeling can help lessen the emotions. For instance, you may have had a lonely childhood and that feeling is coming up for you to look at. If it comes from childhood, you may want to do some therapy to heal the inner child. Or the feeling may be coming from some old lifetimes of being a hermit or an ascetic. Even though in those lives you may have welcomed being alone, just the idea of doing it again in a spiritual practice may bring up all the repressed feelings.

When you have had many lives in a spiritual teaching, you may find that this feeling is something you can pass through quickly. There is an inner knowing that you are never alone and that the teacher and Master, even when not visible, are always there. This certainly lessens feelings of being lost and alone.

You have looked at feelings of being alone or abandoned. Now it is important to look more deeply into these feelings, into the realm of feeling lost. What this means is that no matter how much you strive spiritually, there is no one who has walked in your shoes, and in knowing this comes the strange realization that only you can do this. You certainly have the guidance of the teacher and Master and even those students who have walked before you, but in actuality, it is up to you to take each step. With this realization comes the fear that you will go off and make so many mistakes that you will no longer grow spiritually.

Of course, the negative forces want you to feel this way and will try to persuade you that the best thing to do is to give up. This is a difficult time for every student. It's a time that can become clouded with apathy and discontent, and may cause the student to leave the path. Basically, then the student cannot be helped because he feels lost and even the teacher cannot penetrate this feeling.

How do you help someone who will not reach out or even try to work with the Higher Self for guidance? If you see someone who may be experiencing this, here are the best ways to help:

- Be direct. Ask the person what is wrong. Sometimes just talking helps a student come to a better understanding about what is happening.
- Ask the person if he needs help of any kind, and if the

answer is yes, help the student and even follow through later to make certain the help is working.

If the student is acting very negatively, naturally there is a tendency to avoid any contact with him. Try to overcome the negativity by sending rays of light to him before you contact him. If you try to see him and he is still very negative, do not allow the negativity to come into you. Be certain to protect yourself with a glass bell over your body or armor of some kind. Check with your Higher Self about the best way to protect your aura so that you do not allow the person's negativity to invade you.

In some cases the negativity is so strong that it is impossible to reach the person. If this happens, it is best to send love at a distance, praying that the person will realize how destructive he has become. In general, do the best you can and avoid being sucked into the feelings that are being projected.

When a person goes through feelings of being lost, the outcome usually is the loss of contact with the Higher Self. It is important to establish a way to regain contact when you are not in this feeling; then that process will be a resource when you need it.

Do the following exercise when you are in a positive frame of mind.

Exercise Two:
Ask the Higher Self:
1. *When I feel alone, isolated, or lost, what is the best way for me to regain contact with You?*
2. *Then ask: Is there anything else I can do to help me remember to use the above process?*
3. *When I am negative, how do I reach out to you?*
4. *Is it possible that I can hand those negative feelings over to you?*
5. *Can you warn me before I become negative?*
6. *If the answer is yes, ask: What will be the warning?*
7. *In looking at my feelings for the past six months, were there times when I was feeling so lost that I couldn't let go of the feelings?*

8. *If the answer is yes, ask: What would be a good way for me to process these feelings in order to lessen them?*

All of the above are ways to prepare yourself in case you suddenly find yourself in these circumstances. Trying to deal with the feelings can be very difficult. Just recognizing them is a start, and then choosing to remain neutral so they don't control you is the next step. Lastly, to be in a position to be more analytical about what is happening, ask yourself the following questions:

Exercise Three:
1. *What brought on these feelings of being alone or lost?*
2. *Can I understand how what happened provoked these feelings?*
3. *Did what happened bring to the surface some childhood trauma?*
4. *Did it bring to the surface some past life trauma? If so, should I look at the past life?*

When you have a clearer understanding of what can trigger these feelings, then you are in a disidentified place and can proceed accordingly. Let's take some time now to analyze what could cause these feelings to come up for you in the first place.

Essentially, there are two major causes. The first major cause is that these feelings are an appropriate part of the journey. The second major cause is that some childhood or past-life trauma triggers the feelings.

In both these cases, identifying the feelings and the causes is important in order move through them and continue your spiritual work. Too often a student gets stuck in these emotions and has difficulty recognizing the cause.

Of course, it is always best to recognize those times in your life when you get stuck in feelings. Being alone can make a student either feel good or feel bad. Being alone can be a positive experience, unless the student has huge rejection or abandonment issues, in which case being alone is usually negative.

Let's look at the positive aspects of being alone.

1. Being alone gives you the opportunity to schedule your time and follow through with projects.
2. Being alone gives the student the space to meditate and to follow a spiritual practice.
3. Being alone also gives the student the time to accomplish goals and meet deadlines.
4. Being alone gives the student time to reflect and link more closely with the Masters.
5. Being alone has the potential of giving the student freedom to go anywhere and do anything.
6. Being alone also gives a calm and peaceful feeling to the surroundings and helps the student to concentrate.

All of the above are positive aspects of being alone. If a person is genuinely happy when he is alone or lives alone, then he can enjoy all the above opportunities.

The negative aspects for someone who lives alone, or in general feels alone, are the following.

1. Feeling isolated, with no one to share your feelings with.
2. Feeling there is no one to talk to.
3. Feeling dissatisfied with work because there is no one to show it to.
4. Wanting freedom, but feeling that freedom is for someone else who is more developed.
5. Thinking that it is karma to be alone and resenting the karma.
6. Thinking all the time about lost relationships, or relationships that may happen.
7. Spending too much time on e-mail in order to feel less alone.
8. Procrastinating by filling your time with nonproductive things.
9. Spending a lot of time doing errands or other things that are not essential.
10. In general, feeling depressed because no one is there.

When you have any of the above feelings, you are experiencing aloneness. What needs to happen when you feel that way is to recognize what is happening and then analyze where these feelings of aloneness are coming from. Is it part of your ego self or your lower nature? If it is the latter, then it is important to define whether it is coming from you entirely, or whether it is coming from an outside negative force.

Vigilance is a key word in any spiritual teaching, and it means just that. If you are vigilant you will know immediately where your feelings are originating. If they truly originate within you, then you need to confront them and understand the source. If they originate from a negative force trying to make you feel a certain way, then you need to say no to the negative force and not listen to it. With each obstacle there will be whispers from negative forces. Separating them out makes the obstacles much easier to overcome.

There was a very lovely woman who is a good example of how negative forces operate. This woman, whom we will call Juanita, lived in a spiritual community and was very devoted to the teacher and to her brothers and sisters. Her life was full of tasks. Some were mundane tasks, as she was an administrator of a small shop in the community, and some tasks were spiritually oriented. Juanita was also in charge of changing the food offerings and cleaning up the main shrine in the temple. This task brought her much joy, and she made it a daily ritual that she practiced by chanting many mantras and meditating afterward.

One day, the guru of the ashram called Juanita to a meeting. He told her that she needed to develop her meditation practice more and that he was therefore putting her into a meditation hut for six months so that she could do this. Being in such an environment was very conducive to spiritual development, and it was offered only to students the teacher felt were ready to move to a higher level. Naturally, Juanita was very happy that this was being offered to her, but her heart felt sad about giving up her shrine practice, and she asked the guru if she could continue it during her time in the hut. He said no, that she needed to give up her shrine practice.

When Juanita found herself alone in the hut with no more tasks and no people to communicate with, it was extremely difficult. To be sequestered meant there would be no more contact with anyone; even her food would be passed to her through an opening in the door. During those six months, she was to live in solitude at all times. Initially, she was able to let go of the community and even the teacher, knowing that he, of course, was always with her on the subtle plane. But giving up of the shrine task gave her great anguish. Instead of meditating, she started worrying about who was doing the work and whether it was being done correctly. Then, her thoughts were on whether this important task would be hers when she returned, and that became a constant interruption in her meditation.

One month passed, and then two months passed with this constant turmoil. Then, one day a small mouse came into her hut, and she gave it some food out of her dish. Before long, there was another mouse, and they started coming on a regular basis. Juanita would carefully lay the food out for them, and when she was meditating while they were eating, she would open her eyes and send them love. Soon her thoughts about the shrine task were gone, and all she could think about were the mice.

Then, one day a note was passed to her. It read: "There are mice in your hut. It is all right now, we have set traps and are taking them far away so they will no longer disturb you." Juanita was heartbroken. Where were they taking them, and how would they eat? These thoughts took up another month in the hut, until she let them go. At this point Juanita became very depressed and was more conscious of her aloneness. "What a terrible practice this is," she thought. "I can't wait until it ends." And she started keeping track each day to the time the six months would end. The more depressed she became, the more alone she felt. "No one cares. I'm sitting here alone and unhappy, and no one is even aware of me. They all think this is an honor when it's just horrible."

Her thoughts became darker and darker. In the beginning she could see and feel her teacher with her, but soon he disappeared and now there was no sense at all of him even visiting her. She became more and more resentful and even had thoughts of leaving the teaching as soon as she got out. The only thing that kept her from pounding on the door and demanding to be freed was her pride. She would never show anyone that she couldn't do this, and when she left the ashram, it would be quietly. No one cared, so why even say goodbye? Obviously, she was listening to negative forces, but she had no understanding of this and gave in to all of the negative thoughts.

One day nearing the end of the six months, as she sat there thinking of her future life, another note was passed in. It read: "Remember your practice, remember you are a yogi, and try to find your Higher Self again. You will stay in the hut until you can remember this." The note was signed by her guru. Shocked, she became very angry with him. To stay there longer wasn't fair. He hadn't even asked her. She raged at him until she was tired and then she slept. In her dream her teacher held her hands and told her to look up, and when she did, she saw beauty beyond belief. Then he said to look down, and she saw ugliness and decay. He quietly said to her, "You have been down there, strive to be up there," and he pointed upward. "There you will never be alone. Accept your loneliness now as a blessing, and then you will obtain eternal wisdom. It is but a passageway that leads you upward."

When the dream ended, Juanita woke up and felt his love for several minutes. During the next few days she again sat and thought, but this time she looked at all that had happened to her from a different place. She began to see it for what it really was: constant obstacles that took away the time to pursue her meditation practice, which was why she was in the hut in the first place. She realized how she had been influenced, and she also realized how the community and her teacher had become the family she never had. She looked at who she was in detail and acknowledged some of her false motivations for entering a spiritual practice in the first place. At the same time, she realized that it wasn't about the community, or even her teacher, but was about herself and her inner need to find God Consciousness.

Suddenly, Juanita no longer felt alone, and she began to meditate in earnest. Each day was a joy of deepening her level of being, each day was gone in a wink, and the next, and the next. She slept and ate and meditated and began to see and hear things that were part of the upper planes she was shown.

One day there was a knock at the door and a voice said, "Tomorrow you will leave the hut."

"Oh, no. I want to have more time," she cried.

"You have been in the hut for one year. Your body needs exercise."

"But that can't be. I have not been here a year and I do exercise."

She was just able to stand up in the hut, and everyday she'd stretched and moved her body to keep it mobile.

"Just a few more days, please." There was no answer. The next day the door opened, and standing there to greet her was her guru.

"So, you have discovered the true meaning of being alone. You have done well to learn that lesson. Now you need to keep that understanding in your heart and strive to have it all the time."

When she came out into the sunlight, the community was there to greet her, and she looked at them all with a new kind of love, love without attachment or need, just love. Juanita continued in her practice and became a guru herself. She was one of the few Western women to have achieved that in an Eastern ashram. Her path brought her back to the West to teach esoteric practices and to accomplish the rest of her dharma.

Often a student believes that the state of loneliness is a place to be avoided when, in actuality, it is a very important stage to go through and is an indication that the student is striving and doing very well in the esoteric practice. It is a sign of real accomplishment.

Naturally, loneliness is a difficult concept to accept. How can I be accomplished when I feel deserted by all those I love? How can I realize true inner depth when the outer me feels isolated? These feelings block the truth, but the state of feeling lost and alone is a spiritual passage every yogi has to go through. Without a doubt, it is a step on the path that must be taken, and the student has to realize the importance of that state.

You may ask, why? Why is it a necessary step? The answer encompasses several layers of wisdom. When you are surrounded by the outside world and make that world your life focus, then the focus needs to be reexamined. Spending time without anyone or any outside influence gives you the opportunity to apply your focus on your inner being.

The other main reason is to help you become closer to the teacher and the teaching. The more you focus on both, the more you will grow spiritually, because when you strive, you automatically receive higher wisdom. Being immersed in outside distractions causes you to lose contact with the source. Periods of isolation help you to refocus your energy and, therefore, strengthen the spiritual ties that bind you to the path.

Sometimes the feelings of loss arise when a student is absorbed in the outside world and they are just as strong as if the student were in a place of isolation. It does not require a certain kind of setting for this experience to happen. Since it is a stage in the development of every student, let's explore more closely why this experience is a requirement.

First, it is necessary for you to become more aware of your inner self, which holds many core beliefs and hidden skandhas. On the path to God Consciousness, it is necessary to open all of these in order to grow spiritually, since the goal is to have full knowledge of your innermost being. To find this knowledge, it is important to understand who you are. The real you is very hidden in the mundane world. It is painful to let go of the worldly self to find the inner self. Often the inner self has much to process psychologically. There are inner parts within everyone that need to be examined, understood, and transformed.

During this process a sense of having no identity arises. The identity in the outside world seems false, and the inner self is full of conflict and feelings, which cloud the student's ability to reach the Higher Self. This is when the feelings of being lost occur. It takes courage to face this and to understand that it is all right to be feeling it. To allow yourself to feel the emotion of being lost takes courage. Facing this feeling takes you into the action of striving to discover who you really are.

To help you in this process, try these two things.

Exercise Three:
　　1. *Ask your Higher Self if there is any way you can remember to be positive while in this process.*
　　2. *Ask your Higher Self if you can be given a symbol that will represent your new identity, and use that symbol in your meditation practice.*

On this path, you will encounter others who are going through similar processes. Since everyone is an individual, do not judge or compare their processes with yours. It takes commitment and a sense of truth to let go of this feeling of being separate. You are separate. All people have their own evolutionary paths and no two are alike. But when you are in this place of aloneness, do not forget that there is a bridge that connects all of humanity and makes all one. Yes, your individuality is different, but your spirit is one with others. The source is the same in all people, and that oneness can give you the faith to face the inner self, which is alone.

When you go through this stage of development and reach the other side, you will have a deeper understanding of what true aloneness is and, at the same time, a deeper understanding of your destiny. Before you reach this stage, you may go through a stage of feeling on the outside of the group or sensing you do not completely belong with the others. Even the teacher will seem distant, and you imagine that he does not notice you or even think you are worthy to walk the path. All these feelings come from your inner child, who can feel unworthy, and in that feeling can, for example, take what is an ordinary remark and turn it into something that alienates you from others.

Exercise Four:
If you start to feel this way, it is best to meditate and ask your Higher Self the following questions:
　　1. *Am I being too sensitive to what was said or done?*
　　2. *Was the remark directed toward me?*

If you receive a yes answer for number 1 and a no answer for number

2, then you most definitely are taking what was said or done too personally. If you are uncertain of your answer, then approach the person who made the remark and ask if it was directed toward you. If you should find that unkind remarks are being directed toward you, then you need to sit down and talk to whoever is making the remarks.

Often, when someone is new in a teaching, he feels a little on the outside of the group. It takes two or three meetings for him to start to feel at home. Therefore, it is important that the people in the group make every effort to help a new person to feel welcome, even if there is some karmic tension that hasn't been explored. When someone new comes into any group, it is natural for those in the group to be hesitant about opening themselves to him. A new person is very vulnerable and needs to be accepted immediately, no matter how difficult that is; otherwise, he may not continue coming when he is meant to.

Many people have entered a spiritual path and became stuck in the feelings of loneliness. This feeling can also come from an inner recall of former lives in which the person spent time living in a solitary situation. Those feelings will begin to emerge and block the person, especially if he has sorrow around a particular past life. Starting on a spiritual path will bring recall of past lives, some of which caused the individual much pain and separation.

If you have had such a past life, it is important to ask the Higher Self the following questions.

Exercise Five:
1. *Please give me an indication if I had a solitary and lonely life in the past.*
2. *Am I bringing some of these feelings into this life?*
   - *If the answer is yes, ask for a process to help let go of the feelings.*
   - *If the answer is no, ask whether the feelings will emerge at a later time.*
3. *In both cases, ask the Higher Self for additional ways to recognize the feelings and to be able to let them go.*

When someone comes into a spiritual teaching, a great deal of energy is set into motion. This energy has most often been dormant. The energy can be positive, and it also can be negative, depending on the individual's most recent spiritual lives. If he finds he is having difficulty from the beginning, it may be an indicator that his most recent spiritual life was spent in isolation, causing a deep fear of having to experience that again, particularly if he hadn't achieved God Consciousness in that life.

If he experienced even a little of the energy of God Consciousness, he would not come into a teaching with those feelings of aloneness or being lost. Instead, there would be a deep inner need to experience being alone, mainly because it would bring him closer to God Consciousness again.

Let's look at some of the ways you can overcome the feelings of being lost and alone.

1. When you are by yourself and start to feel very alone, play some beautiful music, or take the time to go out into nature and talk to the elementals or devas.

2. If you feel isolated, telephone a friend and make a date to go somewhere or do something. Just having that on the calendar helps.

3. If you feel very desolate and lonely, try meditating, and if that doesn't work, listen to a book on tape so that your mind focuses on something else.

4. If you are with people and still feel this way, make a point to engage in any conversation with whoever is there. It can just be chitchat and not important.

5. Mainly, try to see the feelings as negative, and give those feelings to your Higher Self or your teacher. Know they are temporary and are never going to be permanent emotions. Just knowing this helps.

6. When you are in the feelings so deeply that you cannot move out of them, go out and see a movie, or go to an art gallery or museum, or even go shopping. It helps to see other people even if you don't know them.

7. Finally, when you are feeling isolated, try thinking posi-

tive thoughts about the teaching and the teacher. Bring those thoughts into your heart and feel how important they are, letting them overshadow the negative ones.

Fortunately, feelings of being lost on the path last only for short periods of time and can dissipate quickly. Know this is true, and do not listen to your lower nature, which wants you to believe you will feel this way forever. Being lost is really not as intense as it sounds; it should be more like being separate for a while, and in that separation comes the opportunity to see things truly and to grow spiritually.

Here is one last story.

Once upon a time in the ancient city of Rome there lived an old woman named Maria. She had had many children. At this time the children were either dead or had moved away with their own families. The children who left Rome never returned, as travel was difficult in those days, and there was no means of communication. Each believed there were others at home with Mother who would take care of her. When the last son left for war, he told her he would be back, but unfortunately he was killed in battle.

Now alone, as her husband had also been killed in war many years earlier, Maria found herself feeling very unhappy. Not a single child or grandchild was near her, and she didn't even know where any of them ended up. Most of her sons had been killed in wars, and her daughters had married and moved to other countries. The only thing she seemed to have left was a chicken that had been her one son's pet. Fortunately, she did have enough money to live on, and she even had a small garden she could handle alone, so there was no lack of food and clothing, only a lack of companionship.

One day, as she sat in her courtyard, Maria remembered all her children, one at a time, and she began to cry, as she hadn't seen any of them for many years. Her heart felt like it was going to break, and, indeed, she even believed that could happen. Maria bowed her head and prayed to her gods that if she could live her life over she would have no children at all, and that way she would have no grief at losing all of them.

Suddenly, her wish was granted, and Maria found herself with her husband back in the early days before he was killed. There were no children, and she was living her life day after day without anyone in the house except her husband. When he left to go to war never to return, again she was alone, but this time, with no memories of others to invade her thoughts. Maria found she felt even more alone than when she had lost her children. Her sense of isolation was much greater, because she had had many years with her children after her husband had died, years in which they all were together.

Again Maria prayed and asked the gods to return her to her true state. Even though the children were gone, she had memories that made her feel less alone. A couple of years later one of her daughters did return to live with her when the daughter's husband died, and the two of them had each other from then on.

The point of this story is that no one is ever alone. Memories keep you from feeling isolated. It is important to build good memories that will be with you all your life, memories that help you to continue your journey alone when that time comes.

Chapter 24
The Journey

The spiritual journey is a long and difficult one. On the path to God Consciousness there are many deviations that cause you to wander off, only to finally find the way back to the main path. To tell you that this path is easy would be false, yet it can be easy, much easier than you realize. Here are a few stories and some advice that may help you understand why this is true.

The main story takes place in ancient Egypt during the rule of the Pharaoh Ramses II. He was a very just ruler and had many children, who were educated to be fine leaders. One of these children was named Ova. Because he was a child by a mistress of Ramses, Ova was not considered royal and, therefore, lived in a house with his mother outside the royal palace. Ramses saw Ova frequently, as he was particularly fond of this child, and was planning to give him, when he grew up, an excellent post in his government.

Like many children, Ova was full of energy and loved to play, but he was also very good at his studies. He trained in the diplomatic field, and was being groomed to be a counselor who would be in charge of certain sections of the kingdom. One day when he was sixteen, he was walking through a small village near his home and entered the village's temple to make an offering to Osiris. Ova had received very thorough religious training from one of the palace priests. Although he was not religious, he had a deep devotion to both Isis and Osiris.

The temple he entered was made of baked clay. It was dry, hot, and very stuffy inside. Oil lanterns were burning, and there was only a small statue of Osiris because it was a temple for the poor and they couldn't afford a grand statue. Sitting in meditation, Ova felt immense joy. The devotional vibrations of this temple were very strong, and they penetrated his whole being, bringing him into a state of bliss. He had never felt this before, and he sat there for several hours just breathing it in. Finally, he arose and asked to see the priest of the temple. He was shown into a small room adjacent to the back of the temple. The priest was a humble man, very devoted to his God and full of love. He immediately recognized Ova as a special man and told him so.

What followed was a strange outcome. Ova, who had no spiritual ambition, decided after one meeting with this priest that his life was to be in the priesthood. He asked the priest to be his teacher, and he went home and told his mother that he was leaving to study for the priesthood.

Ova's mother quickly informed Ramses of this event, and Ramses personally came to see his son to dissuade him. Ova confronted his father and said no, this was his calling. To say no to the Pharaoh was considered a sacrilege, but Ramses, seeing how determined his son was, forgave him and said that he would support this calling only if Ova promised to study with the priests in his palace. Again Ova said no, his teacher was the humble priest who knew the Gods more intimately than any other priest he had met; but he did say that when he had completed his training he would teach at the palace for a time.

In the years that followed, Ova became a great priest, knowledgeable in all the rituals and full of wisdom that came from an inner knowledge and connection with his Higher Self. His character was unblemished, and his striving was full of devotion. He not only taught the wealthy families, but was also the main priest for the royal children.

Once a week he would go back to the small temple and his teacher, and there he would minister to the poor and needy and train young boys who also wanted to become local priests. Ova's path was easy, and he strove with determination to reach the Gods or Masters and become one with them.

The spiritual path is always likened to the journey, the journey is always likened to the way, and the way is likened to one's dharma. In most esoteric religions there is always something that represents the journey, because the journey indicates movement, the movement of traveling from one place to another. It also indicates that in most journeys there will be difficult times and good times.

This last chapter is going to explain more about the actual journey and what is expected on this journey of the neophyte, student, or disciple. No matter what religion, the student begins the journey or path with very little accomplished and ends the path having achieved the Highest. Naturally, many more students start the journey than ever finish it. They leave along the way, having achieved some, but not all, of their destiny.

Why is this, you may ask? Why can't it be easy, an easy journey without the blocks and hindrances that can throw a person off? Why can't you begin and end the journey knowing that you, indeed, walked the path and finished your dharma for a given life? To tell you that it is easy would, perhaps, be the truth for some of you and not the truth for others. Since everyone is an individual with individual karma that has to be dealt with, how can anyone know whether or not the journey will be easy?

The only ones who know this are you and your Master. You can find this information by asking your Higher Self, and your Master can verify it for you. So, why not ask? But before you ask, do you really want to know? If your karma is such that your journey will be very difficult, do you really want to know that? And even if your journey is to be easy, do you really want to understand that when you may be going through an inner struggle?

Before you do the following exercise, ask yourself if you really want to know, or if you are ready to know. Since this journey is very individual, do you want to know that others may have an easy time with it and you may have to face many more difficulties, or vice versa? Do you want to know that you can do it more easily than you have been doing? Just because your path may be easy doesn't mean you will perceive it that way, and, in fact, you may be struggling more than necessary.

If you really know what your dharma is, can you honestly accept it and do it? That is the main question.

Exercise One:

First ask the Higher Self the following questions:

1. *Am I ready to know if my journey is an easy one or a difficult one?*
   - *If the answer is no, ask: When will I be able to know if it is easy or difficult for me?*
   - *If the answer is yes, then ask: Is my journey an easy one or a difficult one?*
2. *If the answer is that your journey is an easy one, ask: Are the obstacles I encounter ones that I am meant to encounter?*
   - *If the answer is yes, ask: Can I move through them more easily? Ask for a process.*
   - *If the answer is no, ask: Why do I encounter obstacles that I am not meant to encounter?*
3. *Going back to the original question, if the answer is that your journey is a difficult one, ask: What karma is causing my journey to be more difficult?*
   - *When you have an answer, ask for a process to ease the karma.*
4. *In the future, when I encounter obstacles, how can I best go through them without being stuck?*
5. *Is there anything else I can do that will help ease the journey for me?*

The spiritual journey can be a long one, taking many lifetimes, or it can be a short one, accomplished in one life. It depends entirely on you. Even if your journey is a difficult one, it can be completed quickly. The key is your desire for God Consciousness. If the desire is strong, you will strive and accomplish it, but if other things pull you away, then it will take longer. These other things are all the attachments of the mundane world as well as all the skandhas that you come in with. Even one small skandha can limit your achievement.

The following story illustrates this.

In the early days of Byzantium, there lived a young man who

came from a very wealthy family. This man, Leros, had some very interesting karma to pay off. Leros was the eldest of seven children, and he had to take care of them all, as his father had died when Leros was still a boy. Leros was very intelligent and worked very hard to keep his family well provided for. While still young, he became a strong administrator of a province that fortunately was under the jurisdiction of his relatives. As his siblings grew up, he gave them good jobs in the province and helped them learn any skills needed for their positions.

Most of Leros's time was spent working, so much so that he had the reputation of never having any fun. His only recreation was horseback riding in the woods, or hunting deer and rabbit.

One day, when Leros was in his late twenties, he stumbled on an old hermit living in a cave in the forest. The hermit was a wise man who devoted his life to God, living with little but a loincloth and berries as his food. When Leros sat and talked with the hermit, he felt that he had come home, and he immediately asked the hermit to be his teacher. The hermit said he would teach him, but only if Leros were willing to give up everything he had, even renouncing his job as administrator. Leros said that he would have to meditate on this and return. When he meditated, he saw that none of his siblings were as yet capable of taking his position.

Leros went back to the hermit and asked him if he could return in a year after he had properly trained a brother to take over his position. The hermit said no, it had to be now or never. Again, Leros thought about it, and he was full of anguish about leaving his family responsibility. He knew that everything would collapse if he suddenly disappeared. Even though his heart longed to be with his teacher, Leros chose to stay and complete his work.

Several more years passed, and Leros had trained two brothers to handle all his responsibilities. When he felt they could take over, he announced that he was leaving on a long journey and did not know whether or not he would return. The whole family protested, cried, and made many scenes, as they loved him and did not want him to leave. Leros saw that he was breaking their hearts, especially that of his mother, who was now old and not well. So, he stayed a few more years until the death of his mother and then once more told his siblings that he was leaving, that he had given them many years of his life, and that now he needed to go his own way alone. This time he left. He was now forty.

The first place he went to was the cave where his teacher had lived, but the hermit was no longer there. Leros thought that perhaps the hermit had died, as it was at least fifteen years since he had seen him. He sat in the cave for several months trying to meditate, doing religious practices, and living as the hermit did on berries from the forest.

One day in his meditation he saw the hermit, who told him to leave, that the cave was not his destiny, and that he needed to travel and find his teacher who would then guide him on his spiritual journey. So Leros wandered through the forest, into towns, and even into other countries looking for another teacher.

He met many hardships along the way. Sometimes there was not enough food, and begging brought him very little. Other times a kindly person would lavish food and clothing on him, and he would be all right. Every place Leros went he asked if there were any spiritual teachers in the vicinity. On several occasions he was told yes, but when he met the teacher he knew in his heart this was not the one. Leros would ask each teacher where he needed to go next to find his teacher and was given many directions. One day he met a wise one sitting by the side of the road. Leros knew this man was not his teacher, but again asked for advice, saying that he had looked for several years with no luck and was feeling sad and distraught about not finding him. The wise one said, "Have you asked your heart?"

"No, what do you mean?"

"Just put in your heart your longing to find your teacher and your heart will guide you."

So Leros found a solitary place and placed the question in his heart and waited. One day he awoke with an image of a statue, and the statue pointed to a map, and on the map was the name of his home. The statue was pointing to his home.

But how could that be, he wondered. The hermit in the cave

was gone. Could he have returned? Should he return home? He put this question in his heart and felt his heart respond. It took Leros several months to make the journey home. The first thing he did was to go to the cave in the forest, but it was empty. When he approached his home, he saw that it looked dull and decayed. At first, none of the servants recognized Leros, as his hair was down to his waist and his skin was dark and leathery from the sun, but when he spoke they recognized his voice and let him in.

What he saw saddened him; everything looked uncared for. There were fewer servants, and he soon found out that his brothers had split up and divided the province, quarrelling about who received what. As a result of the years of fighting, many of the administrative duties had not been done, and the whole province was suffering from lack of direction. Leros immediately fired his brothers and took back his holdings.

For the next three years he worked very hard to restore all that had been before. Everyone was filled with joy at his return. Most of the family was still there, and even his brothers, when they were again under his supervision, settled their differences. Leros again had no time to continue his spiritual journey, and he realized that the statue pointed to his home because he was very much needed there.

This time Leros set up a governing team of people, not just his family, who would be in charge of the province. This way, when he died he could be assured that things would be carried on correctly. Leros led this team for several years before retiring. By now he was fifty-five years old. After he retired, he remained another five years to be certain that everything ran smoothly, and then, feeling assured that he was no longer needed, he again set out on his journey to find his true teacher. This time Leros remembered to ask his heart first and was given an indication to go north to the mountains. There, in a monastery, he found his teacher and spent the remaining years of his life in a spiritual practice.

Leros achieved God Consciousness at the end of his life even though his spiritual practice in the monastery was only for seven years. He was able to do so because his decision to follow through on his responsibilities was the right one. He spent his life putting others before himself, and on his journey he followed the right path, which involved work in the world, thus achieving his dharma. He then followed his heart to the Highest.

This story illustrates that the journey is different for everyone. It is not just about living in a cave, or creating one of your own making. The journey needs to happen in the world, being part of it, but having in your heart the true understanding of what is the most important thing you have to accomplish. Leros always knew that his quest for God was most important, but also that his other work had to be completed because he was born into that responsibility.

Holding the quest in his heart helped him throughout those years of hard work, for he knew that someday, whether or not it would be in this lifetime, he was to fulfill his spiritual dream. His journey was a difficult one, yet he never failed in his goal or gave in to the difficulties. He fulfilled all his responsibilities, and even though his work took him away from his dream, he never complained or felt burdened by it. His attitude was a constant one of following his path, whatever direction it took him. In following it, he returned to the "main road" and realized he had traveled farther than he expected. Because of his attitude the difficulty was lessened, and had anyone asked him if he felt his journey was difficult, he probably would have said, no, it was easy. This was because he followed his heart and looked on life as a constant learning process.

How does a person achieve this attitude? How do you see life as a learning process and not become burdened by the difficulties but instead see them as challenges that can easily be overcome? It is all about attitude.

This book has focused on attitude in many of the chapters, and it will end with some exercises that will inform you more about your own attitude toward life.

Do you see life as a drain on you? Do you want to learn from your mistakes? These are some of the questions that inform you about your basic attitudes. First, let's do an exercise to determine whether your attitudes tend toward the negative or the positive:

Ask yourself the following questions. Be careful in the way you answer these questions, and be honest. Take your time in determining the answers, and try to think of situations that could have provoked an attitude. Take each question and rate yourself from 1 to 10, 10 being the highest. For example, if your answer to question 1 is that you become depressed when confronting a problem, rate yourself from 1 to 10 in terms of how depressed you get; if you approach a problem as a challenge, rate yourself according to that response.

Exercise One:

1. *When you have a problem, does it make you depressed or is it an exciting challenge?*
2. *Do you see yourself as a positive person or a negative person?*
3. *Do others see you as being more positive or more negative?*
4. *Do you have a strong worry pattern?*
5. *When something happens to you that is a hardship, can you overcome it quickly, or do you stay in it longer than necessary?*
6. *When you are alone, do you sometimes think of life as being too difficult?*
7. *Have you ever wanted to die?*
8. *When you look at your friends, do you see their positive characteristics first?*
9. *When you look at your friends, do you give them praise for the positive qualities, or do you always see something wrong in them?*
10. *With each day, do you give thanks for being in the teaching?*
11. *With each day, are you aware of all the beauty around you?*
12. *With each day, can you honestly feel happy to be alive?*
13. *When you visit others, do you feel good to be with friends?*

14. *Are your relationships happy ones?*
15. *If you are in a club or organization, does attending meetings make you happy?*
16. *As you age, do you feel your life has been full and mainly a good one?*
17. *At the end of the day, can you honestly say you have had a good day?*
18. *With each loved one, can you feel what it means to simply have love and give love?*

You should fluctuate on these answers. Obviously, if all the answers are close to a 10 on the positive questions and very low on any questions indicating a negative attitude, then you have what is called a Pollyanna pattern and are not being honest with yourself. Generally, you should be in the 5 to 7 range. If most of your answers are below 5 for positive items, then you see things more in a negative than a positive manner, and if you see things higher than 5, then you generally are more positive about life. If any of the above has a rating between 1 and 3, then you definitely need to work on that question.

Exercise Two:
Take each one of those negative responses and ask your Higher Self the following questions:
  1. *Why am I so negative about this?*
  2. *Does it come from my childhood conditioning?*
  3. *Does it come from a past life?*
  4. *Do I have a core belief around this? If so, what is it?*
  5. *Give me a process and a first step to change this attitude.*

Work daily with the answer you are given, and also do a nightly review and honestly see how a negative attitude can affect your thinking and therefore your life. Negative attitudes are major blocks on the spiritual path. They keep you from experiencing the joy of life and the beauty of nature. They take away your inspiration and creativity and hold you in the lower self.

Sometimes it is important to see things in a very realistic manner. If your ratings are too high, then you live in a dream world and cannot see the reality around you. As part of the Pollyanna pattern, this attitude can block you on the path, because you cannot deal with life at all levels. For example, if you have a genuine psychological problem and think it will just get better on its own, you are deluding yourself. The same is true if you have a physical problem and choose to ignore it, hoping it will change. It is normal to have mood swings and have days when you feel a little down, but it is not good if those days become a week or more. Then it means that you are in a state of depression. Such depression needs to be changed either by outside help, or, if you have a chemical imbalance, you may need some drug therapy.

Spiritual people have a tendency to avoid any outside help, believing that Hierarchy will make everything all right. Hierarchy and your teacher can send healings and help, but if a person has a chemical imbalance, then chemical help is needed. The same is true if someone is suffering from psychological problems stemming from childhood. Psychotherapy, if it is with a good therapist, can really change a person's attitudes and make one more balanced and, therefore, happier.

The spiritual journey is full of surprises. Some can be negative and some positive. The way to approach these surprises is with an open heart. Then if they are negative, you can contain them, and if they are positive, you can accept them with joy.

Let's look at some of the things that can occur suddenly and reflect on whether any of them have happened to you, starting with the negative.

1. You meet someone with whom you have difficult karma and that person does something that is very hurtful.
2. Someone you love ends the relationship.
3. You are afflicted with an unexpected illness.
4. You are disappointed by the actions of someone you respect.
5. In general, there is a cloud over you that looks as if it's not going to lift.

6. Your work goes through a difficult stage.
7. Everything you value gets shaken up.
8. When you want to proceed with a good plan, everything seems to impede it.
9. People you care about are going through difficult crises and you can't help them.
10. When everything seems to be going well, something happens to change that.
11. There is a sudden death in the family.
12. Weather conditions stop you from doing something important.
13. Your spiritual practice can't be followed because of a sudden crisis that takes your time.
14. You have wonderful meditations and suddenly they are terrible.

The following are examples of the positive surprises. Again, take time to reflect on whether any of these have happened to you.

1. You meet someone with whom you have very positive karma.
2. There is a sudden new love relationship.
3. When you meditate, you suddenly see or hear things.
4. At the end of the day, you realize it was an exhilarating day.
5. Your work takes a positive and very exciting turn.
6. When you visit friends, there is a deep feeling of love and compassion.
7. Unexpected gifts come to you.
8. You find yourself in a place where others look up to you.
9. Decisions happen that make your life easier.
10. Your teacher gives you another initiation.
11. Your Master sends you a message.
12. When you work with your buddy, you reach a deeper place of co-measurement.
13. Someone you respect compliments you.
14. You suddenly feel joy.
15. You come to a deeper understanding of the journey.

16. You find your knowledge of the teaching has reached another level.
17. You understand yourself and come in contact with the true sense of Be-ness.

There are other surprises that happen on the journey, surprises that relate to your individual progress. For example, you are always going through spiritual tests, and some of them you pass and others you do not. Some tests that you would normally think impassable you pass easily, and others that seem simple may stop you. These tests help you to come to a better understanding of your striving and your devotion as well as helping you to see areas of your lower nature that need to be confronted and transmuted.

The journey requires discipline, striving, devotion, acceptance, co-measurement, discrimination, and, most of all, the willingness to change and be flexible. It can be a long journey or a short one. It always depends upon you and the way you walk the path. Do you deviate and get caught up in mundane distractions? Do you lose focus and become too undisciplined in your spiritual work? Do you feel devotion some times and other times forget? Are you grateful for the help that is given? If you have a teacher and she suggests something, do you follow the suggestion? Have you remembered to always be linked to your Higher Self? Is the quest for God Consciousness the most important goal in your life? Can you handle change? And can you, most of all, accept your karma, whether it be negative or positive?

All of these factors and many more determine your ability to make the journey a long one or a short one. Examining them brings you to a deeper awareness of who you are and a deeper understanding of the teaching of Higher Self Yoga. May you walk the path and make the journey one that is full of joy, full of compassion, and, most of all, full of heightened awareness of the goal. Let your heart be open to all that happens on the path, let your mind be open to new knowledge and understanding, and let your body be strong to withstand the up-and-down terrain.

The journey has an end. Believe that. The journey has a beginning. Know that. The journey is the only way to reach God

Consciousness. Understand that, and in that understanding realize that it is a journey you can finish. Others have gone before you; let them guide you. Trust and respect them, as they have succeeded. Use their wisdom to help you realize the true meaning of the path. Believe in their love, for only they can give you the ability to change and grow spiritually. When the journey is ended, only then will you understand its full meaning. Trust in your heart, in your mind, and most of all, trust in your Higher Self to always be there leading the way.

You will find the Higher Self in all your fellow travelers. Reach out to them as your true family and know the importance of those relationships. Someday you will all stand together as one and experience the meaning of harmony. The Masters await you and pray that you will be steady on the path. The Masters will always guide you, but you have to take the steps and strive toward the goal.

Remember, it is your journey, and each one's journey has to be taken alone. You will meet many on the path, and many will walk by your side, but each step comes from you alone, and each step changes you. Make the steps small ones so they do not require more effort than you can give. Small steps will achieve the goal as quickly as big ones.

Sometimes on the path you will run, and sometimes you will rest. Try to keep the rhythm of movement always present, even when you sit for a while. Never look back on the journey except to see the lessons you still need to learn. Never judge yourself or others you encounter, as judgments stop or impede progress.

Let your hearts be aflame with love, let your minds be open to wisdom, and let your bodies be renewed with energy, and, most of all, let your Higher Self operate more and more in your consciousness.

Glossary

Adept: One who has achieved the sixth or higher initiation in an esoteric tradition.

AUM: (Sanskrit) A sacred mystical syllable, often intoned prior to a prayer or mantra.

Clairvoyance: The faculty of seeing with the inner eye or spiritual sight.

Devachan: Part of the higher Astral plane where only those spirits who have left their earthly bodies go. When the period of rest is concluded there the soul emerges from the state of bliss for another lifetime on earth.

Devas: The spiritual forces or beings behind nature. Devas follow a separate evolution from humans. Devas are here to work with humans and want to develop a relationship of mutual benefit.

Dharma: The way we live our lives spiritually and ethically, as well as the way we develop our evolutionary paths. This includes the next step on our spiritual path, as well as the work a person chooses to do in a given lifetime.

Disidentify: The ability to detach from the thinking mind, which is constantly labeling, judging, defining, conceptualizing, covering the world up with words rather than allowing an individual to experience the world directly through presence. It is also the ability to detach from desires and ego-needs.

Elementals: Spirits of the elements, forces of nature. They are made of energy and have no separate consciousness. Elementals are guided by the devas and nature spirits, and are influenced by humans. They are in everything.

Esoteric: Secret Teachings based on higher knowledge.

Exoteric: Knowledge that is public as opposed to secret.

Feminine Principle: The nurturing, sustaining, and inspirational influence in the universe. The Masculine Principle initiates action and movement; the Feminine Principle nurtures, inspires and is responsive to those actions and movements.

Fiery World: Cosmic realm that is the source of cosmic knowledge, serving to inspire fiery creativity in people who have developed their creative capabilities and intelligence. This creative fire becomes the inspirational source for inventors, dancers, artists, musicians and all creative people alike.

Gross Body: The physical body.

Guide: The Guardian Angel or personal Guide given to everybody at birth for one lifetime. It represents one's conscience and common sense intuition, thereby providing guidance for daily life situations. As the person evolves, so does the Guide. After a persons death, his or her Guide, according to its development, is assigned to someone else who is ready to be reborn.

Hierarchy: The Masters in the Great White Brotherhood who were formerly embodied on the Earth and learned the lessons of life during their incarnations. They serve as teachers of humankind and act to inspire and motivate our spiritual growth. They follow the cosmic laws and are responsible for maintaining the evolution of the planet.

Higher Self: The Higher Self, often called the Wise Being within, is part of you and also part of the Source - the unknown, the ultimate Reality, the energies that have no beginning and no end. For more, see the Preface and Introduction.

Higher Worlds: The higher subtle planes of existence in the subtle world where Beauty, Love and Truth abide to the highest degree.

Initiate: Some one who has been initiated by a teacher who is themself at least a fourth initiate. It is a sacred ceremony in which the student is bonded with the teacher through the heart.

Initiations: There are a total of 7 initiations, which a disciple has to achieve in order to become a Master. In each initiation there are levels of testing both psychologically and spiritually. A disciple's Master determines when a student is ready for the first and also for each of the others. When a disciple receives her/his full fourth initiation s/he can then become a teacher. When a disciple receives her/his 6th initiation this is called adeptship. Initiations are part of the esoteric tradition but not necessary in order to study Higher Self Yoga.

Kama Loka: A specific place in Devachan where people go to play out their desires fully. After the desires are played out the person continues his journey through Devachan, which has several planes.

Kumara: A very high Being in charge of the evolution of a particular planet. The Lord Maitreya is the Kumara of the Earth.

Mantras: A word or words repeated over and over again during meditation. It sets up a series of vibrations which can create transformation. Aum (Om) is an extremely powerful mantra.

Masculine Principle: The proactive and initiating nature of the universe. The Masculine Principle initiates action and movement; the Feminine Principle nurtures, inspires and is responsive to those actions and movements.

Master: Also called Mahatma, one who has achieved seven initiations. A Master is a Teacher, Elder Brother and Guardian of humanity, overseeing and guiding the planetary and human evolution. The Masters instruct humankind, inspire elevating thoughts and instill beneficial higher impulses.

Monad: The immortal part of man, the seed of the spirit, which reincarnates from lifetime to lifetime. The Monad contains the higher principles and has attached to it the skandhas (attributes from previous lives), which carry the individual characteristics of the evolving human. The seed of the spirit, which is within the Monad, is the fiery energy that propels the soul or individuality to evolve.

Shambhala: The Abode of Enlightened Beings, or Masters, also known as the Ashram of Hierarchy. It exists in the mundane world and in the Subtle World.

Skandhas: The inclinations, patterns and creative powers that a person carries over from past lives.

Subtle World: The planes where a person goes during sleep to restore psychic energies, receive individual instruction and training, and do service. Each individual molds him or herself literally by way of bringing back from the Subtle World new impressions that further personal and spiritual development. Each person goes to the level that is in accordance with his or her spiritual development.

About the Author

Nanette Hucknall is the founder and President of the Higher Self Yoga Association. She has developed and led Higher Self Yoga classes and retreats for over twenty years throughout the United States and Canada.

This is the first of two planned volumes of Higher Self Yoga teachings. There will be other books about Higher Self Yoga and related subjects.

In addition to her work with Higher Self Yoga, Nanette has been a career therapist and psychotherapist for twenty-five years. Her book, *Karma, Destiny, and Your Career*, has been translated and published in four different countries, and was recently made into an e-book and audiotape.

Nanette has designed and facilitated workshops on "Karma, Destiny, and Your Career," and recently "Living From Your Heart," which she has presented in the United States and in Canada. Together with her business partner, Dr. Judith Bach, she has also presented seminars and workshops throughout the United States, Canada, Belgium, Germany and Italy.

Before introducing Higher Self Yoga, Nanette studied Agni Yoga for many years, and was trained in Psychosynthesis.

Index

In this index, the phrase "Higher Self" is abbreviated in subheadings as HS.

abandonment, feelings of
  and aloneness as necessary part of the
    spiritual path, 287, 292
  as emotional suffering, 92
  and lost, feelings of being, 292, 295
Abode of Enlightened Beings, 175
abusive relationships
  child abuse, 94, 134
  and choice of teacher, 266
  emotional abuse, breaking cycle of,
    142-143
  free will and breaking cycle of, 50-51,
    222-223
  victim pattern, 93-94
  See also childhood conditioning
addictions
  alcohol and drugs, 34-35, 121-122,
    211
  defined, 94-95
  as emotional suffering, 94-95
  as impasse, 129-131
  lack of sunlight and, 34-35
  and meditation, 121-122
  sex, 130-131
  See also balance
adept, defined, 321
affirmations, meanings of the words in,
  10
Agni Yoga, 169
alcohol and drug use and abuse
  lack of sunlight and, 34-35
  meditation and, 121-122
  prana and, 211
  See also addictions
aloneness as necessary part of the
spiritual path, 286-306
  accomplishment in path and, 286-
    287, 295, 300-302
  distractions from, seeking of, 53, 287,
    301
  fear of abandonment and, 287, 292
  fear of being alone vs., 53, 286
  and fear of making mistakes, 293
  and the group, feeling outside of,
    302-303
  and identity, 301-302
  as longing of the spirit for God
    Consciousness, 287-288

and love as ever present, 290
negative forces as exploiting, 286, 293
positive aspects of being alone, 53,
  206
stories to illustrate, 288-290, 297-
  300, 305-306
and the teacher/Master, 287, 293
uniqueness of each student's path
  and, 286-287, 293, 302, 314, 320
vs. socializing, and choosing a
  spiritual path, 66-69, 73
See also lost, feelings of being
anger
  and childhood conditioning, 92
  cleansing a space of, 28, 258
  as emotional suffering, 92-93
  expectations resulting in, 273-274
  expression of, 96, 98
  imbalance caused by, 95-96
  of initiate, as more powerful, 248
  nature and, 258
  and speaking consciously, 13, 17
  and tone of voice, 13
  unrequited love and, 204
  vibrations of, 1, 24, 28
  words spoken in, 2
  See also emotions
animals
  and color perception, 40
  extinction of, 45-46
  group souls of, 47
  humans distinguished from, 214
  lack of change over time, 47
  as pets, and development of capacity
    to love, 215
  reduction of numbers of, 46
  on Subtle Plane, 117
  vibrations and, 29, 31
antiques, vibrations of, 109
apathy, as impasse, 143-144
appearance, respect and, 12
arguments
  cleansing the surroundings of, 28, 258
  nature and vibrations of, 258
  and negative karma in family, 20-21
  speaking consciously and, 14
  See also anger
aromatherapy for cleansing, 257-258

artists, and desire for fame, 132–133
asceticism
  assessing amount of, in student,
    212–213
  defined, 211–212
  as invalid for today's world, 212
ashrams
  and desire for private study with
    teacher, 228
  and diet, 122
  as easier but less fruitful path, 245,
    260
  and Path of Devotion, 75
  and sexual abstinence, 122
  as traditional, 84, 212
  See also world: being in it but not of it
asthma, 94
astral body. See subtle body
astral planes
  as beginning of journey, 113
  humanity mostly stuck on, 112–113
  levels within, 113, 114
  Mental and Buddhic Planes
    distinguished from, 112–113
  See also Higher Astral Plane (subtle
    plane); Lower Astral Plane(s)
attachments
  and death, 149–150
  and ease or difficulty of journey, 310,
    319
  expectations as, 272, 284, 285
  giving up to teacher/Master, 284
  and journey as short or long, 310
  to lower nature, feelings producing,
    27
  readiness to release, 70
  and unrequited love, 284
  See also attitudes; change;
    childhood conditioning;
    disidentification; expectations;
    karmic relationships; lost, feelings
    of being; nonattachment; past lives;
    skandhas
attitudes
  glass half empty, 248
  negative or positive, and the journey,
    314–317
  Pollyanna pattern, 316, 317
  procrastination as, 275
  psychotherapy and change of, 317
  and releasing negativity, 27
  spiritual superiority, 74, 76, 81, 129,
    186–189, 191
  withdrawal from the path and, 40–41,

178
  See also expectations; perfectionism
attraction, nature of, and negative
karma
  and boundaries, need for, 205
  fellow student as loved one, 182,
    208–209
  future lives affected by, 8
  and games played by karma, 99
  guidance from HS to check out, 8
  love and hate and, 204
  positive karma as attracting in
    similar manner, 8, 106, 205
  and unrequited love, 204, 284
  and the will, use of, 222
  See also negative karma
auditory sensations, visualization and, v
AUM, 1, 321
aura
  cleansing and enhancing of, 24,
    26–27, 294
  and public success, 181
authority, issues of, 95, 140–141, 280
awareness
  of expectations, 271
  speaking consciously and, 3, 19
  and vibrations, working with, 29

balance
  in life-stage strategizing, 153
  and pleasure, desire for, 139
  in relationships, expectations and,
    273, 275
  in self-discipline, 59
  in social life, 139
  in spiritual discipline, 278
  in work, 139
beauty
  inclusion of, in life-stage strategizing,
    152–153
  self-pity dissolved through, 164
  speaking of, to transform negative
    energy, 161
  surrounding oneself with, 136
Beings. See devas; elementals; entities;
  Guide; Higher Beings; light, demanding
  to see, if a being speaks or appears;
  lower beings; nature spirits; negative
  beings; negative forces
Blavatsy, H. P., 44
blocks. See fears; psychological blocks
body. See desire body; physical body
  (gross body); subtle body
bodybuilding, 130

boundaries, personal
  agreement on, 236
  defined, 227
  disidentified love, attainment of,
    230–232
  exercise to create, 236
  and karmic relationships, 205–206
  offending someone with, 236
  suffering caused by, avoidance of,
    236–237
  time, protection of, 236
  work relationships, 236
boundaries, subtle-world
  checking on the real and not real, 229
  and communication on subtle planes,
    234–235
  defined, 227
  and freedom, expectation of, 227–228
  of the heart, 228–232
  and helping others, 229–230
  and information, 232–233
  and journeys, 234–235
  with Masters, 235–236
  and nature spirits, 233–234
  and teachers, relationship with,
    228–229
Buddha, 72, 115, 119, 203–204
Buddhic Plane, 112, 119
busy-ness, as impasse on spiritual path,
  124–126

calmness, and expectations, 276–277
camphor, cleansing home with, 28, 114,
  258
celibacy/sexual abstinence, 122, 203
cells, light energy and, 34
Chalice, 166, 167
change
  abusive relationships and, 50–51
  disidentification with, 54
  as evolutionary force, 193–194
  fanaticism and rigidity toward, 59
  human vs. animal ability for, 48
  the journey and, 319
  learning through, 48–50
  and life-stage strategizing, 154,
    155–156
  metamorphosis, 46
  near-death experiences and
    acceptance of, 194
  openness to, and spiritual path, 59,
    225, 232
  openness to, expectations and lack
    of, 280
  as opportunity, 52–54
  as seed of karma, 49–50
  spiritual growth resulting from, as
    necessary, 50, 51–52
  spiritual path choice and, 64, 65,
    78–79
  stability and, 49
  and truth as relative, 232–233
  vibrations and, 33
  See also evolution
channeling, 136, 233
chants, checking the meanings of the
  words in, 10
child abuse, 94, 134
childhood conditioning
  and constant need to be entertained,
    138
  core beliefs, 93, 316
  and emotional desires as impasse,
    131–132
  emotional suffering and, 90, 92, 93,
    94, 95, 96
  and expectations, 261–262, 266–267,
    271, 283
  healing of, and overcoming emotions,
    90
  and lost, feelings of being, 293, 295
  negative attitudes and, 316
  and obstacles, spiritual, 177, 187, 190
  perfectionism and, 128
  personality arising from, 127
  and speaking consciously, 13
  and will, lack of, 134
  See also psychological blocks;
    psychotherapy
children
  and choice of spiritual path, 69
  karma and, 220–221
  reprimanding, 258
  vibration of caring for, 29
  See also family
clairaudience, 118, 137
clairvoyance
  and colors of the subtle world, 39
  defined, 321
  and recall of higher world
    experiences, 118
  teacher needed for guidance with, 137
  of teacher, requiring permission from
    student, 83
cleansing the surroundings
  of anger and arguments, 28, 258
  with aromatherapy, 257–258
  aura cleansing, 24, 26–27, 294

Buddha to help with, 115
of depression/negative vibrations, 161,
    257–259
elementals and need for, 27–28
elementals requested to change
    vibration, 32
of entities, 114–115
with incense and burning herbs, 27,
    28, 114–115, 257–258
leaving the space, 28
with light vibrations, 27–28
with mantra, 28s
of murder or abuse, 28
with nature, 258
by repainting the walls, 28
with roses, 25, 114, 257–258
teachers helping with, 28–29, 115
by washing walls with camphor and
    eucalyptus, 28
of workplace, 259
See also protection
clutter, entities attracted by, 115
color
and clairvoyance, 39
and demand to see light when
    approached by a being, 37, 120
for holding the wisdom symbol, 175
and lack of striving, recovery from, 41
luminous, 37–38
and subtle-plane meditation, 38–40,
    117, 120
and symbols, 39–40
commitment, need for, 56, 81
community
as focus in New Age, 65
Subtle Plane and building of, 116–117
See also aloneness as necessary part
    of the spiritual path; service in the
    world; spiritual family; students;
    teachers
compassion, viii, 9, 10, 16, 72, 89, 260,
292, 319
competitiveness, as obstacle, 128,
186–188
concentration, need for, 29, 29–31
control issues (authority issues), 95,
140–141, 280
core beliefs, 93, 316
cosmic law, vs. relativity of information,
233
Cosmic Principles, change and, 46
creativity, as outlet for sexual energy,
209
crowds, protection from negative

vibrations in, 25

Dalai Lama, 232
darkness. See light
death
attachments and, 149–150
flashback of important events prior
    to, 138
ghosts, 28, 115–116, 117, 162, 229
and loved ones, 149–150
near-death experiences, 194
and nonattachment, 147–148, 150–151
of other person in negative karma
    relationship, 164
and tasks, unfinished, 150, 151
of teacher, and ongoing relationship
    with student, 137
as truth, acceptance of, 194
Western denial of, 151
See also death as a stage; grief
death as a stage, 146–156
acceptance of, as process, 148–151,
    156
acceptance of, obstacles preventing,
    149–151
beyond death, stage of, 154–155
change and, 146–147
cycle of life and, and evolutionary
    path of the individual, 147
discrimination and, 154
and divine desire, 147–148
and energy, conservation of, 146
grief of loved ones, as obstacle,
    149–150
grief transformed by awareness of,
    164–165
no beginning and no end of life, 146
and personal desires, 147–148
as renewal, 156
and stages of life, examination of,
    151–156
See also rebirth
decision making
and commitment, lack of, 56
desire body and, 58
ending relationships, 59
excessive thinking about, as waste of
    time, 55–56, 58
failure to make, 61
fear and, 60, 61
gender and, 56
intuition and. See intuition
karma and, 58–62
"maybe" as answer to, 55

mistakes in, learning from, 60–62
others involved in, 59
past-life relationships and, 59–60
patterns of response and, 56–58
and the rational mind, 104, 105, 110
self-discipline and, 58
democracy, 47
depression (sadness), 157–165
action as transforming, 164
emotional suffering as cause of, 90
entity presence and, 114
exercise to prepare for, 164–165
as halting progress on path, 157, 159
and humor, 161
immobility arising from, 96
lack of sunlight and, 34–35
letting go of, 163–165
medication for, 90, 96, 317
negative vibrations of, 161
others' feelings, sympathy with, 165
and physical illness, 90
psychotherapy and, 317
and suicide, 90, 97
teacher removing, 85, 161–162
transforming of, 160–165
trigger subjects and, 162
and the will, strength of, 211
See also grief; self-pity
desire body
and boundaries of the heart, 228–229
decision making and, 58
excessive need for joy as, 138
expectations as, 261, 266
holding the wisdom and avoidance of, 175–176
impersonating the HS, vi–vii
interfering with HS messages, v
Kama Loka and playing out of, 147, 154, 322
and life-stage strategizing, protecting against, 153
and lower being impersonating Higher Being, 120
multiple relationships and focus on, 208
Path of Higher Mind and curtailing of, 73
rebirth and fulfillment of, 147–148
sexual, as stronger in spiritual person, 209
speaking consciously and, 14
See also asceticism; disidentification; impasses; obstacles
destined disciple, 178

destiny, 220–226
changing of, process for, 224–226
energies arising to help return to, 221–222
evolution and, 46
following of, vs. sidetrack, exercise to determine, 222
free will and, 50–51, 221, 222–224
and God Consciousness, achievement of, 244
and karma, 190, 222–225
and negative karma, 222–223
as planned, 222
and the spiritual path, 190, 220–222
and suicide, 96–97
and switching to another path, 140
and teachers, finding, 81–82, 178
and withdrawal from the path, 309
and work, 182, 190, 224
detachment. *See* disidentification; nonattachment
Determination, Path of, 77–78
Devachan, 147–148, 321
devas
defined, 321
elementals as guided by, 321
and lost, feelings of being, 304
and vibrations, healing of, 161
See also elementals; nature spirits
Devotion, Path of, 75
dharma
defined, 321
karma as barrier to knowing, 220–221
and Path of Illumination, 70
See also world: being in it but not of it
diet
eating problems, 134–135
food addiction, 94–95
meditation and, 122
and prana, 211
discrimination
and boundaries of the heart, 228, 229, 230, 232
and death as a stage, 154
to distinguishe between Higher and lower beings, 120
and free will, 51–52
and holding the wisdom, 173–174
and karmic relationships with other students, 86–87
and working in the world, 247
disidentification
and casual affairs, 208

and death, acceptance of, 149–151,
    156
defined, 321
and expectations, reaction to, 276–
    277, 285
from feelings arising from lower self,
    27
and lost, feelings of being, 295
and love, beyond the personal,
    214–215
of love, boundaries and, 230–232
and material objects, 134, 150
from mood, 85
and negative karma, 9
as observation, 53–54
and observation of change, 53–54
and obstacles, spiritual, 191
and the Path of Love, 72
perfectionism and, 129
from physical pain, 89–90
and relationships, 150
from shadow side, vi
suffering as inability to achieve, 89
and truth, 54
from work, youth and, 151
See also attachments; nonattachment
Divine. See God Consciousness
divorce, and negative karma, 101
dreams. See sleep and dreaming

Earth, evolution of, 45, 147, 176
eating problems, 134–135
ecstasy, Samadhi distinguished from,
    130
ego self
    awareness of, as goal, 3
    and belief that a teacher is not
        needed, 80, 81
    and belief that the goal is too difficult,
        190
    and fame, need for, 133
    and fantasy life as impasse, 137
    inflation of, as clouding HS, 180
    and lost, feelings of being, 297
    and pride, spiritual, 269
    and psychological blocks as obstacle,
        179
    and satisfaction in your spiritual
        work, 216
    success and, 180, 181
    See also identity; lower self;
        psychological blocks
elementals
    asking for help from, to clear

vibrations, 31–32, 161
careless speech affecting, 2
and death and rebirth of plants,
    146–147
defined, 321
light vibrations and cleansing of, 27,
    28
negative, commanding to leave, 24
sound moderated by, 1
and storms, 32, 33
See also nature spirits
elements, light energy and, 34
emotional suffering, 90–98
    addiction caused by, 94–95
    anger, 92–93
    attracting abuse, 93–94
    attracting dysfunction, 94
    childhood conditioning and, 90, 92,
        93, 94, 95, 96
    core beliefs, 93
    depression caused by, 90
    dysfunction caused by, 94
    extreme needs, imbalance caused by,
        95–96
    fear, 91, 94
    freedom from, 97
    identification of, and working on,
        97–98
    immobility caused by, 96
    inner wounds, 93, 98
    life-threatening, 96–97
    loss, 91–92
    mental illness caused by, 94
    not expressing feelings, 90, 98
    past lives and, 90, 92, 93, 94
    physical illness caused by, 96
    physical pain caused by, 90
    positive emotions, 97
    self-pity, 92
    stubbornness coming from, 95
    therapy to work through, 98
    See also obstacles
emotions
    asking HS to remove, vi
    control of, need for, as impasse,
        142–143
    dissolving of, and resolution of
        blocked situations, 201
    excessive desires of, as impasse,
        131–132
    and expectations, reactions to,
        276–277
    of initiate, power of, 248–249
    and lower nature, attachment to, 27

of others, sympathy with, 165
positive, achievement of, 97
vibrations of, 1, 24, 248–249
See also abandonment, feelings of;
  anger; childhood conditioning;
  depression; emotional suffering;
  fear; gratitude; grief; insecurity;
  lost, feelings of being; mood;
  negative feelings
energy
  of expectation, vs. energy of
    cooperation, 264–265, 276, 280–
    281, 283
  of HS, as warm and expansive, vii
  information and, 232–233
  of light, 34–37, 43
  as result of entering a spiritual path,
    304
  as result of vibration, 23
  symbols as representation of, 174
  of thoughts, 10
  of words, and conscious speaking, 5,
    7, 9–10
  See also prana; sexual energy
entertainment, need for, 138–139
enthusiasm, waning, 124
entities
  defined, 114
  dirty and cluttered home attracting,
    115
  effects of, 114, 115
  ghosts distinguished from, 115–116
  inner child producing experience
    like, 115
  vs. lower nature, 114
  negativity attracting, 114–115
  purifying against, 114–115
  See also negative forces
environment, as obstacle, 257–259
  See also cleansing the surroundings;
    home; work and workplace
esoteric studies, 166, 321
ethics, and being in the world, 245,
  246–247
eucalyptus, cleansing home with, 28
Euphoric Aroma Diffuser oil, 257
evolution
  and change, ability for, 48–54
  change as underlying force of,
    193–194
  destiny and, 46
  extinction of species and, 45–46
  human condition as hampering, 54
  light energy and, 34, 37

from light to physicality to light
  again, 47–48
physical change over time, 44–45, 46
of the planet, 45, 147, 176
and rebirth, cycle of, 147
of seed strains, 45–46
spirit propelling, 46
subtle world and, 46–47
truth as relative to period of, 232–233
wisdom and, 166, 176
exercise
  excesses in, 130
  lack of, 130
  prana and, 211
exoteric, defined, 321
expectations
  asking and being asked for help
    instead of, 281–283
  as attachment, 272, 284, 285
  balance in relationships and, 273, 275
  and boundaries, establishment of, 273
  childhood conditioning as source of,
    261–262, 266–267, 271, 283
  denial of existence of, 273–274
  disappointment with others, 273–275
  disidentification and calmness and,
    276–277, 285
  energy of, vs. energy of cooperation,
    264–265, 276, 280–281, 283
  of freedom in subtle world, 227–228
  hoping vs., 280–281
  identification and transmutation of,
    266–271
  karma and, 137–138, 283, 284–285
  of love relationships, 284–285
  as obstacle, 265
  past lives as source of, 271–272
  pattern of, overcoming, 142–143, 265,
    266, 269–270, 271–273
  as personal desire, 261, 266
  and resentment of help given to
    others, 264
  and rigidity in life, 278–280
  of self, 277–280
  of self, by others, 268–269, 272–277
  and shift in personal relationships,
    270–271
  and task sharing, 274–276
  of teacher and Master, 262–265
  willingness to let go of, 271
  workaholics and, 275–276
  See also perfectionism
extraterrestrials, Mental Plane and, 119

facing truth. *See* truth
fame, desire for, 132–133
family
  arguments and fighting among,
    20–21, 258
  attachment to, and death process,
    149–150
  and depression, 157–159, 160
  and disharmonious vibrations, 24,
    258
  and entertainment, need for, 138
  excessive emotional needs and, 131,
    132
  speaking consciously and, 20–22
  and will, lack of, 134
  See also childhood conditioning;
    children; marriage; spiritual family
fanaticism
  and boundaries, 236–237
  expectations and, 279
  self-discipline as, 59
  spiritual subpersonality and, 277–278
  and unfulfilled sexual energy, 209
  See also perfectionism
fantasy life
  getting carried away in, as impasse,
    136–138
  judging others on, 138
  and subtle world meditation, 121
  See also truth
fears
  asking HS for a step-by-step process
    to remove, viii
  asking HS to remove, vi
  of decision making, 60, 61
  and difficulty finding a teacher, 82
  entities causing, 115
  ghosts causing, 115
  as obstacle of emotional suffering,
    91, 94
  as obstacle stemming from past lives,
    101–103
  as obstacle to acceptance of death,
    149, 155
  physical ailments caused by, 94
  of power and authority, as impasse,
    140–141
  of revealing oneself to a teacher, 86
  speaking consciously to overcome, 11
  of the unknown, 194–195, 200
  See also emotions; lost, feelings of
    being
Feminine Principle
  defined, 321

HS coming from combination of,
  with Masculine Principle, 109–110
intuition and, 104, 105, 107, 109–110
repression of, 107
fiery world, defined, 321
flowers, as protective, 25, 114, 115
food addiction, 122
free will
  and action based on intuition, 101
  and color, working with, 40
  depression despite strength of, 211
  destiny and, 50–51, 221, 222–224
  focusing of, 249
  heart energy distinguished from, 249
  and heart, used in combination,
    251–256
  and karma, breaking of, 51, 183
  lack of strong, as impasse, 134–135
  and leave of absence, returning from,
    140
  light as activated by, 41
  mistaken for heart, 249
  negative thoughts defeated via, 41
  of nonspiritual partner, 185
  pain control and, 90
  and Path of Illumination, 70
  sexual energy and the development
    of, 209–211
  use of, correct, 51–52
  See also striving
freedom
  of aloneness, 296
  and control of negative emotions, 97
  disidentification as path to, 129
  and expectations, letting go of, 285
  facing of self and, 53
  self-control leading to, 142
  of subtle world, as expectation,
    227–228
  See also free will
friends and friendships
  and adventure, 197
  asking and being asked for help,
    281–283
  and being in the world, 259–260
  and boundaries, 231
  expectations and, 273, 281–283
  and grief as obstacle, 149–150
  and human need for love, 213
  and lost, feelings of being, 292
  with Masters, 265
  and talking about the teaching,
    173–174
  with teachers, 86

and vibrations, 27, 248–249, 258–259
See also relationships

Garden Exercise, xii–xiii
gender
 and personification of HS, v
 use of, in text, iv
 See also Feminine Principle;
  Masculine Principle
ghosts, 28, 115–116, 117, 162, 229
glass bell as protection, 259, 294
goals
 as daily practice, 41–43
 of God Consciousness vs. HS, 63–64
 and God within, 243–244
 seeing as too difficult, as obstacle,
  189–191
God Consciousness
 aloneness arising from longing for,
  287–288
 and death, preparation for, 151
 desire of longing for, and rebirth,
  147–148
 as goal, vs. HS, 63–64
 and God within, experience of,
  243–244
 and the journey, 310–314, 319
 lack of desire for, as impasse, 124,
  126, 135–136
 Path of Higher Mind and fallacies
  of, 74
 See also God within
God within
 difficulty in believing in, 242
 and the Divine as unmanifested
  energy, 241
 experience of, 242–244
 and goal of achieving God
  Consciousness, 243–244
 "God" as term, 238
 and inner beliefs about God, 240–241
 as symbol, 243
 vs. external conceptions of God,
  238–239
 and wisdom, finding of, 239–240, 244
 worshipping as concept and, 241–242
good and evil, representations of, 36–37
good, as term, 4
good deeds. *See* service in the world
gratitude
 as daily practice, 315
 to elementals, 31
 for help given, 264–265
 to Masters, 235, 264

to nature spirits, 258–259
and teacher as pathfinder, 88
greed, as impasse, 133–134
grief
 ghosts and, 162
 healthy expression of, 162–163
 letting go of, 163–165
 and memories, 163–164
 in the presence of the dying, 149–150
 and regrets, 164
 See also death
gross body. *See* physical body
Guide
 assistance given by, 108–109
 defined, 108, 322
 intuition distinguished from, 108–109
 voice of, as never critical, 109
guilt feelings, death and, 164

health
 and ability to access the subtle planes,
  38
 and sorrow, 165
 See also mental illness; physical
  illness
heart chakra
 desires of, and working with subtle
  planes, 40
 linking with, HS appearing in
  response to, vii
 linking with, to reestablish
  communication with HS, vi, vii
 location of, vi
 operation of HS dependent on, vii
 personal love and opening of, 183,
  203–204, 206–207, 213, 215
 sensory forms of HS and essential
  link to, vii
 strengthening of connection with HS
  and, vii–viii
heart energy
 focusing of, 249–251
 mind as distinguished from, 251
 used in combination with focused
  will, 251–256
 the will as distinguished from, 249
heart energy, connection to
 and boundaries, need for, 228–232
 focused heart distinguished from, 250
 and holding the wisdom with symbol,
  175
 love relationships and, 183
 and nature of karmic relationship,
  determining, 99

and neglect of path, 126
and Path of Love, 72
speaking consciously and, 5, 6, 9, 10
spiritual goals coming from, vs.
    subpersonality, 278
and striving, recovery of, 41
and surprises on journey, 317
and truth, assessment of, 39
herbs for cleansing. *See* aromatherapy;
incense
hermit, desire for isolation as, 132
Hierarchy, defined, 322
Higher Astral Plane (subtle plane), 112,
116–118
    asking for help on, 116
    colors on, 117
    community building lessons on,
        116–117
    Devachan, 147–148, 321
    distinguished from lower planes,
        117–118
    as endless, 117
    helper (Higher Being) on, 116
    initiations on, 137
    Kama Loka, 147, 154, 322
    meditation practice to achieve, 118
    memory of, asking for, 118
    nature and, 117
    notes on experiences in, 118
    sounds on, 117
Higher Beings
    and God within, 241–242
    and the higher planes, 112, 116
    impersonated by lower beings, 120
    information from, verifying, 39, 233
    karma of, 119–120
    teacher verifying, 120
Higher Mind, Path of, 73–74
Higher Self
    acknowledgement by self of, viii
    awareness of, as goal, 3
    defined, iii, 322
    energy of, as warm and expansive, vii
    exercises for connection with, ix–xiv
    from Feminine and Masculine
        Principles working together,
        100–110
    forms of, v, vi, vii
    and intuition, 106–107, 109–111
    mirroring, 6
    and other students, karma with, 87
    problems in life assisted by, v–vi
    reestablishing contact with, 294–295
    and the spirit of the individual, viii

strengthening of, via use of, vi, vii–
    viii, 43
strengthening of, with each lifetime,
    110
symbol or saying to remind about, 43
and vibrations, protection from, 25,
    161
See also heart chakra; Higher Self,
    communication with; Higher Self
    guidance, about
Higher Self, communication with
    cold feeling in chest during, vii
    deception and, vii
    delayed answers, v
    disappearance of HS during, vi
    experience of, as sensory vs. verbal, v
    forms of HS and, v, vi, vii
    games of HS and, vii
    as gentle and loving, vii
    information presented during,
        readiness for, vii
    shining a light on HS, to test, vi–vii
    signals for, v
    symbol for HS, asking for, viii
    symbols revealed but not understood,
        vii
    warm expansive feelings as evidence
        of, vii
Higher Self guidance, about
    blocks to making lifestyle changes,
        199, 201
    excessive emotional needs, 132
    expectations, identification and
        transmutation of, 263
    fears stemming from past lives, 102
    free will vs. destiny, 223–224
    holding the wisdom, 175–176
    impasses, overcoming, 145
    intuition, use of, 110–111
    lost, feelings of, 292–293
    sadness, preparation for, 165
    self-pity, 160
    stages of life, strategizing, 152,
        154–156
    teacher, development of relationship
        with, 88
    teacher, verification of choice of, 84
    time frame of progress on path,
        179–180
    truth, recognition of, 37, 84
Higher Self Yoga
    asceticism not part of, 212
    based on Agni Yoga and Theosophy,
        169

as method of union with the Source,
    iii–iv
psychological growth emphasized
    in, iv
See also spiritual path
higher worlds
    defined, 322
    distinguished from lower planes,
        117–118
    gifts of, 117
    See also Higher Astral Plane (subtle
        plane)
holding the wisdom. *See* wisdom,
holding the
home
    in city vs. country, 257
    clean, and communication with
        Masters, 235–236
    dirty and cluttered, entities attracted
        by, 115
    dirty and cluttered, perfectionist
        pattern and, 129
    leaving, to avoid negative vibrations,
        28
    and Path of Illumination, 70
    redecoration of, 197–199
    repainting, 28
    tranquil, need for, 257–259
    See also cleansing the surroundings;
        protection
hoping, vs. expectations, 280–281
House Exercise, xiii–xiv
humanitarianism, 72, 74, 76–77
humor
    depression and, 161
    and negative karma, 206

identity
    and aloneness as part of the path,
        301–302
    and greed, 133–134
    and lost, feelings of being, 301–302
    perfectionism as, 128–129
    See also disidentification
illness. *See* mental illness; physical
illness
Illumination, Path of, 70–71
illusion. *See* fantasy life
immobility, as emotional suffering, 96
impasses, 123–145
    easier path, desire for, 139–140
    emotional desires, 131–132
    emotions, control of, 142–143
    fame, desire for, 132–133

fantasy life, 136–138
God Consciousness, weakened desire
    for, 124, 126, 135–136
greed for material objects, 133–134
Higher Self for guidance with, 145
leave of absence, desire for, 140, 144
leaving a spiritual teaching because
    of, 123
obstacles distinguished from, 177
perfectionism, 124, 126–129
physical desires, 129–131
pleasure, excessive desire for, 138–139
power and authority, fear of, 140–141
recognition of, 144–145
signs of, 124–125
teacher help with, 126, 144–145
and teacher, relationship with,
    124–125
time for overcoming, 145
too busy, 124–126
will, lack of, 134–135
wisdom, weakened desire for, 143–
    144
See also obstacles
incense, cleansing with, 27, 28, 114–115,
257–258
independence, excessive, 132
individuality. *See* soul
information
    source of, discrimination and, 233
    truth of, as relative to evolutionary
        period, 232–233
initiate, defined, 322
initiations
    attachment to, and death process, 151
    defined, 322
    expectations and, 262–263
    first, in physical plane, 137
    psychological blocks as obstacle to,
        178–179
    and satisfaction in your spiritual
        work, 216
    on subtle plane, 137
    and uniqueness of each student's
        path, 286–287
inner child
    addiction and, 95
    and core beliefs, 93
    entity-like experiences produced by,
        115
    and love, desire for personal, 214
    and taking remarks personally,
        302–303
    therapy for work with, 98

wounds of, as emotional suffering,
    93, 98
wounds of, physical ailments caused
    by, 94
inner power, fear of, as impasse, 140–141
insecurity
    and alienation from the group, 302
    and attachment to lower nature, 27
    expectations caused by, 284
    facing, 200
    and spiritual superiority, 188
    See also emotions
instinct, distinguished from intuition,
    106
Internet, 52–53
intuition
    capacity for, exercise to determine,
        105
    defined, 106
    development of, exercises for, 107–
        108, 110–111
    and the Feminine Principle, 104, 105,
        107, 109–110
    the Guide distinguished from,
        108–109
    the HS and, 106–107, 109–111
    instinct distinguished from, 106
    karmic relationships recognized by, 8
    negative karma and, 106
    rational mind combined with,
        105–106
    vs. rational mind decision making,
        104, 105, 110
    strengthened by acting upon, 105
    timing and, 104–105
    truth recognized by, 106
    verification of, via Higher Self, 111
    the will and, 105

Jesus Christ, 115, 286
journal keeping, 103, 118, 121, 126
journey on the spiritual path, 307–320
    and aloneness, 320
    attachments and skandhas and, 310,
        319
    and attitude, negative or positive,
        314–317
    and change, 319
    as easy or difficult, 309–310
    end of, 319–320
    and God Consciousness, desire for,
        310–314, 319
    and guidance, 320
    and judgments, 320

and karma, 319
outside help needed for problems on,
    317
Pollyanna pattern and, 316, 317
and rhythm of movement, 320
as short or long, 310, 319
small steps and, 320
and spiritual family, 320
stories to illustrate, 306–307, 310–314
and striving, 320
surprises on, positive and negative,
    317–319
as symbol, 308–309
and tests of path, 319
uniqueness of, 314, 320
See also spiritual path
joy
    excessive need for, as impasse,
        138–139
    flexibility vs. patterns and, 201–202
    as higher state (Joy), 138
judging others, avoidance of, 138, 320

Kama Loka, 147, 154, 322
karma
    as barrier to knowing dharma,
        220–221
    being in the world and avoiding, 246
    change as seed of, 49–50
    and change in life plans, 154
    decision making and, 58–62
    destiny and, 190, 222–225
    and excesses of one life continued to
        future, 51–52
    expectations and, 137–138, 283,
        284–285
    of Higher Beings, 119–120
    illness as caused by, 223
    as instantly created, 9
    power and authority issues and, 141
    truth distinguished from, 7–8
    vibrations as causing, 1
    See also destiny; karmic
        relationships; rebirth
karmic relationships
    and attraction, nature of, 204, 205
    boundaries as essential to, 205–206
    and choosing a spiritual path, 69
    determining negative or positive
        nature of, 8, 99–100, 183–184
    families and, 20–21
    and finding a teacher, 82, 84
    lightheartedness as helpful to, 206
    as obstacle to overcome, 98–101

with other students of teacher, 86–87
personal love and, 183–184, 204,
    205–206
reflection of old life vs. truth of
    present life, determining of, 7–9
speaking consciously and, 7–9
and vigilance, 9
See also attraction, nature of, and
    negative karma; negative karma;
    past-life relationships; positive
    karma
know-it-alls, 128
Kumara, defined, 322
Kundalini Yoga, 209

Lake Exercise, xiii
language. *See* speaking consciously
laughter, vibrations of, 1
lavender, 257–258
Lavender Aroma Diffuser oil, 257
lemon grass, 258
lifestyle changes
    blocks in making, 154, 155–156
    truth and, 196–199
light
    color of, 37–38, 39
    and creativity, 41
    energy of, 34–37, 43
    as essence of striving, 41
    magnetic properties of, 37–38
    and the subtle body, 38–40, 43
    and subtle world meditation, 120–121
    vibrations of, protecting and
        cleansing with, 27–28
    See also light, demanding to see, if a
        being speaks or appears
light, demanding to see, if a being
speaks or appears
    blocks or fears, removal of, vi
    color seen, 37, 120
    demand to leave if no light shown,
        vi–vii, 39
    and desire body as impersonating HS,
        vi–vii, 153
    heart connection and, 37, 39, 229
    and help asked for by being, 229
    and Higher Self, communication
        with, vi–vii, 153
    knowing one's own level of
        consciousness and, 37
    retesting to ensure light is present,
        vi–vii, 153
    sound heard, 121
    and teacher or Master appearing, 229

technique for, 120–121
truth of, teacher as verifying, 39
waves of light, 120–121
loneliness. *See* aloneness as necessary
part of the spiritual path; lost, feelings
of being
loss, as emotional suffering, 91–92
lost, feelings of being
    and abandonment feelings, 292, 295
    as brief, 305
    childhood conditioning as cause of,
        293, 295
    defined, 292
    experience of feelings, list of, 291
    and friendships, strain on, 292
    and the group, feelings outside of,
        302–303
    helping another student with,
        293–294
    and the HS, reestablishing contact
        with, 294–295
    and identity, 301–302
    and memories, need for, 306
    negative aspects of being alone, 296
    negative forces and, 286, 293, 297–300
    overcoming, methods for, 304–305
    past lives as cause of, 293, 295,
        303–304
    positive aspects of being alone, 296
    recognition of feeling, 292–293, 295
    and relationships, strain on, 292
    sources of, analysis of, 295–297
    stories to illustrate, 288–290, 297–
        300, 305–306
    stuck in the emotion, 295
    withdrawal from path and, 293
    See also aloneness as necessary part
        of the spiritual path; emotions
lost objects, the Guide and assistance
with, 108–109
Love. *See* Source/Wisdom/Love
love, lack of personal, 206–215
    and asceticism, limits of, 211–213
    exercise for assessment of, 214
    fear of, and questioning of spiritual
        path, 219–220
    karmic implications of, denial of,
        207–209
    and negative emotions as impasse,
        207
    and service in the world, 215
    sexual energy and, 209–211, 213
    and teacher relationships, difficulty
        with, 207

and using the teaching as a substitute,
    213–214
  See also love, personal
Love, Path of, 72–73
love, personal, 203–215
  conditional, as need for something in
    return, 230–232
  as distraction, useful, 207
  and emotional excess as impasse, 131
  emotions as part of, 204
  as energy, 284
  enlightenment path and need to
    experience, 203–204, 214–215
  expectations of, 284–285
  and heart chakra, opening of, 183,
    203–204, 206–207, 213, 215
  as human need, 203, 213, 214–215
  hurting the other and, 204
  ideal/genuine relationships, 204–205,
    206
  and insecurity, 284
  karmic relationships, 183–184, 204,
    205–206
  multiple relationships and casual
    affairs, 207–208
  with nonspiritual/unsympathetic
    partner, 182–186
  as obstacle in path, 182–186
  overpowering with, 230
  psychological patterns exposed via,
    183
  rejection, 284
  resentment of partner for spiritual
    path, 182, 184–186
  students, affairs or marriage with
    other, 208–209
  as test of path, 183
  unrequited, 204, 284
  See also attraction, nature of, and
    negative karma; boundaries,
    personal; love, lack of personal;
    negative karma; relationships;
    sexual behavior
Lower Astral Plane(s), 112, 114–116
  and boundaries of the heart, 229
  channeling and, 136
  distinguished from higher worlds,
    117–118
  multiple levels of, 114
  See also entities
lower beings
  impersonating Higher Beings, 120
  as targeting those on spiritual path,
    116

See also negative beings
lower self
  awareness of, as goal, 3
  entities attracted by, 114–115
  feelings that anchor one in, 27
  and free will, 51
  and loss of desire for God
    Consciousness, 135
  and satisfaction in your spiritual
    work, 216
  See also ego self

magnetic properties, of light in the
  subtle world, 37–38
mantras
  AUM, 1, 321
  and cleansing home, 28
  defined, 322
  power of, 10
Manvantara, 37
marriage
  with another student, 208–209
  and depression, 160
  and destiny, 221
  expectations and, 261, 272–273
  and negative karma, 100–101,
    183–184
  See also family; love, personal;
    relationships
Masculine Principle
  defined, 322–323
  HS coming from combination of,
    with Feminine Principle, 109–110
  and intuition, lack of development of,
    107, 110
  and repression of the Feminine
    Principle, 107
Masters
  and aloneness as necessary part of
    path, 293
  appearing during meditation,
    demanding light from, 229
  boundaries with, 235–236
  clean home and communication with,
    235–236
  defined, 323
  and dharma of students, 132–133
  direct messages from, 136–137
  and expectations, 264–265
  as friends, 265
  gratitude for, 235, 264
  as Hierarchy, 322
  initiation readiness determined, by,
    322

jealousy of, as obstacle, 188
and the journey, 309, 320
need for recognition from, as
    obstacle, 188–189
and perfection, 127
striving of, 216
and teacher's knowledge, 127
See also spiritual family; students;
    teachers
material objects
    the death process and attachment to,
        149, 150
    depression and loss of, 165
    disidentification and, 134, 150
    greed for, as impasse, 133–134
    and home decluttering and
        redecoration, 197–199
    lost, finding of, 108–109
    nonattachment and enjoyment of,
        134, 150, 212
Meadow Exercise, x–xi
meditation
    and alcohol or drug abuse, 121–122
    aura cleansing and enhancing with,
        24, 26–27
    and color visuals, 38–40, 117, 120
    forgetting about, 124–125
    and holding the wisdom with a
        symbol, 175
    increase in numbers of people
        practicing, 38
    and lightness/darkness, experience of,
        37–38, 39
    memory of experiences during,
        asking for, 118
    nature spirits as pleased by, 258–259
    pain and discomfort during, 38
    prana restoration, 211
    rigidity and expectations and,
        278–280
    and sexual drive, 209
    subtle body refined through, 142
    and subtle world travel, 113, 116, 118,
        120–121
    and "the Sun behind the sun," 38
    and words in the mind, 9
memory and memories
    death and sadness and, 163–164
    feelings of being lost, and need for,
        306
    forgetting and neglect of the path,
        124–126
    of higher worlds, asking to remember
        experiences of, 118

holding the wisdom and, 170
loss of, and lack of knowledge
    retention, 169
mental illness, child abuse or
conditioning and, 94
    See also depression
Mental Plane, 112–113, 118–119
mind
    combined with intuition, 105–106
    decision making based on, 104, 105,
        110
    esoteric learning and, 166, 169, 175
    freeing of, from words, 9
    and heart concentration, 251
    heart distinguished from, 251
    inner, speaking consciously as
        doorway to, 9
    and the journey, 319, 320
    negative karma and focus of, 8
    Path of Higher Mind, 73–74
    and Path of Love, 72
    See also attachment; awareness;
        decision making; disidentification;
        free will; obstacles; thoughts
mirroring others, conscious speaking
and, 6
missions
    of Buddha, 203–204
    envy of, 186–187
    as factor in spiritual path, 155, 220
    help with, 264
    and losing sight of reality, 136
    negative emotions interfering with,
        186–187
    past lives as basis for, 186
    secrecy of, 186–187
    of teacher, and demands of time from,
        228
    See also service in the world; work
        and workplace; world: being in it
        but not of it
molecules, 23, 34
Monad, 46, 138, 323
mood
    disidentification from, 85
    light energy and, 34
    storms and, 32
    student responsibility for, 85
motion, as cause of vibrations, 23
Mountain Exercise, ix–x
murder, cleansing a space of, 28
music, vibrations of, 31

narcissism, 131–132

nature
  activities in, as outlet for sexual
    energy, 209
  appreciation of, 41–42, 197
  and arguments, vibrations of, 258
  and depression, addressing, 161
  and lost, feelings of being, 304
  Subtle Plane and, 117
  and tranquil home, 257
  use of wisdom gained from, 167
nature spirits
  elementals as guided by, 321
  etiquette of interaction with, 233–234
  and evolution, 46–47
  gratitude for, 258–259
  and meditation as pleasing to,
    258–259
near-death experiences, 194
negative beings
  encountered in meditation, 37
  targeting those on spiritual path, 80,
    116
  See also lower beings
negative feelings
  envy of others' mission, 186–187
  protecting oneself from others,' 294
  working through, 27
  See also depression; emotions
negative forces
  aloneness as part of the path
    exploited by, 286, 293
  channeling and, 136
  entities used by, 114
  holding the wisdom and dealing with,
    167
  lack of, in the higher worlds, 37
  and lost, feelings of being, 286, 293,
    297–300
  and need for teacher on path, 80
  and need to feel special, 137
  and neglect of the path, 125–126
  and Path of Illumination, 71
  procrastination as influence of,
    189–190
  and questioning the path, 219
  and satisfaction in your spiritual
    work, 216
  vigilance and overcoming of, 297
  and worldly success, 181
  See also entities
negative karma
  and arguments in family, 20–21
  death of other person, 164
  decision making and creation of,

58–62
  depression and creation of, 162
  and destiny, 222–223
  determining nature of relationship,
    8–9, 14–15, 99–100, 106, 183–184
  and emotions, need for control of, 142
  ending, 8, 15, 99–101, 183–184
  and esoteric knowledge, abuse of, 174
  and expectations of love, 284–285
  and family dynamics, 157–160
  good deeds as overcoming, 138
  intuition and, 106
  lightheartedness as helpful to, 206
  marriage and, 100–101, 183–184
  and mind, need for focus of, 8
  multiple relationships and casual
    affairs and, 207–208
  playing it out, 8, 183
  seeds of, 101–102
  service in the world as overcoming,
    138
  and sojourn between lives, 147
  speaking consciously and, 8–9, 14
  the will as changing, 222–223
  working with the other person to
    explore nature of, 100
  and the world, being of but not in it,
    246–247
  See also abusive relationships;
    attraction, nature of, and negative
    karma
negative thoughts
  defined, 41
  entities attracted by, 114–115
  the heart and refusal of, 41
  negative past lives and, 101
  and neglect of the path, 125–126
  pull of, and strengthening of HS, vi
  transformation of, vi, 161–162
  the will and refusal of, 41
  withdrawal from path and, 218
neglect of path, 124–126
Nirvanic Plane, 112, 119
nonattachment
  and death, 147–148, 150–151
  and material possessions/success in
    the world, 134, 150, 212
  and striving spiritually, 151
  and work, 151
  See also attachments;
    disidentification

obesity, 122
obsessive-compulsive behavior, 94

obstacles
  entering spiritual practice as forcing
    to arise, 89
  expectations as, 265
  impasses distinguished from, 177
  journal keeping and, 103
  karmic relationships, 98–101
  negative attitudes as, 316
  negative forces and, 297
  and past lives, fears stemming from,
    101–103
  physical environment as, 257–259
  returning in different forms, 103
  social customs, falling into, 256–257
  suffering, emotional. *See* emotional
    suffering
  suffering, physical, 89–90
  "through the obstacles you grow," 89
  and yearning to return to the higher
    worlds, 117
  See also impasses; lost, feelings
    of being; obstacles (spiritual);
    withdrawal from spiritual path
obstacles (spiritual)
  childhood conditioning and, 177, 187,
    190
  disidentification and, 191
  impasses distinguished from, 177
  seeing the goal as too difficult to
    achieve, 189–191
  spiritual subpersonality and
    expectations, 277–280
  too many desires in love
    relationships, 182–186
  too many desires in the mundane
    world, 180–182
  wanting acknowledgment from the
    Masters, 188–189
  wanting prestige and recognition
    from other students, 186–188
  wanting to grow faster than you are
    ready, 178–180
odors, entities causing, 115
opportunity
  alone time as, 53
  change as, 52–54
  taking advantage of, 54
optimism, 11
Origins
  as mystery, 44
  See also evolution

pain
  disidentification from, 89–90

emotional suffering as cause of, 90
teacher removing, during meditation,
    38
the past, observation of, vs. dwelling on,
    49–50
past-life relationships
  consciously speaking and, 7–9, 13,
    14, 20
  decision making issues involving,
    59–60
  See also karmic relationships
past lives
  asceticism stemming from, 211
  emotional suffering and, 90, 92, 93, 94
  excessive emotional needs originating
    in, 132
  fears stemming from, as obstacle to
    overcome, 101–103
  form of HS in guise of, vii
  and God within, 240
  and lost, feelings of being, 293, 295,
    303–304
  negative attitudes and, 316
  negative lives as negative seeds,
    101–102
  power and authority issues and, 141
  religion as destructive in, 219–220
  subtle body as accumulation of, 113,
    122
  therapy for (past-life regression), 102
  and will, lack of, 134
  See also karmic relationships
path. *See* spiritual path
patience, 6, 17
patterns
  awareness of, 56–57
  decision-making, 56–58
  of expectation, overcoming, 142–143,
    265, 266, 269–270, 271–273
  flexibility vs., 201–202
  and holding on to old truths, 201
  love as exposing, 183
  of negative karma, rebirth and, 147
  overcoming, generally, 57–58
  Pollyanna pattern, 316, 317
  victim pattern, 93–94
  See also perfectionism
perfectionism
  arising of, 124
  and authority, issues with, 280
  changing the pattern of, 128–129
  childhood conditioning and, 128
  disidentification and, 129
  expectations and, 128, 275–276, 280

flaws in personality of, 127–128,
    275–276
"holier than thou" attitude and, 127
as identity, 128–129
as impasse, 124, 126–129
know-it-all attitude and, 128
and life-stage strategizing, 154
and other students, 126, 128
self-criticism and, 128
spiritual subpersonality and, 277–280
and teacher relationship, 83, 126–128
therapy for, 128
tone of voice and superior attitude,
    129
workaholics and, 275–276
and the world, being of but not in it,
    260
personal desires. *See* desire body
personality
    as arising from childhood
        conditioning, 127
    shadow side of. *See* negative thoughts
    spiritual subpersonality, 277–280
    of teacher, expectations about,
        127–128
    See also desire body; ego self;
        expectations; perfectionism;
        psychological blocks
pessimism, power of, 248–249
physical body (gross body)
    bodybuilding, 130
    and death, process of, 148–149
    environment of, as obstacle, 257–259
    lack of exercise, 130
    light energy and, 34
    and physical plane, 114
    suffering of, as obstacle, 89–90
physical illness
    child abuse or fears from childhood
        and, 94
    depression causing, 90
    emotions causing, 96
    evolution and curing of, 47
    karma as cause of, 223
    pain, 38, 89–90
physical plane, 112, 113–114
    boundaries and, 227
    work required on, and help from
        Subtle Plane, 116
    See also physical body
planes. *See* subtle world
plants
    death and rebirth of, 146–147
    etiquette of communication with

spirits of, 233–234
home protected by beauty of, 115
on Subtle Plane, 117
vibrations and, 24, 29
pleasers, 6, 283
pleasure, excessive desire for, 138–139
politics
    evolution and, 47
    work in, 245–246, 264
Pollyanna pattern, 316, 317
positive karma
    and attraction, nature of, 8, 106, 205
    determining nature of relationship,
        99
    and friendship and good feelings,
        access to, 8
    and sojourn between lives, 147
positive thoughts
    entities banished by, 115
    negative vibrations dissolved via, 24,
        25
power and authority, fear of, 140–141
Pralaya, 37
prana
    exercise to restore, 211
    healthy routines to develop, 211
    level of, determining, 210–211
    sexual desire and, 210
prayer, for memory of higher-plane
    experiences, 118
pride, spiritual, 269
procrastination
    expectation and, 275
    of goal, as obstacle, 189–190
    skandhas and, 59
protection
    ghosts removed by teacher, 115, 116
    glass bell as, 259, 294
    light vibrations, 27–28
    from negative emotions, 294
    negative forces attracted to students,
        and need for teacher, 80
    from negative vibrations, 24–29,
        32–33, 161–162, 258–259
    plants around home as, 115
    positive thoughts as, 24, 25, 115
    public success and need for, 181
    sending love at a distance, 294
    for speaking negatively about others,
        2–3
    See also boundaries; cleansing the
        surroundings; light, demanding to
        see, if a being speaks or appears;
        wisdom, holding the

psychic communication from teacher, verifying with teacher, 86
psychic energy
fire element and, 35
and Path of Spiritual Labor, 76
See also energy; prana
psychological blocks
addictions, 94–95
and belief that goal is too difficult, 190
growth through, emphasis on, iv
love relationships as exposing, 183
as obstacle, 178–179
and Pollyanna pattern, 317
and teacher, finding, 81–82
See also childhood conditioning; psychotherapy
psychotherapy
for couples, when partner is nonspiritual, 186
for depression, 317
and feelings of being lost, 293
for inner child work, 98
and need for recognition, 187
past-life regression, 102
for pattern of expectations, 266, 271
for perfectionist pattern, 128
for problems stemming from childhood, 317
for procrastination, 275
for workaholics, 275–276
purification. *See* cleansing; protection

rational mind. *See* mind
rebirth
and ceasing to strive, 40–41
as cycle of life, with death, 146–148
desire and, 147–148
and evolution of earth, 147
length of life and, 155
and life-stage strategizing, 154–155
sojourn prior to, karma and, 147
recall. *See* memory and memories
reincarnation
belief in, as basis for mutual understanding of negative karma, 100
belief in, as basis for talking about the teaching, 173
and evolution of planet, 147
and power, fear of, 141
See also karma; rebirth
rejection
fear of, and stubbornness, 95

as karmic, 284
and lost, feelings of being, 295
relationships
adventure and, 197
and death, preparation for, 149, 150
desires for, as obstacle, 182–186
disidentification and, 150
and emotions, need for control of, 142
ending, decision for, 59
and lost, feelings of being, 292
and Path of Higher Mind, 74
and Path of Illumination, 70
and Path of Love, 72
perfectionist pattern and, 128, 129
spiritual path chosen to replace, 69
See also abusive relationships; boundaries, personal; expectations; family; friends and friendships; karmic relationships; love, personal; past-life relationships; speaking consciously
relaxation
balance in, 138–139
death as, 156
religion
ancient, and the sun, 34
as destructive in past life, 219–220
esoteric branch in, 47
fanaticism, and unfulfilled sexual desire, 209
and lightness/darkness, 36–37
Path of Devotion as, 75
as substitute for chosen path, 139
suicide condemned by, 97
respect
speaking consciously and, 11–12
Western lack of, for Eastern yogis, 12
responsibility
and finding a teacher, 81
follow-through on, 313–314
for mood, 85
and spiritual striving, 40–41
for vibrations, 2–3, 25–26, 27, 32–33
right, need to always be, 95
Roerich Pact, 175
roses, rose water, and rose essence, 25, 114, 257–258

sacred sounds. *See* mantras
sadness, extreme. *See* depression
sage, 27, 28, 114, 259
Samadhi, 130
science
longevity and, 47

truth of, as relative, 192
Secret Doctrine, The (Blavatsky), 44
self
  knowledge of, 301
  speaking consciously to, 10–11
self-discipline
  balance in, 59
  decision making and, 58
  excessive emotional needs and, 132
  neglect of path and, 126
  and will, strengthening of, 135
self-flagellation, 130–131
self-knowledge, and stability, 49
self-pity, 92, 159–160, 164, 213
senses
  at birth, 104
  experience of HS forms via, v, vii
  See also intuition
service in the world
  and external conception of God, 239
  and help, awareness of need for, 283
  and help, being asked for, 282–283
  and love, experience of, 215
  need for, and lack of love, 215
  and need to live in the world, 212
  negative karma overcome by, 138
  and pleasure, balance of, 139
  as requirement for adeptship, 84–85,
    87
  Service, Path of, 76–77
  See also work and workplace; world:
    being in it but not of it
Service, Path of, 76–77
sexual abstinence/celibacy, 122, 203
sexual behavior
  abstinence/celibacy, 122, 203
  as addiction, 130–131
  recommended frequency, 130
  and spouse not on path, 130
  thoughts about, 130
sexual energy
  Kundalini Yoga and, 209
  as stronger in spiritual persons, 209
  sublimation of, 209
  and the will, development of, 209–211
shadow side of personality. *See* negative
thoughts
shamanism, Path of Higher Mind and,
73
Shambhala, 175, 232, 323
skandhas
  defined, 46, 323
  and ease or difficulty of journey, 310
  and the Monad, 46

Path of Illumination and, 70–71
procrastination and, 59
and recall of experiences, 118
and the senses, 104
sleep and dreaming
  and death, process of, 148
  and illusion vs. subtle world journeys,
    121
  journaling messages received, 121
  memory of experiences during,
    asking for, 118
  subtle world travel during, 113, 116,
    121
smoking, 121–122
social life
  aloneness vs., and spiritual path,
    66–69, 73
  balance in, 139
  customs of society and peers, falling
    into, 256–257
  and negative vibrations, protection
    from, 161
  and neglect of path, 125, 138–139
  See also love, personal; relationships;
    world
solitude. *See* aloneness as necessary
part of the spiritual path; lost, feelings
of being
sorrow. *See* depression; grief
soul
  of animals, 47
  growth of. *See* spiritual path
  meditation and, 38
  Monad and, 46, 138, 323
  stability of, 149
  young, 110
  See also death as a stage; karma; past
    lives; rebirth
sound
  elementals as moderating, 1
  entities causing, 115
  as pollution, 1
  sacred (mantras), 1, 10, 28, 321, 322
  of Subtle Plane, 117
  and subtle-world meditation, 121
  and vibration, 23
  Word creating, 1
  See also energy; vibrations
Source/Wisdom/Love
  and aloneness as part of the path, 290
  defined, iii, iv
  and the God within, 242
  as Path, 72–73
  return to, as spiritual path, iii

union with, yoga as method of, iii–iv
See also spiritual path
speaking consciously
    analyzing conversation afterward, 19
    apologizing for failures of, 19
    awareness and, 3, 19
    and childhood conditioning, 13
    and consciousness of the person
        spoken to, 12–14
    conveying to someone the
        consequences of their actions, 5
    criticisms and, 5, 7
    difficulty of, 3, 12–13
    and disliked persons, 7, 22
    elementals and subtle planes affected
        by, 2
    emotional content of words, 7, 13,
        17, 19
    energy of words and, 5, 7, 9–10
    exercises for, 6, 9–10, 13, 14, 15, 17–18,
        21–22
    expressing negative feelings about
        others, 2–3
    and focus, need for, 18
    and heart energy, 5, 6, 9, 10
    hurtful words/regrets, 17, 19–22
    and indirect ways of asking for
        something, 5–6
    mirroring others and, 6
    negative karma and, 8–9, 14
    negative talk about others, 2–3
    and past-life relationships, 7–9, 13,
        14, 20
    patience and, 6, 17
    perfectionist personality and need
        for, 129
    to persons who are overly sensitive to
        words, 13–14
    to persons who love an argument, 14
    to pleasers, 6
    and respect, 11–12
    to the self, 10–11
    the telephone and, 3
    vs. thinking words, 10
    tone of voice and, 4, 5, 13, 15–16, 19,
        129
    and truth, 2, 7
    vocabulary development and, 4
    and wisdom, holding the, 173, 175
    word choice and, 2, 7, 9–10, 12–13,
        16–17
    word meanings and, 4–5, 7, 10
    words used to fill pauses, 18
    words, using fewer, 4

spirit
    evolution propelled by, 46
    HS as containing, viii
    light energy and, 35–36, 43
    See also God Consciousness; self;
        soul
spiritual, as term, 4
spiritual family
    acclimation to, 87
    desire for worldly success through, as
        obstacle, 132–133
    feeling outside of group, 302–303
    imediate acceptance of new members,
        303
    and the journey, 320
    and love, denial of need for personal,
        213–214
    and love, excessive need for, 131
    Subtle Plane teachings about, 116–117
    See also Masters; students; teachers
Spiritual Labor, path of, 76
spiritual path
    comparing one's path to others,
        64–65, 225–226
    destiny and, 190, 220–222
    negative creatures targeting those
        on, 116
    questioned by student, 219
    sacredness of, 65
    secrecy as traditional to, 65
    and stages of life, strategizing for,
        152–156
    temptations pulling one away from,
        49
    ups and downs of, 64
    See also aloneness as necessary part
        of the spiritual path; boundaries;
        evolution; impasses; initiations;
        journey on the spiritual path;
        Masters; negative forces; obstacles;
        speaking consciously; spiritual
        path choice; striving spiritually;
        students; teachers; withdrawal
        from spiritual path
spiritual path choice, 63–79
    appeal of various choices,
        understanding the, 69–70
    asking HS for guidance in choice of,
        78–79
    extroverts vs. introverts and, 66
    flexibility and changes in, 64, 65,
        78–79
    God Consciousness vs. HS as goal of,
        63–64

karmic relationships and, 69
and relationships, unfulfilled, 69
and solitude vs. socializing, need for,
    66–69, 73
teacher guidance for, 65, 79
using the HS vs. desire body for, 65
wrong choice in, 65–66, 139–140
See also spiritual path types
spiritual path types
    Path of Determination, 77–78
    Path of Devotion, 75
    Path of Higher Mind, 73–74
    Path of Illumination, 70–71
    Path of Love, 72–73
    Path of Service, 76–77
    Path of Spiritual Labor, 76
storms, vibrations and, 32, 33
striving spiritually
    and death, preparation for, 151
    and help, gifts of, 263–264
    lack of, and negative thoughts, 41
    lack of, using heart connection to
        improve, 41
    and life-stage strategizing, 153
    light as essence of, 41
    maintaining a state of, exercises for,
        41–43
    necessity for, 40, 320
    reality created through, 122
    responsibility to self and, 40–41
    satisfaction in your spiritual work
        vs., 216
    sexual energy and, 209
    and teachers, finding of, 82–83
    and teachers, requirement of striving
        toward, 219
    and teachers, revealing oneself to, 87
    the will and, 211
    and work success, help with, 133
stubbornness, as emotional suffering, 95
students
    affairs or marriage with other, 182,
        208–209
    comparing oneself with other, 88,
        128, 186–188, 225–226, 302
    desire for recognition from, as
        obstacle, 186–188
    with feelings of being lost, helping,
        293–294
    help given to others, and expectations
        for self, 264
    karmic relationships with other,
        86–87
    levels of subtle world accessible to,
        113
    and love, need for, 131
    narcissism of, and conflict among,
        131–132
    need for immediate acceptance, 303
    not yet on physical plane, 117
    as role model, 226
    Subtle Plane and community building
        with, 116–117
    superiority attitude, 74, 76, 81, 129,
        186–189, 191
    unkind comments by, 188, 302–303
    See also community; Masters;
        spiritual family; teachers
subtle body (astral body)
    and emotions, need for control of, 142
    and levels of subtle world, access to,
        113, 114
    light and, 38–40, 43
    meditation as refining, 142
    previous lives accumulated in, 113,
        122
    of the sun, 38
    of teachers, demands on, 84
subtle plane. *See* Higher Astral Plane
    (subtle plane)
subtle world, 112–122
    access to, 38–39, 113
    accessibility of, and increase in
        numbers meditating, 38
    awareness of, opening to, 202
    Buddhic Plane, 112, 119
    defined, 323
    freedom in, expectation of, 227–228
    ghosts causing, 115
    help available to journeyer, 235
    illusions vs., 121
    levels within each plane, 113
    lower planes, humanity mostly stuck
        on, 112–113
    Mental Plane, 112–113, 118–119
    and need for a teacher, 80
    Nirvanic Plane, 112, 119
    physical plane and, 116
    speaking consciously and, 2, 16
    travel in, 113, 116–118, 120–121
    See also astral planes; boundaries,
        subtle-world; Higher Astral Plane
        (subtle plane); Higher Beings;
        Lower Astral Plane(s)
suffering
    boundaries causing, 236–237
    caused by inability to disidentify
        from the problem, 89

See also emotional suffering; pain
suicide
    and depression, 90, 97
    emotional suffering and, 96–97
    karma of, 96–97
    lack of sunlight and, 34–35
sun, 34–35, 38
superiority attitude, 74, 76, 81, 129,
186–189, 191
surprises, embracing, 260, 317–319
symbols
    color and, 39–40, 120
    energy represented by, 174
    God within as, 243
    holding the wisdom and, 175
    as reminder of goal to be one with
        HS, 43
    to represent HS, asking for, viii
    revealed but not understood, vii
    and subtle world meditation, 120

teachers
    accuracy of information received in
        meditation checked by, 39
    and aloneness as part of the path, 287
    appearing during meditation,
        demanding light from, 229
    and choosing a spiritual path,
        guidance from, 65, 79
    clairvoyance and clairaudience,
        guidance with, 137
    cleansing spaces, help with, 28–29,
        115
    false, 80
    ghosts taken away by, 115, 116
    help given by, 263–265
    and Higher Beings, verification of,
        120
    and illusion of subtle world, 121,
        136–137
    and impasses, help with overcoming,
        126, 144–145
    and Masters, knowledge of, 127
    and Mental Plane, 118–119
    and mundane world, lack of
        knowledge of, 127
    pain taken away by, 38, 89
    and Path of Determination, 78
    and Path of Devotion, 75
    Path of Higher Mind and becoming,
        74
    and Path of Illumination, 71
    Path of Love and becoming, 73
    and Path of Service, 76

    and Path of Spiritual Labor, 76
    personality of, expectations about,
        127–128
    psychic messages from, verification
        of, 86
    scholarly education and, 127
    sensitivity to needs of students, need
        for, 12
    withholding answers because student
        not ready, 127
    See also teachers, finding; teachers,
        relationship with
teachers, finding
    and boundaries, 229
    choosing not to seek, 80–82
    exercise for, 82
    and expectations, pattern of, 266
    karma and, 82, 84
    negative forces seeking student, and
        need to protect from, 80
    psychological barriers to, 81–82
    striving of students as required for,
        82–83
    and subtle plane work, need for
        assistance with, 80
    two teachers, attraction to, 84
teachers, relationship with
    after death of teacher, 137
    ashrams and, 84
    asking the teacher for advice on
        developing, 88
    boundaries and, 228–229
    conversations, learning to have,
        85–86
    depression of student and, 85
    differences between teachers, 83–84
    directions from, following, 86
    fear of revealing oneself, 86
    friendship, 86
    gratitude, 88
    HS guidance for, 88
    and love, excessive need for, 131
    and love, lack of personal, 207
    negative moods responsibility of
        student, 85
    negative vibrations dispelled by
        teacher, 85
    and other students, karma with, 84,
        86–87
    and other students or disciples,
        comparing oneself with, 88
    perfection, expectations of, 83,
        126–128
    private study, student desire for,

228–229
respect for teacher's time and energy,
    84, 228–229
and service in the world, 84–85, 87
and spiritual history, 87–88
striving toward, as occult law, 219
subtle body of teacher, demands on,
    84
time spent with teacher, 83
volunteering information about
    oneself, 83
workload of teacher, students helping
    with, 84–85
telepathy
    sensitivity to vibrations, 2
    from teacher, verifying with teacher,
        86
telephone conversations, negative talk
and, 3
television, need for entertainment,
138–139
Theosophy, 169
therapy. See psychotherapy
thoughts
    energy of, vs. audibly spoken words,
        10
    sexual, 130
    spoken word vs., 10
    See also negative thoughts; positive
        thoughts
time
    boundaries to protect, 236
    etiquette of, and nature spirits,
        233–234
trees. See plants
trust, and the journey, 320
truth, 192–202
    and change, 193–194
    of death, acceptance of, 194
    and disidentification, 54
    of energy behind words, 7
    esoteric, as a portion of truth, 193
    flexibility and, 201–202
    guidance from HS to recognize, iii,
        37, 84
    hidden, of esoteric study, 193
    importance of speaking, 2
    of information from beings,
        verifying, 39, 233
    intuition recognizing, 106
    karma distinguished from, 7–8
    and lifestyle changes, 196–199
    and lifestyle changes, blocks in
        making, 199–202

meaning of, as relative, 192–194,
    195–196, 200–201
optimism based in, 11
of psychic messages from teacher,
    verifying, 86
as relative to the evolutionary period,
    232–233
source of information, checking, 233
and speaking consciously, 2, 7
and time, 193–194
and the unknown, embracing,
    195–196
and the unknown, fear of, 194–195,
    200

unconditional love
    and aloneness as part of path, 290
    disidentification and, 230
    exercise to test for, 230–231
    expectations and, 284
    personal love as prerequisite to, 204
    and rejection, response to, 284
    from teacher, as insufficient for needy
        student, 131
unfinished business, and death process,
149, 150

vegetarianism, 122
vibrations
    animals and, 29, 31
    of arguments and anger, 2, 28, 258
    assessment of one's own, 25–26
    of AUM chanting, 1
    avoiding people until returned to
        positive, 32–33
    burning sage and, 259
    changing negative to positive, 32–33
    cleansing the surroundings of
        negative, 28, 161, 257–259, 258
    and concentration, need for, 29
    counter-vibrations, 25
    depression and, 161
    of emotions, 1, 24, 248–249
    of essence of each individual, 32
    fatigue as symptom of inundation
        with, 259
    flexibility and working with, 33
    forms of, 28–29
    and friends, 27, 259
    glass bell visualization as protection
        from, 259
    motion as cause of, 23
    nature spirits as sensitive to, 258–259
    and negative feelings, working

through, 27
and negative talk about others, 2–3
place-related, 24, 27–28
plants and, 24, 29
protection of self from, 24–29, 32–33,
 161–162, 258–259
responsibility for, 2–3, 25–26, 27,
 32–33
sensitive people working with, 33
sensitivity enhanced by working
 with, 29
sound and, 23
storms and, 32, 33
teacher dispelling negative, 85
the telephone and, 3
and time of day, 31
and words/thoughts during
 meditation, 9
victim pattern, 93–94
vigilance, 9, 40, 297
violets, essence of, 258
voices
 demanding light to determine
  positivity of, 39
 and fantasy life as impasse, 136
 of the Guide, as never critical, 109
 See also light, demanding to see, if a
  being speaks or appears
volunteer work. *See* service in the world

war, 46
will. *See* free will
Wisdom. *See* Source/Wisdom/Love
wisdom, giving up the desire for,
 143–144
 See also wisdom, holding the
wisdom, holding the
 attainment of ability for, 166
 consciousness changes and, 169
 defined, 166–167
 and discordant situations, 169–170
 evolution of the planet and, 176
 exercise to prioritize knowledge,
  167–168
 feeling-oriented memory and, 170
 habits that prevent, 171–172
 habits that stand in the way of,
  170–172
 HS as guide to, 175–176
 literal method of, 174
 protecting the wisdom, 173–175
 retention, exercise to assess, 170
 retention of knowledge, 168–171
 right- vs. left-brained people and, 170

speaking about the knowledge to
 others, 173, 175
study habits to improve, 172–173
symbolic method of, 174–176
Wise Being within. *See* Higher Self
withdrawal from spiritual path
 desire to choose an easier path,
  139–140
 discouragement for not being "given"
  things right away, 40
 forgetting and neglect of the path,
  124–126
 "I have other lives ahead" in which to
  grow, 40–41
 leave of absence, request for, 140, 144
 and lost, feelings of being, 293
 negative thoughts and, 218
 opportunity lost in, 140
 pacing oneself properly, 64
 and psychic communication from
  teacher, 86
 responsibility to self and, 40–41
 returning from, as rare, 140, 144, 183
 and satisfaction, pursuit of, 216–219
 and wisdom, loss of desire for, 144
 See also impasses; obstacles
the Word. *See* sound. *See also* energy;
 vibrations
words
 carefulness with. *See* speaking
  consciously
 energy of, 5, 7, 9–10
 freeing the mind of, 9
 meanings of, 4–5, 7, 10
 spoken, vs. thoughts, 10
 truth, importance of speaking, 2
work and workplace
 and balance, need for, 139
 benefiting humanity, 180–181, 264
 boundaries in, 236
 burning sage for cleansing of, 259
 and death, preparation for, 151
 disidentification with, youth and, 151
 entities attracted to, 115
 expectations and, 273–274, 276
 fame, desire for, 132–133
 the Guide and assistance in, 109
 and help given by teacher, 264
 and Path of Illumination, 70
 and Path of Service, 76–77
 and Path of Spiritual Labor, 76
 the perfectionist pattern and, 129
 and pleasure, excessive need for, 138
 right work, 181–182

and vibrations, protection from, 25,
247–249, 259
See also service in the world; world:
being in it but not of it
workaholics, 275–276
world
desires for, as obstacle, 180–182
and fantasy life as impasse, 137–138
teachers' lack of knowledge of, 127
See also impasses; obstacles; service
in the world; world: being in it but
not of it
world: being in it but not of it, 212, 245
customs of society and peers, falling
into, 256–257
ethics as conflict in, 245, 246–247
and friendships, 259–260
and the heart, focused, 249–251
and industry, work in, 245, 246, 259,
264
and karma, avoidance of incurring,
246
as the more difficult path, 260
and negative karma, dealing with,
246–247
and the perfect, nonexistence of, 260
physical environment as obstacle,
257–258
and politics, work in, 245–246, 264
and psychological blocks as obstacle,
179
and right work, 181–182
surprises of life, embracing, 260
values required for, 180–181
vibrations of self in workplace,
awareness of, 247–249
vibrations of self with friends and
family, 248–249, 258–259
and vibrations positive and negative,
258–259
and will and heart used in
combination, 251–256
and the will, focused, 249

youth, and work, disidentification with,
151

Made in the USA
Lexington, KY
25 June 2013